Fundamentals of the Economic Role of Government

WARREN J. SAMUELS

Prepared under the auspices of the Policy Studies
Organization

Contributions in Economics and Economic History,
Number 98

Stuart S. Nagel, *Series Editor*

Greenwood Press
NEW YORK • WESTPORT, CONNECTICUT • LONDON

Library of Congress Cataloging-in-Publication Data

Fundamentals of the economic role of government / Warren J. Samuels ;
   prepared under the auspices of the Policy Studies Organization.
      p.   cm.—(Contributions in economics and economic history,
   ISSN 0084–9235 ; no. 98)
      ISBN 0–313–26778–2 (lib. bdg. : alk. paper)
      1. Economic policy.   I. Samuels, Warren J., 1933–
   II. Series.
   338.9—dc20   89–2133

British Library Cataloguing in Publication Data is available.

Library of Congress Catalog Card Number: 89–2133
ISBN: 0–313–26778–2
ISSN: 0084–9235

First published in 1989

Greenwood Press, Inc.
88 Post Road West, Westport, Connecticut   06881

Printed in the United States of America

The paper used in this book complies with the
Permanent Paper Standard issued by the National
Information Standards Organization (Z39.48–1984).

10 9 8 7 6 5 4 3 2 1

For
> Edward A. Carlin
> Herbert Kisch
> Arthur S. Miller

In memoriam

Contents

Preface

The economic role of government is one of the most important, controversial, and confused subjects in the social sciences, history, law, and philosophy. There are almost as many approaches to the subject as there are scholarly disciplines, schools of thought within disciplines, and perhaps even individuals. Most if not all modern ideologies are characterized by the agenda or nonagenda that they would assign to government—though most if not all tend to be relatively silent about certain fundamental uses to which they would put government, uses which their theorizing takes for granted and even obfuscates. It is very difficult if not impossible to make objective, positive statements about government, especially in regard to its economic role, which are not in some fashion implicitly laden with or channeled by some ideological, normative, or subjective point of view. Moreover, there are enormous disagreements over such questions as (1) what is inevitable or imperative versus optional or problematic about the economic role of government, (2) the ends of economic policy, (3) the substance of desirable economic policy means or techniques, and (4) the relationships between the various means of economic policy to the sundry ends thereof, and so on.

The purpose of this volume is decidedly neither to resolve the great questions of ideology and policy which characterize discussion in this area nor to develop some calculus immediately applicable to questions of policy. The immediate objective is to present and explore a variety of identifications of the most fundamental propositions which one can state about the economic role of government—fundamental in the sense that they transcend the details of specific government actions or policies, indeed, fundamental in the sense that specific policies represent their solution or fruition. The larger objective is to see what generalizations, major themes, and conclusions can be stated, as nonnormatively and nonideologically as possible, about what is fundamental to the economic role of government. As far as I can discern, the only value judgment inherent in this venture is that supporting the public discussion of fundamentals of the economic role of government.

The chapters in this book were commissioned from specialists in diverse fields. Contributors were identified on the basis of the general quality, pertinence, and diversity of their past work. They were asked to respond to the question, what are the most fundamental things you can say concerning the economic role of government? The only requirement was to have their work address this question as they saw fit, within approximately three thousand words. The authors had complete discretion in formulating their presentations. My intention was, first, to have them concentrate on what, in their individual view, was truly "fundamental," and, second, to secure responses from a number of different disciplinary and ideological perspectives.

I indicated to prospective contributors my desire that the fundamentals which they identify be positive and nonnormative, though I was aware that a strict approach would be question-begging and perhaps undesirably narrowing. I also indicated that their responses should not be legal-economic system specific, but again this stricture should not be taken to unduly narrow discussion. Apropos of both ideology and particular legal-economic systems, I indicated that to the greatest extent possible I would like their responses to identify the subjects with respect to which both ideology and specific legal-economic systems take positions. I stressed that the specific points should penetrate to quite deep (fundamental) levels of political and economic organization, to the existential problems that define that level and not with the various positions that can be taken on them. Again, I emphasized that I would not want such a statement to foreclose any serious answer to the question, what are the most fundamental propositions that one can make about the economic role of government?

I also indicated that I would contribute a comparative, analytical, integrative chapter based largely on the other contributions. Among other things, this chapter would attempt to interpret, systematize, and generalize from what the other contributions seem to be saying as to what we know, on the most fundamental level, about the economic role of government, and also the nature and bases of the differences of interpretation.

Accordingly, the bulk of this volume consists of the works prepared by the invited contributors presenting what they believe constitutes the most fundamental statements which they think can and/or should be made about the economic role of government. These chapters are followed by my interpretive chapter.

The authors responded to their charge with considerable diversity and also with great common sense, much thoughtfulness, and perceptivity, as well as with some idiosyncrasy derivative of their particular interests. But let us first have the authors speak for themselves. In the absence of any other organizing principle that was both obvious and commanding, the works are presented in alphabetical order by author.

One final matter. From the beginning I was equivocal as to whether I should contribute a chapter comparable to the others, one presenting my own answer to the question posed to all contributors. On the one hand, it seemed superfluous, given that I would be writing an integrative and interpretive chapter. On the other hand, it seemed desirable to enable the reader to distinguish my own personal views from those presented in my concluding chapter, to the extent that there is a difference which after all may be negligible. There were other pertinent considerations, such as the presumed general affinity of my own views to those, at least, of A. Allan Schmid and James D. Shaffer, with whom I have published work in the field of law and economics. (Both an outline and a draft of my contribution were prepared prior to my receipt of their contributions.) On balance, it seemed desirable to enable the reader to see where I stand, quite independent of the other contributors, if only so that they could be in a better position to assess the interpretation I give in the concluding chapter. The reader will find my personal contribution in its alphabetical place.

Warren J. Samuels

Fundamentals of the Economic Role of Government

1

Government and Competitive Free Enterprise

Walter Adams and James W. Brock

"Bad governments are of two sorts," James Wilson reminded his colleagues as they struggled with the constitutional blueprint for American democracy: "First, that which does too little. Secondly, that which does too much: that which fails thro' weakness; and that which destroys thro' oppression" (Madison, 1987, p. 222).

The dilemma Wilson identified is particularly apropos to the governance of a competitive free enterprise society. Here, the state must steer a peculiarly complex course between the Scylla of too much government and the Charybdis of too little. On the one hand, it must abjure direct control over economic affairs; instead, it must delegate this responsibility to an effectively competitive market. On the other, government must establish, and enforce, the kind of ground rules that will permit the competitive market to perform its regulatory function; it must protect the integrity of the free market process and safeguard its survival against possible depredation and subversion.

Clearly, this requires the concentration of considerable coercive force in government which, in turn, sets up an almost irresistibly tantalizing temptation for private interests to try to manipulate government for favors and special privileges, and to subvert it to their own anticompetitive, antisocial ends. Hence, government power must, at one and the same time, be the greatest bulwark for preserving competition as a regulatory mechanism and for preventing the erosion of this mechanism by itself becoming a mask for private privilege and monopoly.

THE ROLE OF COMPETITION

In designing a structural framework for economic activity, every society must confront the core questions of political economy: Who shall make what decisions? On whose behalf? At what cost? With what benefits? For whom? And with what assurance that the outcome will be congruent with the national interest and the common good? Every society, in other words, must face up to the question of how economic power shall be distributed and what safeguards must be erected to prevent its abuse.

In a free enterprise society, the competitive market is the prime principle of economic organization. It is at once a mechanism for allocating society's resources—deciding which goods and services shall be produced, in what quantities, at what prices, and by what techniques—and a regulatory system for controlling private power. Like the political framework prescribed by the Constitution, a competitive market system is founded on distrust of concentrated power and on a belief in the maximum possible diffusion of economic rights and opportunity. Decision-making power over such vital matters as price, production, and investment is to be decentralized and scattered into a multitude of hands rather than concentrated in a few. Although private enterprisers are free to assume primary responsibility for organizing the productive activities on which the life of the community depends, they have to pay a price for that freedom: they have to submit to the discipline of competition. They have to heed the voice of the community, as expressed in the market, rather than serving it merely as they might themselves deem fit and proper. A free enterprise society grants individuals the privilege of economic freedom only because competition imposes the checks and balances required to harness that freedom and turn it to the public good.

Competition, then, is first and foremost a system of freedom and decentralized economic power.

THE ROLE OF GOVERNMENT

Maintaining this system—fostering it and ensuring that it obtains in practice—is the fundamental role of government. But contrary to simplistic libertarian preachments, this does *not* mean anarchy and absence of government. It does *not* imply absolute individual freedom and opposition to any government intervention in economic affairs. Instead, it requires active government involvement in order to achieve a system of ordered liberty. The reasons should be obvious.

First, harmony between individuals pursuing their own self-interests, and between those self-interests and the common good, is neither natural, nor spontaneous, nor self-generating. As Thomas Hobbes recognized three centuries ago, "during the time men live without a common Power to keep them all in awe, they are in that condition which is called Warre; and such a warre, as is every man, against every man. . . . In such condition, there is no place for Industry; because the fruit thereof is uncertain; and consequently no Culture of the Earth; no Navigation, nor use of the commodities that may be imported by Sea; no commodious Building; no Instruments of moving, and removing such things as require much force; no Knowledge of the face of the Earth; no account of Time; no Arts; no Letters; no Society." Instead, this "state of nature" is tantamount to a *bellum omnium contra omnes*, characterized most prominently by "continuall feare, and danger of violent death; And the life of man, solitary, poore, nasty, brutish, and short'' (Hobbes, 1968, pp. 185–86).

Second, as good Enlightenment thinkers well understood, the lust for power is endemic to the human condition. Said Edmund Burke in 1777:

Power of all kinds has an irresistable propensity to increase a desire for itself. It gives the passion of ambition a velocity which increases in its progress, and this is a passion which grows in proportion as it is gratified. . . . The root of the evil is deep in human nature. . . . Power will sometime or other be abused unless men are well watched, and checked by something they cannot remove when they please'' (Quoted in Adams and Brock, 1986, p. 87).

Third, in civil society, therefore, individual freedom can never be absolute. ''All that makes existence valuable to anyone,'' John Stuart Mill wrote, ''depends on the enforcement of restraints upon the actions of other people'' (Mill, 1972, pp. 73–74). Or as William Blackstone put it:

no man, that considers a moment, would wish to retain the absolute and uncontroled power of doing whatever he pleases; the consequence of which is, that every other man would also have the same power; and then there would be no security to individuals in any of the enjoyments of life. Political therefore, or civil, liberty, which is that of a member of society, is no other than natural liberty so far restrained by human laws (and no farther) as is necessary and expedient for the general advantage of the publick (Blackstone, 1987, p. 88).

Fourth, in a civil society, then, the relevant question is what kinds of laws will promote what sorts of freedoms and for whom. In a free society, an irreducible element of government force, coercion, and intervention is essential in order to create and to maintain a system within which collective freedom can flourish—freedom not just for a few, but for all. Government must enforce a free economic system—a pattern of economic freedoms distributed within an economic power structure. Government must establish the boundaries within which individuals will be free to do as they please, and it must enforce those limits. Above all, government must ensure that the system remains free—that the freedom of some is not used to destroy the freedoms of others, or even to subvert the entire structure of freedom. As Lord Robbins observed: ''The invisible hand which guides men to promote ends which were no part of their intention, is not the hand of some god or some natural agency independent of human effort; it is the hand of the lawgiver, the hand which withdraws from the sphere of the pursuit of self-interest those possibilities which do not harmonize with the public good'' (Robbins, 1952, p. 56; Samuels, 1966). The invisible hand is the hand of government acting in the role of rulemaker and umpire—creating the framework in which economic freedom can perform its assigned social task.

Fifth, in a free enterprise system, individuals enjoy a wide latitude of freedom in making decisions, but this freedom is not, and cannot be, absolute. It cannot be permitted, for example, to include the freedom to eliminate competition; nor the freedom to control the market; nor the freedom to usurp the market as society's regulatory instrument. It cannot be permitted to include the freedom to collude, to create cartels, to merge with rivals, or to monopolize. It cannot be permitted to include the freedom to destroy the discipline imposed by competition, nor the freedom to deny to others economic opportunity and their freedom to compete. Carried to such extremes, individual freedom would destroy the collective *structure* of freedom which it is the object of the system to achieve and retain.

Sixth, as the preceding considerations suggest and as economic experience amply affirms, the competitive market is *not* an immutable artifact of nature. Nor is it automatically self-perpetuating. Instead, the competitive market is susceptible to destruction from within by private interests who chafe at its discipline, who refuse to submit to its control, and who aspire to arrogate its planning function unto themselves. Some concoct cartels and collusive pricing schemes. Others play the merger game in order to immunize themselves from the dictates of the competitive market. Others forge Brobdingnagian corporate power structures that undermine the market's authority by virtue of their sheer size and their disproportionate impact on society as a whole.

Seventh, once such private economic power complexes arise, they are no longer under social control. They are no longer socially accountable or socially responsible. As Justice William O. Douglas warned, such private economic power ineluctably gravitates toward industrial oligarchy. (Douglas, 1948, p. 535). It becomes a government unto itself, an *imperium in imperio*, which renders the community's fortunes dependent on the whims and caprice, the political prejudices, and the emotional stability of a few self-appointed masters. Then, private decisions (and mistakes) are made in furtherance of private ends but with no built-in assurance that they will promote the national interest. Then, power is arbitrary and, hence, irresponsible.

Eighth, in a free enterprise system, government must therefore intervene, in order to protect and sustain the integrity of competition as an effective social regulatory mechanism. Government must ensure that the structural prerequisites for effective competition are in place:

that all persons engaged in business dealings with one another are basically equal in status and are not hopelessly unequal in bargaining power. None is favored by a preferential position at law nor by avoidable special privilege. None is exposed to ganging-up, that is, to coercion or exploitation growing out of concerted action by others. Though single concerns are likely to differ in size, wealth, and power, there must be some limit, even though an ill-defined one, to the bargaining advantages that grow out of such differences (Edwards, 1949, p. 3).

Government must arrest, neutralize, and remove accretions of economic power so great that they obstruct competition, destroy the freedom of opportunity to compete, and operate outside the checks and balances of the competitive market.

These, then, comprise government's fundamental role in a free enterprise society. Moreover, to the degree that the state performs this role, the overall extent of government involvement in the economy is minimized. As long as the market functions effectively in controlling private power, there is no need for massive government intervention. Nor is there a need for an overarching, detailed blueprint mapping out the precise end at which the economy is targeted to arrive. Enforcing ordered economic liberty, Walter Lippmann pointed out, allows the economy to develop in the directions toward which individual creativity and ingenuity move it, wherever they may lead. It commits society's economic destiny, not to the determination of a few, but to the whole genius of humankind (Lippmann, 1937, pp. 364–68).

SOME PERENNIAL DILEMMAS

At least three vexing dilemmas perennially confront a free enterprise, representative democracy:

First, private interests will almost inevitably be attracted to government. They will almost inevitably contrive to usurp government power and bend it to their own devices. As Richard T. Ely observed long ago, it is "a necessary outcome of human nature that those persons who are to be controlled should enter politics in order that they may either escape the control, or shape it to their own ends" (Ely, 1903, p. 231). But the results are seldom, if ever, in the public interest.

In his day, for example, Adam Smith surveyed the crushing panoply of mercantilistic, government-imposed restraints on imports, restraints on exports, state bounties and subsidies, and royal grants of monopoly privilege at home and abroad. "It cannot be very difficult to determine who have been the contrivers of this whole mercantile system," he wrote; "not the consumers . . . whose interest has been entirely neglected; but the producers, whose interest has been so carefully attended to." The cruelest of revenue laws, he ventured to affirm, "are mild and gentle in comparison of some of those which the clamour of our merchants and manufacturers has extorted from the legislature, for the support of their own absurd and oppressive monopolies" (Smith, 1937, pp. 612, 626).

The problem persists in our own day. Merchants and manufacturers—typically allied with organized labor—still lobby government to obtain antiproductive, state-imposed restraints on import competition, government-enforced cartels, direct and indirect subsidies, and outright government bailouts (Adams and Brock, 1986).

Two factors tend to attenuate the ability of private power groups to exert concentrated political force on the state and to frustrate their efforts to capture total control of the state. One is the maintenance of a competitively structured economy. The other is a splintered political system wherein governmental powers are divided among a multitude of branches, bureaus, and departments.

Second, although the separation of governmental powers and a system of political checks and balances complicate the task of usurpers who would capture the state, these structural peculiarities simultaneously weaken government authority and make it vulnerable to manipulation by special interest groups. By creating an enormous apparatus of byzantine complexity, Hans Morgenthau has observed, and by dividing and subdividing political functions, and parcelling them out to a plethora of administrative agencies often working at cross-purposes, government power is fragmented and the sum total of public power is diminished. As one result, "government, instead of speaking with one strong and purposeful voice, speaks in many voices, each trying to outshout the others, but all really weak as well as contradictory." More problematically, a decomposition of government power is concomitant with a weakening of public authority, and this makes government more prone to manipulation (Morgenthau, 1962, p. 286). In the process, decentralization of government, but without a corresponding decentralization of the private economic power structure, becomes a recipe for erosion of the state as the guarantor of a free system.

Third, a representative democracy, designed to respond to pressures exerted on it, is continually vulnerable to what Henry C. Simons called the orderly routine of democratic corruption, because every interference by government on behalf of one organized economic interest group elicits additional government intervention on behalf of other groups. Once underway, private groups feel compelled to lobby government for favors and privileges, in order to counteract those granted others. But the cumulative tendency is not merely to neutralize one special interest favor by granting another. Nor does the combined result secure or promote the common interest. Instead, the long-term tendency is "an accumulation of government regulation which yields, in many industries, all the afflictions of socialization and none of its possible benefits; an enterprise economy paralyzed by political control; the moral disintegration of representative government in the endless contest of innumerable pressure groups for political favors." The drift is toward "a miscellany of specialized collectivisms, organized to take income away from one another and incapable of acting in their own common interest or in a manner compatible with general prosperity" (Simons, 1948, p. 87–88). Eventually, only an inordinately powerful state verging on dictatorship would be strong enough to ride herd on a collectivity of special interests constantly conspiring against the national welfare.

Together, these dilemmas comprise the perennial challenge confronting a free enterprise society intent on preserving democratic institutions. How can we prevent private concentrations of power, organized into potent political pressure groups, from achieving dominance over the economy and, eventually, over the state? And how can we do so without creating an omnipotent government, strong enough not only to control private oligarchies but also to become an instrument of oppression beyond public control and accountability?

REFERENCES

Adams, Walter, and James W. Brock. *The Bigness Complex*. New York: Pantheon, 1986.
Blackstone, William. "Commentaries." In Philip B. Kurland and Ralph Lerner (eds.),
    Founders' Constitution. Chicago: University of Chicago Press, 1987.

Douglas, Justice William O. *United States* v. *Columbia Steel Corp.* (Dissenting Opinion). 334 U.S. 495 (1948).

Edwards, Corwin D. *Maintaining Competition*. New York: McGraw-Hill, 1949.

Ely, Richard T. *Studies in the Evolution of Industrial Society*. London: Macmillan & Co. Ltd., 1903.

Hobbes, Thomas. *Leviathan*. Baltimore: Penguin Books, 1968.

Lippmann, Walter. *An Inquiry into the Principles of the Good Society*. Boston: Little, Brown & Co., 1937.

Madison, James. *Notes of Debates in the Federal Convention of 1787*. New York: W. W. Norton, 1987.

Mill, John Stuart. *On Liberty*. London: Everyman's Library, 1972.

Morgenthau, Hans J. *The Purpose of American Politics*. New York: Alfred A. Knopf, 1962.

Robbins, Lionel. *The Theory of Economic Policy in English Classical Political Economy*. London: Macmillan & Co. Ltd., 1952.

Samuels, Warren. *The Classical Theory of Economic Policy*. Cleveland: World Publishing Co., 1966.

Simons, Henry C. *Economic Policy for a Free Society*. Chicago: University of Chicago Press, 1948.

Smith, Adam. *The Wealth of Nations*. New York: Modern Library, 1937.

2

Power, Politics, and Economics

Andrew Altman

Among the central issues of modern social science are those that concern the relations between political and economic power. Both normative and descriptive questions about the economic role of government are deeply intertwined with issues about the relation of political to economic power. In the course of modern Western social thought, several competing theoretical approaches have emerged to address these complicated issues and their implications for questions about the role of government in economic affairs. In this chapter, two such approaches are examined and some conclusions are drawn about the economic role of government from that examination.

THE BASIC THEORETICAL ISSUE

Perhaps the simplest way to put the basic theoretical issue of the relation of political and economic power is as follows: Which of the two is the more fundamental form of social power? The question stands in need of clarification.[1]

The clarification may begin with a point on which a wide range of thinkers would agree: in stratified human societies, the groups that tend to have the lion's share of economic power also tend to have the lions share of political power. Conversely, the groups that tend to have little economic power also tend to have little political power. What accounts for this correlation of economic and political power? One approach adopts the hypothesis that the correlation is explained by the fact that groups with a great deal of economic power use it to establish and perpetuate their control over a dominant share of political power. Let us call this the "economic hypothesis." The most well-known social theory incorporating this hypothesis is, of course, Marxism.[2]

Another approach adopts the hypothesis that the correlation is explained by the fact that those groups with dominant political power use it to gain and perpetuate their control of a dominant share of economic power. Let us call this the "political hypothesis." The understanding it represents of the relation of political and economic power can be found in thinkers as diverse as James Madison and Mikhail Bakunin. Madison relied on it in arguing in *The Federalist Papers* No. 10 and No. 51 that the constitutional framework of the United States ought to insure the division and dispersal of political power so that no single group or coalition could gain permanent control over it and thus over the economic resources of society. Anarchists such as Bakunin relied on the political hypothesis in arguing that government, that is, political power, ought to be permanently destroyed, since it would inevitably fall into the hands of a few, who would then use it to subjugate society, economically and otherwise (Bakunin, 1953, pp. 263–301).

The economic hypothesis can be thought of as proposing that economic power is a more fundamental form of social power than political in this sense: The distribution of political power is to be explained in terms of the way economic power is distributed and exercised. The political hypothesis can be thought of as proposing that political power is more fundamental than economic in this sense: The distribution of economic power is to be explained in terms of the way political power is distributed and exercised. The question of which kind of power is more fundamental is the question of which type of power provides the terms with which to explain the forms and patterns taken by the other. Both hypotheses presume that there is a one-way explanatory relation between the two kinds of power. (I.e., the distribution and exercise of one kind explains the distribution and exercise of the other but not vice versa.) It is possible to accept both hypotheses but only as long as one claims that they apply to different societies or to the same society at different times.

THE PRIMACY OF THE ECONOMIC: MARXISM

In Marxist theory, the economic hypothesis is conjoined with the thesis that government serves to reinforce and extend the control of the economically dominant group in society. The thesis follows from the economic hypothesis in conjunction with the premise that a group that controls state power will use it to advance its group interests. Moreover, within Marxism, the economic hypothesis is conjoined with the thesis that those groups that have little economic power will not be able to work within the existing political system and use lawful means to gain substantially greater control over economic resources relative to the control exercised by the dominant group. This thesis is connected to the Marxist postulate that in any class-divided society there is a fundamental conflict of economic interests between the economically dominant and subordinate classes. Short of revolutionary overthrow of the existing political and economic order, there is no way for subordinate economic classes to employ government power in order to liberate themselves from their subordinate status, or even to substantially ameliorate that status in any way that works to the serious detriment of the dominant classes.

Moreover, Marxist theory holds that no subordinate class, or coalition of such classes, will be able to mount a successful social-political revolution unless it is capable of exercising control over the economic resources in a way that would dramatically increase the level of economic productivity reached by society. The bourgeosie was able to mount a successful revolution against the feudal nobility only because its mastery of state power meant such a breakthrough would be forthcoming. Similarly, the proletarian revolution can be successful only when a proletarian state promises to break through the fetters on productivity which capitalist relations of production eventually come to constitute.

Marxist theory thus sees economic power as more fundamental than political power in both stable and revolutionary periods in the history of a society. In the stable periods, it is more fundamental in that the de facto distribution and exercise of economic power accounts for the distribution and limits of political power. In revolutionary periods, it is more fundamental in that a revolutionary group's potential for exercising economic dominance in a way that achieves higher levels of productivity dictates whether it will be successful in its revolution and gain political dominance during the next period of stability.

On Marxist theory, then, there is a crucial subordination of the political to the economic. Variables relating to the control of economic power and what may be accomplished with that control place crucial limits on what politics—revolutionary or normal politics—may accomplish. Economic relations place crucial constraints on the role government may play in shaping the social world.

THE PRIMACY OF THE POLITICAL: ANTI-MARXIST THEORIES

Those who embrace the political hypothesis reject the Marxist notion that the limits of nonrevolutionary, or normal, politics is invariably set by the basic interests of the group currently holding dominant economic power and that the limits of revolutionary politics is invariably set by the basic interests of the social group that will generate higher levels of productivity if it gains political and economic dominance. In their view, the power of politics to shape society and even to create a new social world is, in the end, limited only by whatever is incompatible with human nature. Although there are a variety of views on how severe the constraints of human nature may be, the approach represented by the political hypothesis generally accords far greater potential power to politics than does a Marxist approach. Even though Marxism is committed to the notion that human nature is highly malleable, ultimately it is the economic, and not the political arrangement, that dictates which form human nature will take in any given social-historical context. The political hypothesis, on the other hand, sees politics as a power with the potential to create and re-create the shape of social life in a way that is largely autonomous from the existing patterns of economic power.[3]

Adherents to the political hypothesis who are living in a society which they see as good, or even tolerable, thus seek to put severe limits on government so that the potential of politics to remake society is largely crippled. Historically, they have been especially concerned to limit the role government may play in dictating and manipulating the distribution of economic power. For even though they regard political power as the more fundamental form of social power, they have seen the virtues of existing arrangements as tied closely to the existing distribution of economic power. Radical shifts in economic power would harm society in substantial ways, and so the potential of politics to effect such shifts has to be blocked by institutional devices (such as those devised by our Constitution's framers) designed to eliminate the potentially radical power of government.

The approach is quite different for those proponents of the political hypothesis who do not believe that their existing society is good or even tolerable. They seek to unleash, rather than defuse, the radical potential politics. Since the distribution of economic power typically seems to be at the heart of what is intolerable about society, they advocate that the power of government be used to create and stabilize a new economic order. In many instances, this involves the appeal to revolutionary politics. But the acceptance of the political hypothesis is fully consistent with the idea that, in some political systems at least, normal politics provides a means to shift radically the distribution of economic power.

ASSESSING THE APPROACHES

The history of the twentieth century has amply demonstrated Marxism's flawed view of the limits placed on politics by economics. Government has been used to smash existing economic orders in ways quite incompatible with Marxism. Revolutions have led to the dominance of groups much less capable of raising the level of economic productivity than other potential ruling classes. As many commentators have pointed out, an exemplary and ironic instance of the latter phenomenon can be found in the Bolshevik revolution. However, the deeper lesson for social theory behind the events of the twentieth century goes beyond the discrediting of the Marxist version of the economic hypothesis. The deeper lesson is that politics has the radical potential which people such as Madison and the other framers feared. Government can be used to smash economic orders and to create radically new ones, and there appear to be no substantive claims one can make a priori about the character of the new orders. They may achieve the kind of economic breakthroughs which Marxism postulates but they may also stifle economic productivity. They may increase economic inequality, or they may decrease it. They may create entirely new patterns in the distribution of economic power, or they may reconstitute old patterns.

To talk of the potential of politics to destroy and create economic orders is not to say that the typical role of government in human history has been to engage in such activities. The truth is that government tends to function in the way Marxism postulates and for largely, though not entirely, Marxist reasons: Government typically serves to reinforce and perpetuate the economic power of the dominant economic classes, and it does so because economic power is an important lever for directing the deployment of state power.

Defenders of the political hypothesis could, of course, accept the idea that government typically serves to reinforce the power of the economically dominant class, but they could not account for this phenomenon ultimately in terms of the influence of the economic over the political. Instead, it would insist on the primacy of political power. This seems to be as unwarranted as the Marxist's insistence on the primacy of the economic. Economic power provides great leverage over the actions and policies of government. It is not necessary to deny this capability in order to agree that, in the final analysis, the power of government can become unleashed from the control of the economically dominant class. Most of the time, things do not operate as they, in the final analysis, have the potential to operate.

THE BIG QUESTION AND A SMALLER ONE

The big question concerns the conditions under which politics will become unleashed from its normal subordination to the economic. No one has an answer to this question that is even remotely adequate. If and when one emerges, we may have to rethink the whole issue of the economic role of government and the relation of the political to the economic. Such an answer could show that the economic is really more fundamental after all: for it might show that there are economic factors, as yet undiscovered, that determine when politics becomes unleashed from its usual subordination to the interests of the dominant economic class. In such a case, the economic hypothesis would be vindicated but only as integrated into some non-Marxist theory.

In a paradoxical manner, however, the discovery of such a theory may lead to its immediate or eventual falsification. For once it becomes known which economic conditions cause politics to become unleashed, that knowledge could become integrated into the political process so that those conditions would be deliberately instituted, or deliberately avoided, by state action. The primacy of politics would then replace the primacy of economics. If knowledge is power, then knowledge integrated into and deployed within the workings of the political process is political power.

More manageable than the big question we have just posed is a question that has proved to have a good deal of practical and theoretical significance. The question is whether the politics of liberal democratic states can generate countertendencies that overcome the typical tendency of government to reinforce and perpetuate the economic power of the dominant economic class. It can be taken as granted that the politics of absolutist, totalitarian, and fascist states can generate such countertendencies. Revolutionary politics can generate such countertendencies. The question is whether they can be generated in the normal politics of liberal democracy.

Early in this century, European social democracy adopted in practice, if not always in theory, an affirmative answer to the question. The social democratic strategy was to adopt the path to socialism through normal, rather than revolutionary, politics. The European experience thus provides a test, albeit a limited one, of the idea that the normal politics of liberal democracies can become unleashed from the control of economic power. The social democratic premise was that universal (manhood) suffrage had made it possible to bring about radical shifts in the distribution of economic power without political revolution. This path to socialism was called the evolutionary path: It was so regarded both because of the lawful means it recommended and because of the supposition that such means would involve the gradual, rather than abrupt, introduction of socialism.

Despite the plausibility of the social democratic picture of liberal democratic politics, radical shifts in the patterns of economic power did not take place (Parkin, 1971, pp. 114–21). Moreover, liberal democratic politics has not moved Western societies toward socialism to any significant degree, if socialism is understood to involve the eradication of private ownership of the means of production and the elimination of markets as the principal mechanism for the distribution of goods and services, capital, and labor.

Perhaps it is a good thing that European social democracy failed, but our concern here lies with the implications of the failure for the ideas of social theory and not with the moral or political judgments to be made about it. In light of the evidence provided by the experience of social democracy, it is reasonable to draw the conclusion that liberal democracy hamstrings the power of government in a way that makes it very difficult for nonrevolutionary political activity to effect substantial shifts in the patterns of distribution of economic power. Social democracy appears to have greatly overestimated the extent to which universal suffrage would unleash politics from the control of capital. Some thinkers go further and contend that it is actually impossible for nonrevolutionary politics within liberal democracies to become unleashed from the control of economic power (Unger, 1987). Although we do not know nearly enough about political and economic power to accept such a contention, history has provided enough evidence for us to conclude that liberating the normal politics of a liberal democracy from the control of economic power is, at best, no easy matter.

CONCLUSION

This brief review of some of the theoretical and practical issues surrounding the relation of economic and political power can be summarized in the following descriptive claims about the economic role of government:

1. Government tends to reinforce and perpetuate the control that the dominant economic class exercises over the key economic resources of society, and it does so largely because of the leverage that economic power provides over the direction of deployment of state power.

2. Government has the potential to be used to smash the existing economic order or to effect major shifts in the patterns of economic distribution, but nobody has a good theory explaining when and why political power becomes unleashed from the economic constraints under which it normally operates.

3. In liberal democracies, the evidence fails to show that political activity within the confines of the law can induce government to effect major shifts in the patterns of economic distribution.

NOTES

1. The question presupposes that an intelligible distinction can be drawn between political and economic power. The presupposition is not self-evident, though it is usually taken for granted. Indeed, there are good reasons to reject an absolute distinction between political and economic power because in virtually any political society the control of economic resources will be inextricably intertwined with the rules of property and contract that the government enforces (Cohen, 1927). Nonetheless, it is sensible to distinguish conceptually a form of social power that operates essentially through the (legally sanctioned) control of land, labor, and/or capital and a form that operates through the organs of government in a way that carries no analytical connection to control of land, labor, or capital.

2. None of my claims regarding Marxism should be construed as denying that there are many possible, competing interpretations of the accounts of history and society in the writings of Marx. The principal texts underlying my interpretation are Marx and Engels, 1947; Marx and Engels, 1948; McLellan, 1977; pp. 192—94 and 389–90.

3. There are two distinct ways to elaborate the political hypothesis. In one version, the state is seen as an instrument that social groups, definable independently of their connections to state power, fight over and employ in order to promote their own interests. This version shares with Marxism the idea of the state as a tool of society, although it rejects the Marxist thesis that it is invariably a tool of the economically dominant class. In the other version, those who operate the state apparatus constitute a group that is independent of the groups that constitute society and is dominant over those groups. The importance of the differences between these two elaborations of the political hypothesis are noted in Theda Skocpol (1979).

REFERENCES

Bakunin, Mikhail. *The Political Philosophy of Bakunin*. G. P. Maximoff (ed.). New York: Free Press, 1953.

Cohen, Morris R. "Property and Sovereignty." *Cornell Law Quarterly* 13, No. 8 (1927).

Hamilton, Alexander, James Madison, and John Jay. *The Federalist Papers*. New York: New American Library, 1927.

Marx, Karl, and Friedrich Engels. *The German Ideology*. New York: International Publishers, 1947.

———. *The Communist Manifesto*. New York: International Publishers, 1948.

McClellan, David. *Karl Marx: Selected Writings*. New York: Oxford University Press, 1977.

Parkin, Frank. *Class Inequality and Political Order*. York: Praeger, 1971.
Skocpol, Theda. *States and Social Revolutions*. New York: Cambridge University Press, 1979.
Unger, Roberto. *False Necessity*. New York: Cambridge University Press, 1987.

3

Government and the Economy: What Is Fundamental?

James E. Anderson

Governments in the United States have always intervened in the economy and probably much more extensively in the eighteenth and nineteenth centuries than many people realize. Over time the economic role of government has greatly expanded, although the rate of expansion has varied from one historical period to another. The national government, which is the primary focus of this chapter, is now doing vastly more than it was a few decades ago, let alone a century ago. Its economic policies and programs are directed at an economic system that has also expanded greatly in size, scope, complexity, diversity, and interdependence. Government action has stimulated and facilitated the growth of the economy and at the same time has subjected it to social control in support of such values as equity, equality, efficiency, humaneness, social justice, and democracy.

The expansion of government's economic role has been attended by much political controversy and struggle, which sometimes has become quite bitter in style, as during the 1930s. People obviously differ greatly in their beliefs and notions concerning the proper role for government, whether as promoter, regulator, coordinator, or owner of economic enterprise. At the extremes of the ideological spectrum there are the strong libertarian, who would deny almost everything to the hand of government, and the Marxist, who would assign almost everything to the state (until, one supposes, it withers away). Most persons, however, would place themselves closer to the middle of the ideological spectrum. This still permits considerable diversity of opinion, and many bases for conflict between conservatives and liberals of various pedigrees. On the whole, however, Americans have been more practical than ideological concerning the use of government to deal with economic problems.

A good notion of the extent and variety of economic activities engaged in by the national government can be gained from a perusal of the *Budget of the United States Government* or *The United States Government Manual*. Although all represent responses to needs, demands, or interests of one sort or another, no one would assert that all are fundamental. How then does one differentiate between those sets of activities (or policies and programs) that are fundamental and those that are merely useful or convenient, or that serve the interests of particular groups? There is no easy method, no clever formula for solving this riddle. Ideological responses lack persuasiveness for nonbelievers.

In recent years economists and others have frequently relied on the theory of market failure found in welfare economics to determine when government intervention is appropriate. A perfectly functioning market provides for the efficient allocation of goods and services. However, the theory holds, markets in actuality may "fail" for various reasons—information disparities, externalities, public goods, natural monopolies, competitive failures. In such instances government intervention (regulation, production of goods, provision of information, etc.) is necessary to correct these failures. For example, public utility services can be most efficiently provided by permitting a single company to serve a given area. This "natural" monopoly can be controlled either by taking it into government ownership or by government regulation if it is left in private hands.

Although the theory of market failure is not without utility as an analytical technique, it has a number of limitations. First, many market failures, as specified in the theory, will exist in a modern economy, ranging from the severe to the trivial. The theory does not indicate at what point government action is justified. Second, the theory depoliticizes economic problems by treating them as technical failures. Information disparities, as between lenders and borrowers on true rates of interest and loan costs, are important because of their distributional and other consequences. Strong political struggles may develop among groups that may vary greatly in political power and resources, as to whether government action is required and the form it should take. Third, the theory assumes that efficiency is the only value that should guide government intervention. Other important values—equity, equality of opportunity, democratic accountability, freedom— are neglected. Fourth, the theory of market failure does little to explain why the present set of government policies was adopted. Historically, most public problems that have led to government public policies were not identified, debated, and acted on as market failures. Here the theory is at best a rationale rather than an explanation. In sum, the theory of market failure is too narrowly focused and incomplete to be of much help in specifying the fundamental aspects of government's economic role. Nor is it as "objective" and precise as its proponents contend.

How then does one handle this task? First of all, what is fundamental about government's economic role depends on context—time, place, and circumstance. Thus, the fundamental role of government could be more narrowly described in Adam Smith's time for a society characterized by a small-scale economy and predominantly individual-to-individual economic relationships. In a modern society like the United States with its complex industrial economy, widespread group activity, and interdependence in economic relationships, a larger role for government may be required. This seems commonplace. A closer look at American society will be helpful.

In the United States, both democratic government and a largely capitalist (or private enterprise) economy are firmly in place as integral parts of society. People want and expect government to be responsive to their needs and interests; simultaneously, they want the economy to provide opportunity and economic well-being. Both government and economy in operation are expected to be consonant with such widely shared values—for example, freedom and equality. As society and economy have changed over time, so have the definition of such values. Whereas in the nineteenth century freedom was viewed as the absence of governmental restraint, now it is much more likely to be viewed in terms of "the absence of obstacles to the realization of desires." If on the one hand government can restrain, on the other it can act to liberate, to protect people from economic or social restraints on their freedom. In its actions government often confronts the difficult task of satisfactorily balancing the rights (or freedom) of groups and individuals. It is in this sort of context, only rudimentarily sketched, that one must search for the fundamental economic role of government.

Government has to be viewed as an important means which people can call on to solve problems and meet needs ranging from the profound to the trivial. Governments have been both responsive and creative, as illustrated by the myriad economic policies of the national government referred to earlier. On the basis of a consideration of these policies within the American context, together with some reflection and exercise of judgment, we can identify seven "basic" tasks (or purposes) that collectively comprise the national government's fundamental economic role. (All of them, with the exception of the maintenance of competition, seem generally applicable to other modern nations.) The discussion will indicate generally why they are considered basic and what they involve. Their reach is flexible, subject to changing conditions and demands, and the play of political forces.

Providing Economic Infrastructure. Markets are not natural phenomena; rather, they depend on government for their very existence. The national and state governments in the United States provide the basic institutions, rules, and arrangements necessary for the satisfactory operation of a modern, capitalist economic system. These include the definition and protection of property rights, the enforcement of contracts, the provision of a standard currency, the establishment of uniform weights and measures, the issuance of corporate charters, and the creation of bankruptcy procedures (for those who have exercised, for whatever reasons, their "freedom to fail"). Such matters are so accepted, so much an ordinary part of the environment, notwithstanding their importance, as to make their listing seem commonplace. It also seems appropriate to include here protection of the domestic market by the protective tariff because of its two centuries of existence (although theoretical free traders, among others, will balk) and the encouragement of innovation through the granting of patents and copyrights. Finally, the maintenance of law and order must be noted.

Provision of Various Collective Goods and Services. Included here are such items as national defense, roads and bridges, aids to navigation (the fabled lighthouse and much more), flood control facilities, sewage disposal facilities, and traffic control systems. Many are characterized by their broad use, indivisibility, and nonexcludability. Such goods and services are essential for the well-being of a modern society and its economic system. Conceivably, some of them could be provided by private enterprise or offered by government on a fee-for-use basis. Others by preference have become standard governmental duties. Occasionally they are, as in the instance of toll roads. However, it would be exceedingly cumbersome and inefficient to try to operate an extensive highway system on a toll basis. Adam Smith viewed the provision of such facilities as a basic task of government.

The national government also maintains a variety of informational and advisory services for businesses and farmers. It also develops commodity and product standards that are sometimes voluntary, sometimes mandatory. Such standards should not be regarded as a fundamental task for government. Although they are useful and may contribute to predictability and efficiency in the operation of the economy, they seem less than indispensable. Others may disagree. This example illustrates that how a basic task is handled is somewhat discretionary in nature.

The Resolution and Adjustment of Group Conflicts. A basic reason for the existence of government is the need to resolve or ameliorate conflict in a society in pursuance of justice, order, and stability. Economic activity is a major source of conflict; as an economy becomes more complex, people become more interdependent at the same time that their interests become more numerous and distinct. Conflict increases and becomes more disruptive because economic relationships are likely to be group relationships. Thus, disagreements develop between labor and management, creditors and debtors, retailers and manufacturers, commercial and sport fishermen, craft and industrial unions, railroads and shippers. Government may act to regulate group relationships, to arbitrate differences, or to equalize group power. Judges handled much of the task of conflict resolution under the common law in the nineteenth century, under such categories as torts, nuisances, and master–servant relations. Subsequently, legislatures and administrative agencies became ever more involved through the adoption of laws and regulations.

This task may also include actions to protect the economically weak against the economically strong. According to Professor George Steiner, this protection "has always been a function of government in the American code of political morality" (Steiner, 1953, p. 136). Government may seek to replace exploitation with equity through child labor laws, minimum wage legislation, or worker compensation programs.

The Maintenance of Competition. Americans strongly support competition in the abstract and for others, if not always for themselves. Competition, which is a crucial component of a capitalist economic system, is also an alternative to government regulation as a form of social control of business. Competition does not always maintain itself, however. Unlimited competition may result in the destruction of competition, or competitors through merger or collusion may cease to compete. Consequently, for nearly a century the national government has used antitrust policy, with varying vigor and effectiveness, to help maintain competition. Although there is broad if not total agreement on the need for antitrust, there is some debate as to the form and focus it should take. Thus, the Reagan Administration acted vigorously against collusive behavior (price fixing and bid rigging, especially) while going easy on corporate mergers, to the distress of some of the administration's critics.

Protection of Natural Resources. History has demonstrated that competitive forces cannot be relied on adequately to prevent the wasteful use of natural resources, to protect against degradation of the natural environment (air, water, scenic vistas, etc.), or to care for the interests of future generations. The problem of the commons is endemic here. For instance, in the absence of government action many more species of wildlife would likely have gone the way of the passenger pigeon. Since the late nineteenth century, resource protection has been a major national concern.

Initially, the focus was on conservation, on the wise use of natural resources which, in effect, were viewed as commodities. Land, water, forests, and minerals were to be carefully developed, managed, and productively used. In the post–World War II era, an environmental movement has emerged that is concerned with protecting the environment against degradation by air and water pollution, by hazardous and solid waste disposal, and other misuse. Viewing the environment as a natural and human habitat to be protected rather than as a series of commodities to be exploited, environmentalists have sometimes come into conflict with conservationists, as over the use of the national forests. Both may come into conflict with various producer interests over the use of natural resources and the environment.

Provision for Minimum Access by Individuals to the Goods and Services of the Economy. The operation of the market sometimes produces results that are cruel or socially unacceptable—poverty, unemployment, malnutrition—in their impact on people. Others, because of illness, old age, illiteracy, or whatever, may simply exist outside the market economy. Few would now agree with the nineteenth-century sociologist and adherent of "the survival of the fittest," William Graham Sumner, when he proclaimed that "Root, hog, or die" was the appropriate social philosophy (Hofstadter, 1955, p. 54). Since the early 1930s, the national and state governments have developed a variety of economic social welfare programs—social security, unemployment compensation, supplementary security income, aid to families with dependent children, housing assistance, food stamps, medical care programs, and so on. Controversy continues over such matters as their necessity, scope, cost, and adequacy. Support is stronger for those that benefit the middle class than for those that serve mostly the poor.

Stabilization of the Economy. Capitalist economic systems have always been characterized by fluctuations in the business cycle, by periods of boom and bust. Distressful in an agrarian society, these fluctuations are much worse for a modern industrial society in which individuals are interdependent and non-self-sufficient. No longer could a president acceptably say, as Warren Harding did to a conference on unemployment in 1921: "There has been vast unemployment before and there will be again. There will be depression and inflation just as surely as the tides ebb and flow. I would have little enthusiasm for any proposed remedy which seek a palliation or tonic from the Public Treasury" (Gordon, 1974, p. 22). None was forthcoming. No longer is it believed that the economy is governed by natural economic laws. Since 1946, the national government has been committed by legislation (the Employment Act) and usually also by inclination to act positively to combat inflation and recession. What form the action takes in a particular instance—fiscal policy, monetary policy, monetarism, wage and price controls—its timing and its extent, are open to choice. The public expects the government, notably the president, to act and to act effectively. This has become another basic task of government.

In the last decade and a half much debate and controversy have arisen concerning the role of government in the economy. Always, of course, there has been controversy over particular policies, actual or proposed, and ideological proclamations concerning what governments should do or not do. Two recent efforts to reduce the scope of government action have been somewhat more systematic and broadly focused in form. These are, first, the deregulation movement overlapping the Ford, Carter, and Reagan administrations and, second, the Reagan Administration's attempt (based on conservative ideology) to reduce both the number of domestic and social welfare programs and spending on them. Together, these can be used as a crude empirical test of the "basic" nature of the tasks sketched in this chapter.

The deregulation movement had considerable legislative success, especially during the Carter Administration. Deregulatory legislation almost eliminated economic regulation of commercial airlines (mergers still require approval) and reduced the regulation of railroads, motor carriers, depository institutions, and intercity buses. Other actions have been taken administratively, especially during the Reagan years, to lessen social regulatory activity. Success here was limited by political opposition to some of the administration initiatives. The Reagan Administration's fiscal retrenchment effort bore small fruit; the rate of growth in government spending was slowed, and spending for some social welfare programs, notably for the poor, was reduced. No major programs were eliminated, with the exception of revenue sharing with local governments.

In conclusion, the major contours of government's economic role, as defined by the seven basic tasks, are much the same today as they were in the mid-1970s. Some alteration has taken place in the ways in which some of the tasks are handled or in their scope, which are not unimportant. The basic tasks remain obligations of government in the United States. Their persistence over time, and the broad political support or acceptance that exists for them, are further indication of their basic nature.

REFERENCES

Alt, James E., and K. Alec Chrystal. *Political Economics*. Berkeley: University of California Press, 1983.

Bator, Francis. "The Anatomy of Market Failure." *Quarterly Journal of Economics* 22 (August 1958): 351–79.

Clark, John Maurice. *Social Control of Business*. New York: McGraw-Hill, 1939.

Freidman, Milton and Rose Freidman. *Free to Choose*. New York: Harcourt, Brace Jovanovich, 1980.

Gordon, Robert Aaron. *Economic Stability and Growth: The American Record*. New York: Harper & Row, 1974.

Hofstadter, Richard. *Social Darwinism in American Thought*. Boston: Beacon Press, 1955.

Hughes, Jonathan R. T. *The Governmental Habit*. New York: Basic Books, 1977.

Nelson, Richard R. "Roles of Government in a Mixed Economy." *Journal of Policy Analysis and Management* 6 (1987): 541–57.

Reagan, Michael D. *The Managed Economy*. New York: Oxford University Press, 1963.

Redford, Emmette S. *American Government and the Economy*. New York: Macmillan, 1965.

Steiner, George A. *Government's Role in Economic Life*. New York: McGraw-Hill, 1953.

Williams, Robin M., Jr. *American Society*. New York: Alfred A. Knopf, 1961.

4

The Role of Government in a Market Economy

Robin W. Boadway

THE ECONOMIC OBJECTIVES OF GOVERNMENT

Government is the collective authority of its citizens. The liberal view of government, which is that to which most economists seem to subscribe, holds that the ultimate economic objective of government is to improve the economic well-being of individuals in society; that is, individuals alone matter, and not any corporate bodies per se. More than that, an individual's economic well-being, or *utility* as it is called, is something that is best gauged by the individual involved. Individuals know best what will make them better off and worse off. This individualism implies that, wherever possible, decisions affecting individuals ought to be decentralized to the individuals themselves. In those situations in which collective action is involved, the preferences of the citizens should be paramount.

The precept that individual preferences alone should "count" leads to one of the great organizing principles of modern welfare economics and is at the heart of much policy discussion. This is the so-called Pareto principle, which economists take to be second nature, so much so that its limitations are often not recognized. The principle is very seductive. It says simply that if some persons are made better off as a result of an economic change and none are made worse off, society benefits. The Pareto principle is taken to be almost self-evident by economists who accept the paramouncy of individual preferences, but it is presumably more controversial if applied to spheres of action other than economic. For example, it could be taken to conflict with notions of fairness or equal treatment advocated as principles of law.

The Pareto principle ultimately accounts for a surprisingly large proportion of economic policy justifications. In particular, it accounts for those policy prescriptions that fall under the broad heading of *efficiency* in the economic sense. One way to view government policy is as a way of facilitating those "gains from trade" among individuals which markets, for whatever reason, have been unable fully to exploit. This constitutes the so-called market failure view of government, which is discussed further later in this chapter. According to this argument, if there are unexploited gains from trade, it ought to be possible to exploit them in a Pareto-improving way. If so, economic efficiency will have improved. The argument is taken a step further by allowing economic efficiency to encompass not just actual Pareto improvements, but also potential Pareto improvements. These are changes in which some persons gain and others lose, but in which there are overall net gains in the sense that the gainers hypothetically could compensate the losers and still be better off. This principle has been relied on to justify the universal practice of measuring the gains and losses from economic changes simply in dollar terms regardless of to whom the gains and losses accrue. There is an extensive, and largely inconclusive, literature on the use of the compensation principle as a device for gauging economic efficiency. It is philosophically unsatisfactory as a basis for simply aggregating dollar gains and losses because if the compensation is not actually paid, the change being evaluated will not actually be a Pareto improvement. It is also operationally unsatisfactory because conventional ways of measuring gains and losses have been shown not to coincide with the ability of gainers to compensate losers. Nonetheless, economists rely on monetary measures of gains and losses to judge economic efficiency, despite its highly unsatisfactory basis.

Unfortunately, efficiency alone cannot be the sole arbiter of government policy for two fundamental reasons. The first is that, even when efficiency gains are possible, the process of exploiting them almost inevitably leads to some persons being made better off and others worse off. Only an unreasonable set of compensating transfers could ensure that all policies are Pareto-improving. The second is that, even if all gains from trade could be exploited so that society was operating with economic efficiency, this would not constitute a sufficient criterion for choosing among economic policies. The reason is that there are a large number of economically efficient allocations of resources, each of which differs from another by the distribution of individual utilities. Choosing among them inevitably involves interpersonal comparisons.

Economists who view themselves collectively as objective scientists cannot easily contemplate interpersonal utility comparisons. But the practice of economic policy would not get very far if one were not prepared to vest the making of interpersonal judgments in policymakers. What economists can offer is a framework for making such decisions, including identifying the ultimate gainers and losers as well as the constraints and efficiency of achieving various outcomes. One can discern three different approaches to interpersonal welfare comparisons in the literature (over and above simply treating a dollar as a dollar), each of which accepts the basic liberal individualistic assumption about the paramouncy of individual preferences.

The first approach uses the formal tool of a *social welfare function* developed in the 1930s by Abram Bergson and popularized in the works of Paul Samuelson.

Society's well-being can be considered to be an aggregate of individual utilities, the aggregator being the social welfare function. Unfortunately, the use of a social welfare function involves much more information than does the application of the Pareto principle. In one of the more devastating insights of modern welfare economics, Kenneth Arrow showed that if the only information we allow ourselves is the preference orderings of individual households (which is sufficient to apply the Pareto principle), it will not be a sufficient basis for a social welfare function that satisfies reasonable properties. Either we must restrict the permissible preferences of individuals, which would be inconsistent with individualism; or we must loosen the restrictions on the properties that the social welfare function must satisfy, which is also unattractive; or we must allow more information about individual utility functions. This last alternative, which is the more reasonable, is accomplished by imposing some assumptions about measurability and comparability on utility functions. It has been shown, for example, that imposing some minimal requirements on the measurability and comparability of utility functions allows us to obtain classical utilitarianism as the social welfare function. Accordingly, utility functions must be measurable in a cardinal fashion, and changes in utility must be comparable among individuals. This seems to be a fairly minimal form of interpersonal comparability and one that can be technically implemented with well-developed money metric measures of utility, such as the expenditure function suitably adjusted for family circumstances. Of course, it can be no more than a framework, because some judgment must be made about measuring utility. The framework is a feasible one to use, however, and readily admits of sensitivity analysis concerning different views about interpersonal equity comparisons. It has also been widely used in the context of welfare measurement in less developed countries. The fundamental political problem is how to obtain a consensus on the actual form of the social welfare function to be used. In the case of utilitarianism, this problem boils down to how rapidly utility diminishes as the money metric indicator increases.

A second approach to interpersonal welfare comparisons is the *property rights approach*. It substantially reduces the necessity for interpersonal welfare comparisons by making existing property rights sacrosanct. According to this view, taxation is treated as equivalent to the confiscation of property which is to be condoned only to the extent that it is agreed to voluntarily. The role of decentralization of economic decisions to individuals is emphasized. Indeed, in the extreme form of the property rights approach, the government would be restricted to Pareto-improving policies. This does not rule out redistributive transfers entirely, but it restricts them to those that can be justified by altruism on behalf of the donor groups. Even the property rights approach cannot completely dispense with interpersonal welfare comparisons. Such comparisons must be made at least implicitly when distributing the surplus (gains from trade) of collective action per se. Obviously, the property rights approach leads to a much more restrictive view of government than does the social welfare function approach since it limits the government to be essentially a device for improving the efficiency of the economy. The "equity" role of government is ruled out by making existing property rights inviolable.

A third approach offers something of a reconciliation of the social welfare function approach with the property rights approach by attempting to devise a method whereby equity judgments are made on the basis of individual choice. This is the social contract or the *contractarian approach* to collective choice. This approach could be used to account for much of the redistributive role of government as well as the growing role of government as "insurer," as discussed later in this chapter. According to this approach, we are invited to evaluate policies by placing ourselves "behind the veil of ignorance", that is, by imagining ourselves not to know our place in society relative to others. It is as if we are to assume we have an equal chance of being in anyone else's circumstances. The purpose of this hypothetical procedure is to take collective decisions from a perfectly objective point of view, without taking personal circumstances into account. Collective preferences are still guided by self-interest, however, since preferences over different social choices are such as to maximize their expected utility.

Given the aversion to risk which people are assumed to have, this approach can be used to give a philosophical justification to some form of utilitarianism. Operationally, it can be used to give precedence to government's role as a provider of "social insurance." The term *social insurance* is used to capture redistributive transfers made among individuals according to characteristics that are beyond their control (i.e., are not revealed behind the veil of ignorance). Such characteristics could include endowed ability, natural state of health, as well as "demographic draw." For example, some people are lucky enough to be born with a high IQ and good health, in a time of peace and high productivity, and to be part of a relatively small population of the same age. Social insurance, then, could be viewed as providing interpersonal redistributive transfers, some assistance for health expenditures, and transfers across generations to smooth out fluctuations of opportunities by cohort. A great deal of government activity could be viewed as falling under this rubric.

Whatever view one takes of the ultimate objective of government, at the heart of actual policy decision is the tradeoff between equity and efficiency. Attempts to redistribute utility from one group of persons to another inevitably induce adverse incentive effects that detract from economic efficiency. Where one prefers to be along this tradeoff depends jointly on the value one puts on interpersonal equity (which is a matter for value judgment) and the empirical extent to which redistributive transfers actually do induce inefficiencies. Some observers argue that the difference between left and right political views hinges not so much on different underlying value judgments about redistributive equity as on different degrees of recognition of the importance of the constraints on redistribution. That is, the right is more aware of the efficiency costs of such transfers than is the left. In principle economic analysis should be able to sort out the magnitude of the equity-efficiency tradeoff. Thus far, it has not yet been able to do so.

Whatever philosophical view one embraces, government can be seen to have essentially two roles: by means of collective action, to exploit the gains from trade and increase the efficiency of the economy; and to improve equity. The persistence with which government should pursue one goal as opposed to the other, the two roles being to some some extent conflicting, is a value judgment on which reasonable persons may disagree. Given these overriding objectives for government, let us turn to what they mean in practice.

THE ROLE OF GOVERNMENT IN THE ECONOMY: THE MARKET FAILURE APPROACH

The conventional argument for the economic role of government consists in identifying ways in which the free market fails to achieve socially desirable outcomes and in viewing this failure as a prima facie case for government intervention. Traditionally, four classes of market failures have been identified: public goods and externalities; noncompetitive markets; unemployed resources; and equity.

Public Goods and Externalities

Commodities that yield benefits to several individuals simultaneously are difficult to allocate through the market. In their purest form, individuals cannot be excluded from enjoying their benefits, so the price mechanism cannot be used to ration their use. Even if exclusion were possible, it would not be desirable because it is typically not costly to admit more users. Thus, public provision with no user cost to the consumer is appropriate. In addition, the phenomenon of publicness can apply in lesser degrees to a wide variety of situations. If the use of a resource or commodity unintentionally benefits (or unintentionally harms) a third party, the resource will not be allocated efficiently and government intervention may be helpful. Depending on the strength of the external effect, the remedy may take a wide range of policies. In the extreme, it could involve public provision. For less emphatic external effects, it could take the form of corrective subsidization (or taxation), or direct regulation. If only a small number of parties are involved, resort to damage claims in the courts may be used.

Whatever the remedy, two fundamental problems are involved in determining what amount of government intervention is appropriate. The first is that, by their very nature, the benefits (or costs) of external effects cannot be measured and are not revealed on markets. This absence of information means that judgment is inevitable, and different persons may come to different judgments about the quantitative importance of a particular sort of external effect. Thus, the appropriate role of government in providing education, encouraging research and development, correcting pollution, and so on, is a matter of judgment on which well-informed persons can disagree. The second problem is that the process of correcting for external effects induces its own inefficiencies. For example, the raising of revenues to finance public goods introduces tax distortions in markets. The size of these inefficiencies has come under increasing scrutiny and is now thought to be larger than was previously assumed.

Noncompetitive Markets

Markets can be efficient only if they are competitive. If either the buying or the selling side of the market is dominated by one or a few participants, some monopoly power will ensue which may be inefficient. Governments have responded to this problem in a variety of ways. In the United States, the tendency has been to regulate the pricing policies of those firms that are prone to be natural monopolies, as well as to enforce through general laws a prohibition of noncompetitive practices by any firm. Outside the Untied States, natural monopolies are more often operated as state-owned firms. The enforcement of competition through government regulation, nationalization, and decree has received less favor in recent years for a number of reasons. For one, the globalization of markets has reduced the capacity of firms to achieve monopoly power. For another, market power is seen as having a beneficial side to it in the form of greater potential to innovate and grow in the Schumpeterian fashion. Finally, the absence of economic incentives within the public sector has been viewed as detracting from the efficiency of public intervention in this and other areas.

Unemployed Resources

The existence of unemployed labor or capital may also reflect a failure of markets which can be offset by government action, though even here there is some dispute about government's role. Subsequent to the Keynesian revolution, government was assumed to be the manager of aggregate demand in the economy. Fiscal and monetary policies were viewed as tools to be used to maintain the level of aggregate demand that would ensure as high a level of employment as was compatible with relative price stability. Recently, it has been recognized that unemployed resources reflect more than simply deficient demand. They also reflect structural changes and supply-side changes to which the economy takes time to adjust. Some have even argued that much observed unemployment was not involuntary but was equilibrating. In these circumstances, the role of aggregate demand management is reduced and the role of government should be more directed to ensuring that labor markets are as flexible and adjustable as possible.

Equity

The previous three rationales for government all involve primarily efficiency considerations. As discussed earlier in this chapter, the other arm of government intervention involves redistributive equity. Governments use a combination of tax-transfer policies and universal public services to assist less affluent persons. The vigor with which the government pursues these issues depends jointly on the weight one puts on redistributive equity in the value system and on the ability to pursue redistributive policies without foregoing economic output. The former depends purely on value judgments, whereas the latter ought to be a matter of verifiable fact. Although economists are far from settling the precise extent to which redistributive measures are constrained by the economy's adverse reactions to them, a growing body of literature suggests that income redistribution is not as cost effective as was previously thought. Given the level of marginal tax rates that exist in most countries, additional increments of revenue are very costly to raise in efficiency terms both because of the large marginal distortion imposed on taxpayers and because of the increasing ability to evade or avoid taxes on both labor and capital income. In addition, personal taxes may not be a very effective tool for redistributing welfare, partly because of incentive effects and partly because annual income is a very poor indicator of lifetime welfare. Redistribution in kind through such variables as education, health, and various measures of social insurance may be much more effective redistributive devices.

RECENT REFINEMENTS IN THE MARKET FAILURE APPROACH

As implied by the above discussion, there has been a growing agnosticism among academic economists about the ability of the government to succeed where the market has failed. Thus, we may talk about "public sector failure" as well as market failure. Much of this public sector failure stems from a simple lack of incentives in government and from a growing recognition of the role that constraints play in tempering the government's ability to achieve the ideal social allocation of resources. It is this recognition of constraints rather than a fundamental change in ethical thinking that has led to a tendency to place less reliance on government, though the property rights approach has made some inroads. At the same time, public sector economics has made some significant advances which have implications for government.

The first of these advances is the recognition of the role of uncertainty and information, particularly imperfect information. Uncertainty and asymmetric information are features of most markets. Furthermore, they plague the public sector as much as the private sector, if not more. The recognition that the public sector is not likely to be better informed than the market tends to reduce the role for the public sector.

At the same time, uncertainty is at the basis of what is perhaps the one growth area of government, social insurance. It could be argued that social insurance motives should account for a sizable proportion of government activity, especially that related to redistributive policy. The role of government as provider of social insurance follows directly from the contractarian view of government and can be viewed as the basis of such diverse policies as health insurance, education, welfare, unemployment insurance, and pensions, all of which involve a significant redistributive component.

5

Economic Systems, Government, and Group Interests

Tom Bottomore

The economic role of government has been very diversely conceived and has varied enormously in practice, both historically and between countries. This role has been greatly extended during the twentieth century, in two different ways. First, in socialist countries, beginning in the Soviet Union in 1917, a large part of the economy is publicly owned and in greater or lesser degree centrally planned by government agencies. Second, in capitalist countries since the end of the nineteenth century, but especially since the end of the Second World War, governments have intervened in the economy to provide a much greater range of public services (as is also done, of course, in the socialist countries). This intervention is reflected in the increasing proportion of gross domestic product (GDP) now spent by government. (In Britain, for example, government expenditure as a proportion of GDP increased from about 10 percent before the First World War to just over 20 percent in the 1930s and to 50 percent in the mid–1970s. Although it has declined again during the past decade to about 42 percent as a result of re-privatization and the curtailment of public spending, it remains historically high. The trend in other capitalist countries is broadly similar.) At the same time, many of these countries, especially in Europe, moved toward a "mixed economy" (public and private) as a result of the postwar nationalization of some basic industries and services.

These developments have been interpreted in various ways. A broadly Marxist view (but one also taken by some non-Marxists) conceives them as the manifestation of a general trend toward socialism. Marx himself (*Capital*, Vol. 3, Ch. 27), discussing the emergence and growth of joint-stock companies, wrote of the gradual "socialization" of the economy, and of "the abolition of the capitalist mode of production within capitalist production itself . . . a phase of transition to a new form of production." Rudolf Hilferding (1910) developed this idea further in his analysis of "finance capital" and the modern corporation, and subsequently of "organized capitalism" as a "planned and consciously directed economy'' (1927). It also played a fundamental part in the non-Marxist interpretation of the ''decline of capitalism'' by Joseph A. Schumpeter (influenced, however, by the work of the Austro-Marxist school in which Hilferding was a prominent figure), who likewise argued that ''the economic process tends to socialize *itself*'' (Schumpeter, 1942, p. 219; see also Bottomore, 1985, pp. 66–68).

Schumpeter went on to suggest that the ''march into socialism . . . the migration of people's economic affairs from the private into the public sphere'' (1942, p. 421) might come to a halt at some halfway house, under the influence of various countervailing forces. It appeared to some social thinkers that this situation had in fact been reached during the 1960s, at least in the Western European countries where the ''mixed economy'' and the ''welfare state'' came to be regarded as constituting a new, relatively stable, and durable type of economy and society. In Japan, on the other hand, a different form of active government intervention in the economy has become established in a distinctive cultural context that is characterized by a strong group loyalties and paternalism (Dore, 1987). In contrast, in North America there has been little development of a mixed economy and a much slower, less comprehensive development of a welfare state. Moreover, during the past decade, there has been a notable change in the economic climate and economic policies in Western Europe, with an increasing emphasis on the virtue of free markets and the so-called enterprise economy. This has meant in practice the decline of the mixed economy through the reprivatization of nationalized industries, and the setting of limits to the welfare state by restrictions on public spending. The emergence of this new process of ''desocialization,'' which initially involves massive government intervention, will be considered more fully later in this chapter.

In the socialist countries a different process of change, involving modifications and restrictions of the scope of central planning, has been taking place during the past four decades. It began in Yugoslavia in 1950 following the break with Stalinism; there it has developed into a complex system of workers' self-management and regulated markets (Broekmeyer, 1970; Horvat, 1982). A further stage was marked by the introduction of the carefully prepared ''new economic mechanism'' in 1968 in Hungary, which decentralized economic decision making within the framework of a general plan. Hungary freed enterprises from central control and created conditions in which they would respond to market indicators, especially the price system, with respect to labor and investment as well as consumer goods (Hare, Radice, and Swain, 1981). The Hungarian reforms went beyond anything that had been attempted elsewhere in Eastern Europe at that time. They were followed by the restructuring of the Chinese economy, which drew on the Yugoslav and Hungarian experience, and more recently still by the implementation of a program of radical economic reform in the Soviet Union.

The changes that have been taking place in the socialist economies have become increasingly radical and wide-ranging during the past decade. They have occasionally been interpreted as some kind of ''restoration of capitalism'' in these countries, but this seems to be an erroneous view. The crucial factor is that the major productive resources of society continue to be publicly owned. In Schumpeter's phrase "people's economic affairs" are still firmly located in "the public sphere." What the changes involve is far more a recognition, at a new stage of economic development, of the diverse possible forms of social ownership, the value within this general economic system of various types of private production by individuals and small groups (which may be cooperatives), and the advantages of markets and a price system as regulators of production in what is now frequently referred to as a socialist market economy, compared with comprehensive and detailed central planning.

Undoubtedly, the current reforms in the socialist countries tend to diminish the role of central government (and to some extent the role of regional or local government) in the economy. In particular, they reduce the power of direct and detailed intervention by officials in the planning institutions. Nevertheless, five-year and annual plans still constitute the framework of the economic system. The problems of thus combining planning with the market and developing appropriate macroeconomic institutions in a socialist society have been interestingly discussed by Branko Horvat (1982, pp. 328–67). The process of decentralizing economic decision making by creating markets and introducing forms of self-management has not been easy, and in recent years some of the socialist countries have begun to experience serious problems of inflation, unemployment, and a slowing down of economic growth. It must be added, however, that these problems stem partly from their involvement in the world economy through foreign trade and loans, in conditions of general economic recession, and it does not seem probable that the maintenance of a rigid central planning system would have produced better results.

This preliminary discussion indicates two main areas of interest and controversy in considering the economic role of government. First, we have to distinguish the different levels at which the actions of government affect economic life. In all modern societies it has become a major function of government to provide, maintain, develop or regulate the infrastructure of economic activity. This infrastructure includes not only the physical means of communication and a national system of education and training, but also the framework of rational, "calculable law"—regarded by Max Weber (1923, pp. 208–209) as one of the presuppositions of modern capitalism—which makes possible an orderly and sustained production and exchange of goods and services.

Beyond this level, governments intervene actively and extensively in the economy through monetary and fiscal policies designed to manage demand, control inflation, encourage investment, stimulate economic growth, and so on. During much of the postwar period, it was also a major objective of governments to maintain a high level of employment, for both economic and social reasons. In the past decade, this goal has ceased to be such an important cornerstone of policy in many of the capitalist countries and in Western Europe particularly mass unemployment has reemerged. Fiscal policies also affect the distribution of wealth and income between social groups. In the past decade, following a period of modest reductions in inequality, there has again been increasing inequality, at least in Britain (Stark, 1987) which is directly related to government policy.

At still another level, government policies are concerned with national economic interests as they are perceived at a particular time or by a particular government. Hence, there is more or less continuous intervention to influence or regulate foreign trade and the balance of payments, exchange rates, and interest rates, and to restrict or exclude foreign investment in areas of economic activity that are regarded as being of crucial national importance. In the modern world, however, supranational institutions have their own interventionist policies, a notable example being the European Economic Commission (EEC). This organization spends a major part of its budget to maintain, for various reasons, an artificially high level of agricultural production, though it also supports, on a smaller scale, diverse economic projects in the less developed regions of Western Europe, and in a relatively minor way, educational and cultural development. There is also intervention at the international level by the Group of Seven (the seven leading capitalist countries), which acts to maintain, as far as possible, stable exchange rates (or controlled variations) and to regulate international trade and the balance of payments in the capitalist part of the world.

The counterpart of the EEC in Eastern Europe is the Council for Mutual Economic Assistance (CMEA or Comecon), which has moved toward closer integration of the national economies through the coordination of national plans and the development of an "international socialist division of labour." In the early postwar period the main emphasis was still on industrialization, but increasing attention was later given to the supply of consumer goods and the development of markets. The creation of three specialist committees in the 1970s (for collaboration in planning activity, scientific and technical collaboration, and collaboration in material and technical supply) was intended to promote further integration and modernization of the socialist economies (Brus, in M. C. Kaser, 1986; pp. 231–45).

Finally, governments may intervene in a much more radical way to change the whole economic structure. This kind of intervention occurred in the immediate postwar period when basic industries in some capitalist countries were nationalized and the welfare state began to be constructed. Yet more recently, particularly in Britain, enterprises have been reprivatized and welfare services cut back, whereas in the Soviet Union and other socialist countries a large-scale program of restructuring the economy is underway. It is in this context that we have to consider a second, most important aspect of the economic role of government—namely, its relation to the interests of specific social groups, especially classes.

Government, and the state apparatus as a whole, which includes the higher levels of administration and the judiciary, cannot be regarded simply as a disinterested element in society, concerned only with solving technical problems in a value-neutral way. On the contrary, every modern government is the creation of a political party or coalition of parties (or sometimes of a military faction), which has a more or less definite economic and social policy, and is supported by particular interests. In Western Europe since the early nineteenth century these interests have been class interests, opposing workers to the owners of capital. The present-day socialist societies in Eastern Europe and elsewhere are themselves the product of class politics. The United States, where class interests have never been as clearly defined or as salient in political life, for reasons that have often been debated (Sombart, 1906; Laslett and Lipset, 1984), has not had class-based politics to the same extent. The differences between the United States' two major parties, however, are similar in some respects to those between "left" and "right" in Europe.

The class orientations of governments in Western Europe are evident in the differences of economic and social policy between countries and between historical periods. For example, in Sweden, social democratic governments have been in power for a long time, whereas Britain during the past nine years has had Conservative government. It may be that over the whole postwar period the political awareness, and hence the significance, of class interests has diminished (more, certainly, among the working class than in the capitalist class), as a consequence of rapid economic growth and full employment. Finally, in the 1970s, Western Europe experienced rising levels of living, the growth of service occupations and the middle classes, and the expansion of social services, itself largely brought about by the actions of social democratic governments and the more general influence of left-wing parties. Nevertheless, in all the capitalist countries—and nowhere more than in present-day Britain—the class character of politics and of government policies is still very evident.

It would be excessively simple, and indeed quite misleading, to consider the economic role of government only from a very general and unhistorical standpoint. To be sure, as noted earlier, governments have to perform some universal functions in modern industrial societies (some of which were also carried out in earlier types of society). Notably, they have to ensure an adequate infrastructure, demand management, encouragement of research and development as part of the investment in new technology, defense of what are seen as vital national, or regional, economic interests, and in recent years especially, the protection of the environment. The growing interdependence of national economies has led to a considerable increase in supranational regulation on an intergovernmental basis, not only on a regional level, but on a still wider scale in the relations between the industrialized countries in the Third World.

The extent and nature of the governmental role in the economy differs greatly between countries, depending on the political complexion of the government in power (and the duration and stability of its rule), and on historical cultural traditions that may favor a more active role for the state (as in Japan or in France) or on the contrary may tend to restrict it (as has generally been the case in the United States). The most significant difference, however, is undoubtedly that

between the two major economic systems—capitalist and socialist—which co-
exist in the world today. (We will leave aside here the special case of Third
World countries, which are themselves to some extent divided between capitalist
and socialist models.) In these two systems, beyond the basic functions which
governments can be seen to perform in all the industrialized societies, there are
very different levels and modes of government involvement in the economy. On
one side, we have a general regulation of predominantly market economies in
which the bulk of productive enterprises are privately owned; on the other, we
have comprehensive national planning of economies in which most enterprises
are publicly owned and markets play a smaller part.

Both systems, however, have undergone important changes in the postwar
period. Perhaps the most interesting question we can now pose about the economic role of government is whether a secular tendency for that role to expand
is still discernible. As mentioned at the beginning of this chapter, the Marxist
view, which was also adopted subsequently by Schumpeter, is that in the industrial societies, the economy tends to socialize itself, and this is a major factor
in the "march into socialism." In the immediate postwar years, this process
seemed to be accelerating, first with the emergence of the new socialist systems
in Eastern Europe and in China (which influenced many Third World countries),
and then with the nationalization of basic industries in many countries in Western
Europe, along with a rapid increase in government expenditure which came to
account for some 50 percent of GDP. Therefore, in the 1940s and 1950s, it
appeared that a conscious process of socialization was well underway in which
socialist economies, and those that were moving toward socialism, were acquiring a much greater weight and importance in the world economy as a whole.
The direction of economic affairs came to be seen increasingly as a matter of
deliberate political choices and of the actions of governments. To a large extent
that remains the case. If the current reforms in the socialist countries are successful in stimulating a renewed burst of economic growth, the importance of
these economies will probably continue to increase and to change further the
balance of influence in the world between planned and market systems.

At the same time, in the capitalist countries the socialization of the economy
has been proceeding in quite a different form with the continued rapid growth
of large corporations, and particularly multinational corporations. This can be
seen as a further stage in the development of an organized economy, but it shows
little sign of leading toward socialism. On the contrary, during the past decade,
the privatization or re-privatization of public enterprises and the severe restrictions imposed on public expenditure have created a situation in which economic
affairs are increasingly returned to the sphere of private capital, and the role of
government is redefined, to some degree at least, in terms of the nineteenth-
century conception of the "nightwatchman state." As Charles Beard (1914, p.
53) put it in describing the changes in American society at the end of the
nineteenth century, the men of affairs and political leaders "believed in the
widest possible extension of the principle of private property, and the narrowest

possible restriction of state interference, except to aid private property to increase its gains.''

In present conditions it would be extremely rash to make any confident predictions about the long-term future development of the role of government in economic life. In the capitalist countries the postwar trend toward greater government involvement in the economy has been arrested, or even reversed. At present there seems to be little enthusiasm among the majority of their populations for any renewed extension of public ownership, though there is much support for a higher level of government spending on the social services. On the other hand, the economic weight of the socialist countries in world affairs seems likely to increase and to produce some changes in social attitudes, though we cannot be sure what the eventual outcome of the current reforms will be. In any event we should remember that social and political attitudes are very prone to change, as a glance back at the 1960s will remind us. It may be that in the next decade, under the influence of cyclical movements in the capitalist economies, which seem now to be in a phase of decline, the appeal of a broadly planned and consciously directed economy will revive and lead to new forms of government intervention.

REFERENCES

Beard, Charles A. *Contemporary American History, 1877–1913*. New York: Macmillan, 1914.

Bottomore, Tom. *Theories of Modern Capitalism*. London: Allen & Unwin, 1985.

Broekmeyer, M. J. (ed.). *Yugoslav Workers' Self-Management*. Dordrecht: D. Reidel, 1970.

Dore, Ronald. *Taking Japan Seriously: A Confucian Perspective on Leading Economic Issues*. London: Athlone Press, 1987.

Hare, Paul, Hugo Radice and Nigel Swain (eds.). *Hungary: A Decade of Economic Reform*. London: Allen & Unwin, 1981.

Hilferding, Rudolf. *Finance Capital*. London: Routledge & Kegan Paul, 1981. (1st ed. 1910.)

Horvat, Branko. *The Political Economy of Socialism*. Oxford: Martin Robertson, 1982.

Kaser, M. C. (ed.). *The Economic History of Eastern Europe 1919–1975*. Vol. 3, *Institutional Change Within a Planned Economy*. Oxford: Clarendon Press, 1986.

Laslett, John H. M., and Seymour Martin Lipset (eds.). *Failure of a Dream?* Rev. ed. Berkeley: University of California Press, 1984.

Schumpeter, Joseph A. *Capitalism, Socialism and Democracy*. 6th ed. London: Allen & Unwin, 1987. (1st ed. 1942.)

Sombart, Werner. *Why Is There No Socialism in the United States?* English trans. with an introductory essay by C. T. Husbands. London: Macmillan, 1976. (1st ed. 1906.)

Stark, Thomas. *Income and Wealth in the 1980s*. London: Fabian Society, 1987.

Weber, Max. *General Economic History*. New York: Collier Books, 1961. (1st ed. 1923.)

6

The Changing Economic Role of Government

Jesse Burkhead

The economic role of government must always be specified in an appropriate historical context. That role most obviously is different in primitive societies of hunters armed with bows and arrows than in technologically advanced nations armed with atomic weaponry.

The historically specified context must therefore include appropriate attention to such concerns as the stage of economic development, the relation of one nation-state to other nation-states, and societal sympathy for the underprivileged, for the promotion of economic growth, for disparities in income, and for a host of other concerns. None of these concerns is unchanging. For example, in one decade the economic role of government may appropriately extend to a "war" on poverty; two decades later the war is abandoned. Those in poverty are neglected, and the number of persons in poverty increases.

Finally, it must be stressed that the economic role of government, in any country, is shaped by custom and traditions. These traditions include religion, language, tribal structure, and ethnicity, and may include attitudes toward centralized versus decentralized administration, or toward unitary versus federal governmental systems. This last consideration is particularly important. Every country (with the exception of Singapore) has some degree of devolution of public authority. This devolution, as in federal systems such as the United States and Brazil, probably brings the allocation of resources closer to the preference patterns of citizens of subnational governments and thus may be more efficient in terms of economic welfare. But whether the public sector is larger or smaller in a federal system in contrast with a more nearly unitary system (England), is by no means clear. However difficult such noneconomic influences are to quantify, they do exist and can be appraised and evaluated, if not by an economist or political scientist, then perhaps by an anthropologist or ethnologist.

Thus, the economic role of government is continuously changing. The perceptions of citizens and their administrative and politically elected leaders with respect to the appropriate division of resources between the public and the private sectors will shift from year to year. The distribution of resources within the public sector and its division between national and subnational governments is likewise subject to continuous alteration.

THE BUDGET

At any one time, the complexities of public resource allocation are reflected in the patterns of expenditure and revenue as set forth in government budgets. These budgets, in turn, are complex creatures. There are national and subnational budgets. There are credit budgets, tax expenditure budgets, and regulatory budgets. There are budgets based on national income accounting definitions. There are budgets that project future year outlays and revenues. There are budgets linked to development plans. Some government activities are "off-budget," controlled if at all by relatively autonomous agencies that are neither wholly public nor wholly private.

Government budgets define and describe, well or badly, the economic role of government. Some generalizations about their procedures and characteristics are now in order. These generalizations are applicable only to relatively developed countries, with relatively sophisticated budget systems.

1. Budgets that are comprehensive of public sector activities will embrace three organizational forms:

a. Trust funds in which revenues are segregated and legally "owned" by specified beneficiaries, as with old age pensions. Outlays are frequently transfer payments, but some trust funds may also purchase goods and services.

b. Public enterprises that conduct their activities more or less similar to firms in the private sector. Enterprises may generate surpluses of revenue over expenditure or may incur deficits financed from general revenues. In most governments there is a tradition, sometimes honored, that enterprises should "break even" with revenues at least equal to outlay. In other countries or in other circumstances, enterprises may be expected to generate surpluses to support other activities or their public purposes may justify continued deficits.

c. General government, which embraces traditional functions such as the administration of justice, the collection of revenue, the provision of health and education services, and national defense. There are no price tags attached to general government services. Payments for general government output are compulsory on the citizenry. Costs are the private goods and services that taxpayers forego. There are no distinct units of output, unlike the private sector, which makes for all manner of difficulty in defining an optimum allocation of resources between the public and the private sector (see below).

2. In many countries the organizational forms for public sector activities were reasonably well defined. There have been rather sharp lines, particularly in the Anglo-Saxon tradition, between the public and the private sectors. This is no longer the case in developed countries, and it never obtained in less developed countries. Public enterprises are typically a mixture of public and private authority with widely varying degrees of public control. Trust funds, supported by earmarked revenues, may be dedicated to private purposes. General government, most predominantly "public," may contract for services with the

private sector. The economic role of government increasingly serves a mixture of public and private purposes.

3. In most governments, regardless of the relative size of the public sector, there is an executive budget and a reasonably well-defined relationship between the executive, which prepares and proposes the budget, and the legislature, which has responsibility for authorizing the budget.

This means that there is a budget cycle:

a. The chief executive, with the assistance of staff, prepares and submits the budget to the legislature.

b. The legislature reviews the submission and may have the authority to increase or reduce executive proposals for either revenue or expenditure but ultimately authorizes the executive, or departments and agencies to obligate resources.

c. The executive has the responsibility for budget execution, that is, for the purchase of factors—land, labor, capital—to implement the budget decisions that have been made by the legislature and approved by the executive in acts of appropriation.

d. The final phase of the budget cycle is audit. The accounts for revenue and expenditure in a well-ordered government are reviewed by an agency that is usually under the control of the legislature or perhaps independent of both the legislature and the executive. This audit may be financial, extending only to the legality of obligations in relation to authorizations or appropriations. It may also extend to performance, where the auditing agency judges the efficiency and productivity of programs conducted by departments and agencies.

The budget process, if it is reasonably comprehensive and if there are reasonably good relations between the executive and the legislature, will articulate the interactions among diverse government organizations and provide the necessary linkages among last year's programs, current year programs, proposed programs, and future projected programs.

The foregoing cursory view of government organization and budget procedures by no means exhausts the mechanisms through which the economic role of government is determined. One major omission is regulatory agencies, which in every advanced country may be national or subnational, with authority to control a very wide range of economic activity from securities transactions to pollution abatement to land use. Neither does the foregoing cursory view indicate the importance of a government's revenue policy. The level and character of the tax system will have quite significant impacts on the private sector, on the allocation of resources therein, and on income—family income, regional income, national income. It is a commonplace but important observation that the economy has an impact on the budget and the budget has an impact on the economy. The level of private economic activity will affect the revenue side of the public budget. Revenues are positively elastic with respect to the price level. Similarly, if the level of GNP is relatively constant, a large public budget will encroach on and limit the level of private economic activity. Where revenues are less than expenditure—a deficit budget—there is resulting stimulus to the private sector.

It would be much too simplistic to assert that public programs always encroach on and limit private economic activity—that "government is the problem and not the solution." Many public programs have a positive and purposive character that contribute to an improved standard of living and an extension of human freedom. Programs for resource development, public housing, and public health and nutrition, to name a few, will contribute to an advancement of human dignity and personal liberty. Modern government is not simply a coercive mechanism that restricts and confines.

Nothing in this cursory view of budget characteristics and procedure suggests the complexity of the choices that are made. V. O. Key (1940) posed the problem five decades ago: "On what basis shall it be decided to allocate x dollars to activity A instead of activity B?"

Some progress has been made in answering Key's question. Benefit-cost analysis is helpful in choosing among physical resource development projects when the choice set is narrow, where projects are roughly similar in purpose with about the same volume of externalities. But benefit-cost may be positively misleading in comparing projects of vastly different scale or with different kinds of externalities.

Economic efficiency measures in terms of national income gains have their limitations for use in the public sector. The most significant is that efficiency measurements do not extend to distributional considerations, where this is broadly defined in terms of income class, ethnic status, occupation, or geographic location. No government programs are distributionally neutral, and economists cannot specify a "proper" distribution of income. However, economists do have the responsibility to estimate the distributional consequences of proposed programs. This, at least, should assure that such consequences are reviewed by political decision makers.

Benefit-cost limitations are especially pronounced in application to human resources programs such as education and health. When discounted lifetime earnings are the benefit-cost technique, outcomes are biased against those whose participation in the labor force is far in the future or will be limited in one way or another—the very young, the elderly, nonwhites, and women. Such outcomes are offensive to ethical values.

THE CLASSICAL VIEW

Adam Smith was reasonably certain as to the fundamental economic role of government. It was, of course, to be noninterventionist. In Book V, in defining the proper objects of expenditure "the Expence of Defence" comes first. The second duty of the sovereign is "the Expence of Justice," and the third and last duty is "the Expence of Public Works and Public Institutions." To this Smith added, almost as a footnote, "the Expence of supporting the Dignity of the Sovereign."

Public institutions include those for the education of the youth and those for the instruction of people of all ages. Public works embrace those that facilitate commerce in general (roads, bridges, canals) and those necessary for particular branches of commerce. With progress from "nations of hunters, the lowest and rudest state of society" outlays under each of these heads become larger. In the promotion of commerce great care must be taken to discourage inefficient monopoly by domestic or foreign grants of trading privilege. In the education of youth public expense should support the essential parts of education—"to read, write and account" even for those who are "bred to the lowest occupations."

Throughout his long discussion of the proper expenses of the sovereign and hence the proper economic role of government, Smith, without using the terms, is concerned with both efficiency and income distribution. Identifiable beneficiaries of specific public works—canals, bridges, roads—should pay for their upkeep by appropriate tolls (user charges). "When the toll upon carriages of luxury . . . is made somewhat higher in proportion to their weight, than upon carriages of necessary use . . . the indolence and vanity of the rich is made to contribute in a very easy manner to the relief of the poor" (Smith, 1937).

The contemporary reader of the *Wealth of Nations* must always be impressed, not only by Smith's erudition, but also by his sense of the dynamic of the public finances. Nations of hunters and of shepherds do not require a large expense by the sovereign. As nations develop, public sector requirements expand and increase in complexity—a preliminary version of Wagner's Law. For Smith the economic role of government continuously changes and principles are subject to exceptions. In some circumstances it would even be desirable to extend grants of monopoly to foreign trading companies "for a certain number of years."

THE NEOCLASSICAL VIEW

This chapter is not the occasion for tracing thinking and practice on the "proper" economic role of government from 1776 to 1989 (Burkhead and Miner, 1971). For present purposes it will suffice to leap from the *Wealth of Nations* to the predominant, contemporary mainstream view. That view is very largely the product of Richard A. Musgrave's *The Theory of Public Finance* (1959). Paul Samuelson's earlier contributions (1954/1955) are also very important.

The neoclassical approach that emerged in the 1950s came at a time when public budgets, in both developed and less developed countries, were expanding. The Keynesian Revolution had put public finance in the center of public policy, with an emphasis not on allocational efficiency but on economic stabilization. The task of fiscal theory was now to incorporate stabilization concerns with traditional concerns for economic efficiency, with appropriate attention to distribution.

Musgrave formalized this approach as a normative or optimal theory of the public household, and not as an attempt to explain existing public policies. The Fiscal Department is conceptualized as being composed of three branches: Allocation, Distribution, and Stabilization. The imaginary manager of each branch pursues reasonably well-defined objectives. The Allocations manager reads the preferences of the citizenry and apportions resources between the public and the private sectors and within the public sector. The Distribution manager arranges for income and wealth transfers to effect a "proper" distribution of control over resources. The Stabilization manager establishes policies to secure full employment and price level stability.

No attempt will be made here to enter the intricacies of the Stabilization and Distribution Branches, but some comments are warranted on the Allocations Branch.

This branch is concerned with public goods (social goods) and the exclusion principle does not apply. That is, one person's consumption of a public good does not restrict another person's consumption (and enjoyment) of that good. Thus, preferences for public goods need not be revealed by individuals since supply provided by one can be enjoyed by all—"the free-rider" phenomenon. The absence of a mechanism for preference revelation and the resulting inability to vary quantity in accordance with preferences make it impossible to apply market solutions to public sector allocations.

Given the nonexclusion characteristics of public goods, the effort to define a partial equilibrium for social goods alone, or a general equilibrium for both public and private goods, is a difficult and challenging task (Burkhead and Miner, 1971).

In the world of budgetary practice, governments do not separate the three branches but do adopt fiscal policies that embrace allocation, distribution, and stabilization objectives. Conceptualizing these three objectives as separate responsibilities has provided a systematic approach to the analysis of the economic role of government.

CONCLUDING COMMENTS

The economic role of government is incapable of a definition that is independent of specific circumstances at any one time. This is the case with both central governments and subnational governments. Moreover, the basic budget objectives, as defined in the neoclassical approach, are frequently in conflict, one with another. An aggressive pursuit of high employment stabilization may generate inflationary consequences, with an unintended upward redistribution of income. An allocations policy that favors a large national defense establishment may also contribute to an upward income redistribution.

Within the public sector there are further difficulties. For resource allocation decisions there are different signalling devices than are available in private markets. Private markets do not allocate resources, as is so often contended, but they do send signals (for example, prices, sales volume) to households and firms that facilitate allocation decisions. The budget process in governments generates a very different kind of signal. Political leaders and interest groups reveal the intensity of their demands, although not their willingness to pay, in influencing the size and composition of the government's budget.

In this country, the economic role of the national government is further confused by a number of factors that have contributed to disarray. One is the lack of control over large portions of the budget—the entitlements for Social Security, Medicare, Medicaid, agriculture, and interest on the national debt. Whether or not such programs should be increased or reduced is not the issue. What is important is that they are outside the appropriations process. A second source of disarray is procedural—the failure of the administration and the Congress to develop a routine that produces budgets on time and with reasonably articulated objectives. Perhaps the current state of affairs simply underscores the major point of this chapter: A description of the fundamental economic role of government is most elusive.

REFERENCES

Burkhead, Jesse, and Jerry Miner. *Public Expenditure*. Chicago: Aldine, 1971, pp. 16–23; ch. 2, 3.

Key, V. O. "The Lack of Budgetary Theory." *The American Political Science Review* 34 (1940): 1137–44. Reprinted in *Public Budgeting & Finance* 1 (1981: 86–92.

Musgrave, Richard A. *The Theory of Public Finance*. New York: McGraw-Hill, 1959, pp. 3–57.

Samuelson, Paul A. "The Pure Theory of Public Expenditures." *Review of Economics and Statistics* 36 (1954): 387–89.

———. "Diagrammatic Exposition of a Theory of Public Expenditures." *Review of Economics and Statistics* 37 (1955): 350–56.

Smith, Adam. *The Wealth of Nations*. New York: Modern Library, 1937, Book V, and p. 683.

7

The State: Power and Dichotomy

William M. Dugger

Alas, the time for doing good has not yet come.

—Robespierre

FUNDAMENTALS

The Dual Nature of the State

From an institutionalist point of view, the state reflects a basic dichotomy. The state is a parasitic institution that drains off community resources for its dynamic politics and its ill-fated imperialist schemes, and that dominates the underlying population through force and fraud. The state is also a productive institution that creates resources for community use and for peaceful development, and that establishes a framework of socially beneficial working rules for enlarging and protecting the rights of the common citizen. The state is both of these things, at the same time. When viewed in the concrete, the state's basic dichotomy is its single, most significant feature.

Looking at our own concrete state—the United States of America—it is the largest and therefore the most aggressive of the "banana republics" in the Americas. It was founded by druggers (tobacco), treasure seekers, slavers, and religious zealots, whose "manifest destiny" was greatly to be feared by the underlying populations both inside and outside its original borders. It is run by imperial presidents who rise to power through wars and military exploit (Washington, Jackson, Grant, Eisenhower). It is a depository for the excreta of great revolutions elsewhere, an embranglement of emigres full of anticommunism and fantasies of revenge, a haven for emigrants lusting for fame and fortune and anxious to leave their social responsibilities and personal obligations conveniently behind them. This same United States of America, however, is a host to the United Nations and a welcome refuge for millions, where every race, creed, and nationality have struggled together to make it the source of a long legal tradition of civil rights, equality, and democracy. It was founded by independent farmers, sturdy mechanics, and free thinkers, and is to be greatly admired by egalitarians everywhere. Generations of its brave young men have sacrificed their lives and their limbs on distant shores in the name of high principle. Furthermore, the United States of America is not only run by Hollywood cowboys, but also by statesman presidents who exercise power on behalf of the wretched of the earth (Lincoln, Wilson, Roosevelt). The dual nature of the state is fundamental. The United States lifts up, and it pushes down the common people, usually at the same time.

At the concrete level, then, the state is always dichotomous, being both predatory and productive—making war and making peace, building up and tearing down, wasting lives and saving them. The United States has brought forth both a city on a hill and a neon wilderness, and it partakes heavily of them both, simultaneously. Furthermore, the substance of the state can be grasped best when the state is analyzed in its full context and complexity. This means that the state should be studied in its social and historical context, not as an isolated datum.

Power: The Fundamental Function of the State

At the most fundamental level, the state has but one function—it exercises power. The state usurps for itself the right to use physical force, sometimes giving a little bit of it back to parents for disciplining children and to teachers for disciplining students. Even though the state is jealous of its right to use physical force, it will from time to time lend that right to large employers to control employees. In the United States, this is done by state governors calling out their national guard to help break strikes. But power is far more than the ability to physically restrain or attack. Power is the ability to get people to do what you want them to do, whether or not they want to do it. In the hands of the individual, power is tenuous and is the ability to control the behavior of others by imposing one's will on them. Individual power in stateless societies was limited by traditional, informal sanctions. Predatory individuals could always be shunned or banned, and in the worst cases, they could be stoned by the group being preyed upon. The rise of the state changed all that, however. Institutionalized in the hands of the state, power is not tenuous. State power is awesome and is feared by those subject to it. Constitutions, treaties, conventions, and charters have sprung up to limit state power. The founding fathers of the United States went so far as to virtually conjure up the doctrine of separation of powers to set the branches of government at cross purposes.

In the worst cases of predatory states, state power is limited only by revolution or by the power of other states—that is, by war, civil or international. State power is the ability to exercise social control over the behavior of individuals either directly through the state's own mechanisms, or indirectly through shaping other institutions, which in turn directly control individual behavior. State power is social control, not just individual control. It is power in the large. In so-called primitive societies, where war was unsystematic and the economic surplus small or absent, social control was essentially traditional and the state unnecessary. Power in the large did not exist. But we all left that Eden long ago.

The state is an arena for power struggle and an instrument for power application. As an arena for power struggle, the state's judiciary provides the legal procedure for argument and counterargument; its legislature provides the mechanism for writing new law; its executive provides the high office for statesmanship; and its police provide the threat-incentive to reach agreement in internal struggles, whereas its military provides the threat-incentive to reach agreement in external struggles. As an instrument for applying power, the state's legislature passes laws against deviance; its judiciary finds the necessary facts to convict, its police apprehends the miscreants, and its executive pardons those falsely caught up in the juggernaut.

When the state applies power, particularly in offense or defense against other states, the executive waxes as the largest of the government's branches. When the state serves as an arena for the power struggle of other interests within the society, the legislative or judicial branches wax large. During the early stages of revolutionary upsurges, the executive generally resists the upstarts, so in successful revolutions, the old executive is replaced. On the other hand, the legislative branch frequently serves as a conduit for popular discontent, as the Long Parliament did in the English Revolution and as the National Assembly did in the French Revolution. So the revolutionary legislature enjoys a rise in its power and prestige, until the executive reemerges in the guise of a champion of the revolution—witness the careers of Cromwell and Napoleon.

Purpose: Whose Interests Are Served

The battleground on which demand ultimately meets response is the state. It can be captured by one class or the other and is usually captured by the class whose interests have vested. Capturing the state means to turn it to serve one's own special or class interests—and the state can serve very well, indeed. To say that the state has been captured by the vested interests is to be redundant, for it is the state that vests the interests in the first place. In internal disputes, the different branches of the state can create, destroy, and redistribute income and wealth; create, destroy, and redefine rights and privileges; and recognize or fail to recognize the rights, privileges, and immunities of engaging in collective action instead of mere individual action. In external disputes, the state can defend or fail to defend against the physical attacks of other states or against the commercial inroads of foreign citizens. State tariffs and subsidies can hurt foreign producers and help domestic ones. State regulation of international trade can create or destroy domestic monopolies. For these and many other reasons, the state is a great prize, worthy of much effort and expense. The state must not be underestimated, however. The state is much more than a class mechanism. The mechanisms of the state are important in their own right. They can pursue their own interests against each other and in alliance with class interests or with special interests. The state is not just a dependent variable in a class equation of power. It is more than just an arbiter between classes. It is not just corrupt. The state is also a wielder of power on its own behalf and in its own right. The same holds even for the different mechanisms or branches of the state.

Nonetheless, a basic question is, on whose behalf and for whose benefit does the state exercise its power? To whose purpose is state power turned? The existence of class divisions, of haves and have-nots, implies two different kinds of answers to that question—so too, does the basic dichotomy between the predatory and productive state. On one hand, the modern predatory state in the West exercises power on behalf of entrenched capitalists, on behalf of the haves against the have-nots. Such a state is a corporate state, girded to defend the vested interests of corporations against both internal threats (labor unions, consumer movements, and critical intellectuals) and external threats (rising protectionism, Third World demands, and liberation movements). On the other hand, the modern productive state in the West exercises power on behalf of the workers, on behalf of the have-nots. Such a state is a welfare state, loaded with programs to redistribute income to the poor, power to the workers, and a new international economic order to the Third World. The corporate state protects the vested interests and represses the demands of the lower strata for more. The welfare state promotes the demands of the lower strata against the self-righteous outrage of the vested interests.

The tone of the corporate state is unmistakable in much of the English-speaking, contemporary world, where smugness and arrogance now dominate. From every social organ seems to ooze the righteous self-approval of the upper strata and the same strata's indignant disapproval of the unwarranted claims of the ignorant and slovenly masses. To the privileged, protected as they are by their inheritances, trusts, dividends, old school ties, and social positions, the welfare state seems a useless appendage, at best. At worst, they see it as a corrupter of an otherwise respectful, eager to please, and hard-working labor force. From the point of view of the privileged, the masses can never be satisfied. Any yielding to them not only negates the moral lessons they should be learning from their hard lives, but also encourages them to demand ever more coddling, at the expense of you know who. The unquenchable masses, at various times and places, have demanded that the state enforce a whole series of so-called rights: the right to vote without owning property, the right to go to school without paying tuition, the right to organize unions without their employer's permission, the right to receive income without working, and the right to respect of their person, without demonstrating the proper background and breeding. As the state struggles to meet all of these demands it overburdens the creative classes and dries up the fountainhead of material progress and spiritual grace. The elite know that meeting all these demands would leave everyone worse off, including the masses who mistakenly make the demands in the first place. Privilege seldom yields gracefully, because the upper strata seldom realize that their favored position is due to class privilege rather than individual merit. The upper strata seem uniquely unable to distinguish privilege from merit. To them, their ignorance is bliss. Racism, sexism, and jingoism thrive in this environment of privilege and are enforced by the laws of the predatory state.

The predatory state, in paternalistic, or corporate, or apartheid form, provides the privileged few with a shelter from life's storm, and channels the largest portion of the economic surplus into their comfortable little corner of the world. Though the storm rages, life for the privileged is sweet. As long as their storm shelter holds, respect for authority is widespread. Their traditions and their establishments are accorded great respect. Personal servants are plentiful, cheap, and respectful. Industrial wages are low; dividends high. Income taxes are low, wealth levies subversive. Unions illegal or irrelevant. Regulators friendly; consumers unorganized; intellectuals silent or sycophantic. But when privilege is challenged seriously, the easy sweetness turns to hard paranoia, giving a different tone to a challenged elitist state than to an unchallenged one.

Although paranoia is the tone of the elitist state in decline, great expectations set the tone of the welfare state on the rise. In extreme cases of revolution, the smell of millennialism is unmistakable. Whether dope-smoking Rastafarians or bible-thumping Baptists, when led by revolutionary states, at least some of the people demonstrate faith in a great overturning where the first will be last and the last will be first. In more moderate cases of reform-oriented welfare states, society is characterized by rising expectations and rising demands, and by an erosion of the props to privilege. Racism, sexism, and jingoism come under attack. A lively skepticism emerges, along with a lack of respect for established authority and traditional status. The rich and the successful are no longer automatically accepted as worthy of their good fortune. Most important of all, economic limits are lifted. The old beliefs that there will never be enough to go around are questioned. Even the poor think of having enough—enough food, comfortable shoes, nice clothes, and maybe a little apartment or room of their own. Improvement seems possible; more things are up for grabs. Committees and popular organizations of all kinds proliferate. Grassroots democracy catches fire with proclamations, demands, rallies, marches, and generalized excitement.

In revolutionary upsurges, the vested interests are divested. The state abruptly wrenches the economic surplus away from the privileged through peasant-backed land redistributions, through nationalizations, expropriations, and wealth levies. In moderate upsurges, the vested interests are made to share. The economic surplus is redirected away from the privileged through full employment, low interest rates, high income and inheritance taxes, state-sanctioned collective bargaining and affirmative action, utility regulation, wage and price controls, Social Security pensions, public education, public housing, and public health.

In sum, today's predatory state serves the interests of the corporate elite as it bears down on the lower strata, and sets a certain tone for the whole society. Todays productive state, on the other hand, serves the lower strata as they push up against the higher strata, and sets a different tone for the society. One or the other states can become predominant from time to time. Of course, they remain one and the same state. It is just that separating the two aspects of the dichotomous state is an analytical convenience. The different states—actually, the different aspects of the same state—will be discussed in the following two sections, the productive state first. Focus will be on economic symbols, legal forms, and relations to resources.

THE PRODUCTIVE STATE

Symbols

The contemporary productive state in the West is the welfare state. It stands for lifting the limits of participation that have kept most of the human race from living the good life and from taking an active part in political decisions and community activities. The welfare state symbolizes hope to the downtrodden. The most symbolic groups in the United States are the Southern Christian Leadership Conference of the civil rights movement, the Students for a Democratic Society of the U.S. peace movement, and the National Organization for Women of the women's liberation movement. Although it may not be as influential, the American Indian Movement is also highly symbolic of the U.S. productive state. What these groups have in common is they all symbolize pushing past old barriers that kept the dispossessed from their rightful places. All were organized groups pushing up from below, for free speech, peace, integration, and fair treatment of women. What the welfare state did, at least in the 1960s and 1970s, was respond positively to the pushing up from below, by removing some of the legal barriers and by boosting the underdogs through some of the other barriers with civil rights legislation, affirmative action, and more. Viewed from the bottom, these were restrictive barriers to equal participation needing to be broken by the state. Viewed from the top, however, these were the protective supports of decent civilization needing to be defended by the state.

The welfare state symbolizes equality, not the empty legal equality of everyone being equally free to sleep on top of warm air grates in front of New York's finest restaurants, but real equality to participate fully in the life of the city and polity. Because many are coming up from slavery and oppression, it is foolish to expect everyone to be equally worthy and able at the very outset. Under these unfavorable conditions, handed down from past inequities, equality cannot be enforced as a formal law or as an absolute value. Under these unfavorable conditions, pursuing the form of equality destroys its substance. Instead, equality must be understood in the context of a stratified society. Properly understood in its context, equality becomes a moving and a changing target. The substance of equality is to be found in some more here for the underdog and some less there for the topdog. The substance of equality is also to be found in never accepting some more here and some less there as enough, but just as a starting point for more—always more, until no longer can any particular group be identified as the underdog. In this substantive sense, demands for equality truly are explosive. The role of the welfare state is to facilitate and to further those demands.

Equality is explosive. It lifts limits. Most importantly, most fundamentally, equality creates abundance. Abundance, then, is the premier symbol, the ultimate value of the welfare state. When shared, the good life expands. When limited to a privileged few, it shrinks. Sharing the good life means teaching and learning new skills, building and using new tools, distributing more food to more hungry people, innoculating more babies, opening more schools and hospitals, opening more hearts and minds to the prospects of making a better life. Sharing the good life means reaping the rewards, the higher productivity that comes from making more room. Limiting the good life to a privileged few means losing the higher productivity that comes from making more room. The welfare state's role is to make room, to bring into the sharing process the new people with new drives and new ideas. The new people are the underdogs. The underdogs are the special responsibilities of the welfare state. The responsibility is not just to maintain them, but to uplift them—more precisely, to help them uplift themselves.

Legal Forms

The productive state legalizes the forms used by the underdogs in their struggles to uplift themselves, or fails to do so, depending on the circumstances. During the dark days of slavery in the United States, the productive state should have legalized such forms as the underground railroad. But it did not. It gave us the Dred Scott decision instead. During the dark days of conquering the American Indians, the productive state should have legalized the tribe. But it did not. It gave us the Indian Agent instead. During the dark days of industrial strife that followed the Civil War, the productive state should have legalized the co-op and the union. But it did not. It gave us the injunction instead. And we reaped what we sowed—the Civil War, the land grab, and the Hay Market. The point is an important one, so it has been exaggerated. The forms of organized activity which the state decides to legalize, and the forms which it decides to ignore or to criminalize, become extremely important in determining who can and cannot exercise power through collective action. Two examples from U.S. economic history drive home the point: When the actions of an American Indian tribe— organized to possess tribal lands collectively—are struck down in order to enforce an individual Indian's "right" to contract with a capitalist corporation—organized to drill for oil—the tribe is dispossessed and the corporation is made rich. Likewise, when an individual scab's "right" to execute a labor contract with a capitalist corporation—organized to raise the wealth of stockholders—is upheld against the "right" of a union—organized to raise the wages of workers—the union is beat down and the corporation raised up.

Resources

The productive state, in its contemporary welfare state form, creates community resources through public investment. The public investment is in health care, education, recreation, mother and infant nutrition, transportation, housing, power, and communication. These community resources are social infrastructure; they are not natural resources, and their supply is not strictly limited. Instead, they are manufactured resources. Unless the welfare state fails to finance and deliver them, they are not scarce. When financed by the central state with its ability to tap the wealth and income of the vested interests, and when controlled by the community that needs them, these resources provide the framework for economic growth and community development. They help deliver on the promise of abundance. Providing them runs up against the organized resistance of the vested interests, because it is the vested interests that must help pay for their provision. Without the provision of these resources to the community, however, growth is slower, and making room for the upstarts and the dispossessed is much more difficult.

THE PREDATORY STATE

Symbols

The predatory state, in its contemporary corporate form, is symbolized by just rewards, but only for those who deserve them in the real world of scarcity and limited opportunity. The false expectations of the unskilled and unmotivated masses must be moderated by the realities of the competitive world economy where resource scarcity and the global spread of high-tech industry have drastically altered the realm of the possible. Limits have been ignored or denied for too long. Now they are unavoidable. Room for more people at the top simply does not exist. There is not enough pie to go around, and promises of more in the present only create demands which, if met, will reduce the size of the pie in the future. The poor cannot have more, because to give them more the state must take away from the rich. And since the rich are the source of new investment and of new ideas, taking from them will reduce what is available to all. In place of false hopes and demands, the state should encourage discipline and humility. State schools should therefore teach people their place and teach them to be content with it. Youngsters should learn respect for property and hard work.

Legal Forms

The modern predatory state in the West is called the corporate state for good reason. It has given Westerners a very particular legal form for conducting our economic affairs. It has given us the capitalist corporation. During the formative years of rapid industrialization, the labor union was generally defined by the predatory state's courts as an illegal conspiracy. The predatory state then attacked the union with physical force. The corporation, however, was defined as an artificial person with all the legal rights, privileges, and immunities enjoyed by natural persons. The predatory state then protected the corporation with all the armor of the citizen. So, with a stroke of the judiciary pen, the interests of a corporate capitalist class were vested and the interests of a working class were divested. The legal forms allowed and protected by the state, or disallowed and attacked by the state, always determine the boundaries within which the economy develops. Clearly, a modern economy is not a natural growth but a controlled growth. And the role of the corporate state is to control that growth to benefit some at the expense of others.

Resources

The corporate state needs a vast array and a steady flow of resources for its dynastic politics and imperial adventures. Dynastic politics require large construction contracts and weapons systems to trade back and forth in the logrolling processes of the legislature. The predatory state feeds on spoils, and spoils require heavy taxes and heavy borrowings. Care must be taken to tax the right people and to borrow from the right people, too. In my own predatory state, the regional incidence of the dynastic politics of the 1980s is striking. The Midwest, the industrial heartland of the U.S. economy, has been heavily drained, turning it into the so-called rust belt. At the same time, the southern states, Massachusetts, and California have been the recipients of huge defense contracts, turning these regions into the so-called sun belt. The pattern of defense spending has done much to deindustrialize the old heartland and to invigorate the new high-tech defense sector by redirecting the flow of resources in the economy away from basic industry into star wars technology.

In sum, the corporate state taps into the industrial community's resources to feed the spoils system and to pursue the corporate state's imperial designs.

CONCLUSION

The state, when viewed in the concrete and when analyzed in historical and social context, is dichotomous. On one side of the dichotomy, the state is feminine. It partakes of motherhood and caring. It uplifts the poor and makes room for all our children. This state nurtures. On the other side of the dichotomy the state is masculine. It partakes of the fatherland and conquest. It defends the rich against the poor, and strong against the weak. This state exploits.

8

The Three Faces of John Locke: Fundamental Ambiguities in Government's Economic Functions

John E. Elliott

In a classic motion picture, *The Three Faces of Eve*, Joanne Woodward portrays the ambiguities and tensions associated with multiple personalities within an individual: the very proper Eve White, the very naughty Eve Black, and, guided by the psychoanalytic prowess of Lee J. Cobb, the emergent, middle-of-the-road, Eve Gray.

Similarly, though typically less clearly and dramatically, students of seventeenth-century philosopher John Locke have noted elements of ambiguity and tension in his interpretation of political society. C. B. Macpherson (1987, 1977, 1973, 1964) insightfully roots these ambiguities in Locke's views of property and inequality in emerging capitalism. A useful, albeit somewhat exaggerated, way of examining these themes is by depicting Locke's views on economy, society, and government as if they were embodied in three distinguishable "models"—Radical Locke, Conservative Locke, and Liberal Locke—instead of simply three facets of one overall theory.

For this exaggeration, we beg the reader's indulgence, because our interest is not in Locke per se but in fundamental propositions about government's economic functions. Because of Locke's seminal role in political economy and the contradictions in his thought, however, the "three faces of John Locke," in both its omissions and commissions, provide a useful framework for explicating basic ideas concerning the ends of government and comparing fundamental notions about relationships among economy, social class, and politics.

RADICAL LOCKE

A radical characterization of Locke follows easily from consideration of the first of his two stages of the "state of nature." For Locke, society and economy are understood as logically (indeed, historically) prior to politics. Although such a state may degenerate into war and chaos, it need not do so, for men are at least semisocial creatures guided significantly by reason, rooted in religion and moral values, to live and let live. Such a prepolitical society would be characterized by "perfect freedom" and "equality" because of the absence of differential political powers. The first stage of this state of nature is a simple proprietary economy. Each individual, owning and controlling his own person, labors, thereby transforming the common inheritance of nature into private property. Supposing that each individual uses only such land as will leave "enough and as good" for others and appropriates only such produce as he can use "before it spoils," economic inequalities are also likely to be very small (Locke, 1952, Ch. 5, para. 31–33).

In effect, this is a vision of a "one-class society" (Macpherson, 1977) in which all proprietors are laborers and all laborers are proprietors. In such a society, there would be no economic need to protect the property of one class from incursions by another class, that is, there would be no need to protect the rich and powerful from the envy and redistributive fervor of the poor, or to protect the poor from the oppressions of the rich.

Instead, the economic functions of government would be essentially nonclass in character: Political society would be instituted essentially to protect property in the broad sense of "life, liberty, and estate," not merely of possessions. Because of the relative equality in small-scale proprietary economy, the protection provided by governmental authority would be that extended to individuals relative to other individuals essentially independent of social class. On the one hand, government would adjudicate or serve as umpire in relations among individuals. On the other, it would protect citizens against the threat of external invasions from other societies. Both functions are class-independent and yield benefits to all individuals.

The "radical" character of political economy in such a society would not lie in what government did. Indeed, given the citizenry's semisociality and capacity to reason and the very mild inequalities of a one-class society, government's economic functions might well be very limited in scope. Instead, the radical quality of political life would lie in the fact that the electorate—empowered in Locke's theory both to establish and, when justified, to disestablish (through the "right of revolution") organized political authority—would presumably consist of all "free men," which, in a proprietary economy, would be comprised of the overwhelming majority of adult males in the population. The major conserving economic function ascribed to government by the American Founding Fathers and Karl Marx alike—protection of the propertied against the propertyless masses—would be unnecessary. Capture of government through the class struggle and its use as an agency to foment substantive changes in class relations (for example, bourgeoisie versus landed aristocracy, labor versus business) are similarly redundant if the society is not class-structured to begin with.

Of course, Locke does not stop with the first stage of the state of nature. It is instructive, however, to ask whether such a simple, proprietary economy and associated one-class society would demand additional economic functions of government beyond internal order and protection against external aggression.

Certainly, many of Locke's contemporaries and successors thought so. Rousseau, for example, believed that the institutional framework of society was subject to potential disintegration and transformation and that socioeconomic stability and continuity presupposed protection of the institutional framework itself. Thus, society and economy are *not* prepolitical, and the individual is *by nature* a political animal. In *The Social Contract*. Rousseau argues that a democratic community must minimize inequality of wealth. Regarding the employer-employee relation, "no citizen shall ever be wealthy enough to buy another, and none poor enough to be forced to sell himself." Concerning landed property, "a man must occupy only the amount he needs for his subsistence" and may rightfully take possession only by "labour and cultivation" (Rousseau, 1950, pp. 20, 50). In his *Discourse on Political Economy*, Rousseau states that "One of the most important functions of government is to prevent extreme inequality of fortunes; not by taking away wealth from its possessors . . . but by securing the citizens from becoming poor." To prevent wealth inequalities, and their resulting proclivity to create class structures of propertied employers and poor workers, governments should promote equal geographic distribution of the population and encourage agriculture and "useful and laborious crafts" relative to commerce and the "purely industrial arts" (Rousseau, 1950, p. 306).

Reference to Rousseau enriches our understanding of the fundamental bases of government's economic functions in another way. For Locke, government is a mere instrument, adopted by rational beings in terms of their separate and independent individual self-interests. It serves as a kind of insurance policy against the risk that others will not invariably be fully reasonable. In contrast, for Rousseau, civil society, with its processes for governance, constitutes a community— that is, as Robert A. Nisbet (1966, p. 47) aptly puts it, a set of social relationships "which are characterized by a high degree of personal intimacy, emotional depth, moral commitment, social cohesion, and continuity in time." The "civil state" changes its participants. Justice is substituted for instinct, duty for impulse, and "moral liberty" for "natural liberty." Human faculties are "stimulated and developed," ideas are "extended," feelings are "enobled," and souls are "uplifted" (Rousseau, 1950, pp. 18–19). As a corollary, both the demand for and the supply of collective action are extended. The needs of human beings as members of community are different—and richer—than those of isolated individuals, and human potentialities for coparticipation in common activities are also enhanced by the experience of collective life. Thus, for Rousseau, government is not a necessary evil but (at least in part) is itself a social good.

Finally, Locke presupposes that labor and property must be private and individual, partly, perhaps, because of his agricultural model. Hence, the first stage in the state of nature must be that of a proprietary economy and one-class society. But cultural anthropologists tell us that labor and property in primitive hunting and gathering societies were often collective in character. These typically tribal communities needed (and created modes of social organization to meet those needs) an "organizing authority" to "regulate the common affairs of the community for the benefit of all'' (Draper, 1977, p. 240), despite the absence of separate individual private properties. In addition to maintenance of internal order and protection against potential external aggression, such simple societies were engaged in a struggle with nature. Hence, a decision-making authority was needed to organize hunts and fishing expeditions, regulate and distribution of labor and products, and construct public works, for example, dams. Presumably, the scope of government's economic activities was quite broad and was not limited to adjudication of conflicts among individuals.

The major difference between the ''protopolitical authority'' in simple tribal communities and the clearly political authority of modern states is that coercion in the tribal communities is provided by the community as a whole (as in the villagers' stoning of the wayward widow in *Zorba the Greek*), whereas, in the modern state coercion is exercised by separate, specialized institutions such as the armed forces, the police, and the public bureaucracy. Although such specialized agencies, according to Marx and Engels among others, reflect divisions in wealth and power among social classes, they are also based on growing complexity in the division of labor and are rooted in the common, public needs of society. Collective agencies, after all, still hunt for lost babies and put out fires in highly class-stratified societies. The economic functions of government, however, take on a modified character in a class-structured society, that is, a society with more than one class. This brings us to Conservative Locke.

CONSERVATIVE LOCKE

A conservative characterization of Locke begins with his second stage in the state of nature. Although still prepolitical, this stage depicts a complex, commercial economy with differential accumulations of land and capital. Use of money overcomes the spoilage limitation on property differentials. Not all people are now landowners, but greater productivity based on accumulation is assumed to raise the standard of living for all. Property rights to the fruits of labor now include ''the turfs my servant has cut'' (Locke, para. 28). Although the wage system puts the free laborer under the discipline of the employer, it does so only temporarily and by free consent and contract.

Locke's second stage in the state of nature is thus a vision of a class-structured society and commercial capitalist economy. A small number of owners of land and capital employ essentially propertyless laborers who constitute the majority of the population. In such a context, the fundamental bases for organized political society and the economic functions of government inevitably take on a class character. There is now a clear and pressing need to protect the properties of the rich and powerful against the incursions of the poor and propertyless. Government is instituted not simply because of general uncertainties in the state of nature, but primarily because of the expectation by the propertied that the ''greater part'' of society are ''no strict observers of equity and justice,'' and property is consequently ''very unsafe, very insecure'' (Locke, viii, para. 123). The resulting government still protects life and liberty and guards against external invasion. But its central functions are protection of property owners from non-property owners and adjudication of differences among the propertied.

Because "government has no other end than the preservation of property," its institution is properly accomplished by, as well as on behalf of, men of property, and its operation is properly conducted in accordance with the methodologies and procedures of the government which they establish, whether more or less democratic. This "necessarily supposes and requires" that the people who form government and hold it accountable "should have property." As a corollary, propertyless wage workers—against whose potential unreasoning incursions governments are instituted—are put, like children, under the "parental power" of their "masters" and exercise no decision-making or voting rights (including that of disestablishment of political society) in the government of the owning class (Locke, para. 85, 94, 138). Government protects the properties of the rich against attacks by the poor, adjudicates among the members of the owning class, and protects the lives and liberties of all members of society, including wage laborers, against internal or external aggression. But it does not adjudicate between the owning and nonowning classes. The working poor are integral to society and economy (and thus are potentially subject to government regulation as an economic resource), but are divorced from political participation or independent influence on government's economic functions.

Locke's eighteenth-century successors continued his emphasis on government as protector of the propertied against the propertyless. According to James Madison, government should "protect the minority of the opulent against the majority" (cited in Farrand, 1937, p. 431). Similarly, John Adams wrote: "It is essential to liberty that the rights of the rich be secured; if they are not, they will soon become robbed and become poor" (cited in Commager, 1964, p. 210). Government, Adams proposed, should consist of a "natural aristocracy" of the "educated, well-born, and wealthy." Allowing "those who have no landed property," stated Benjamin Franklin, "to vote for legislators is an impropriety" (cited in Randall, 1976, pp. 348–49). Adam Smith summed up this interpretation with admirable clarity by saying that governments "in every case" constitute a "combination of the rich to oppress the poor, and preserve to themselves the inequality of goods which would otherwise be soon destroyed by the attacks of the poor" (1978, Vol. 4, para. 23). "Civil government, so far as it is instituted for the security of property, is in reality instituted for the defense of the rich against the poor, or of those who have some property against those who have none at all" (1976, Vol. 2, p. 236).

Securing property against expropriations by the propertyless, however, is not the only economic function of government, even from a conservative perspective. Here, Adam Smith provides the classic formula. In addition to internal order and defense, government has the "duty" of

erecting and maintaining certain public works and certain public institutions, which it can never be for the interest of any individual, or small number of individuals, to erect and maintain;

because the profit could never repay the expense to any individual or small number of individuals, though it frequently do much more than repay it to a great society (ibid., p. 209).

Although he wrote from a different ideological perspective, Marx made a similar point. The executive of the modern representative state, he and Engels declared, "is but a committee for managing the common affairs of the bourgeoisie" (Marx and Engels, 1948, p. 11). This supposes that the bourgeoisie has "common affairs," that is, public needs consistent with but extending beyond securing private property against the working class per se. Paul M. Sweezy (pp. 248–49) identifies three such needs: (1) common problems posed by the particular stage of economic development; (2) policies clearly in the interest of the capitalist class as a whole; (3) policies that run counter to some components of the capitalist class but that are essential to the long-run preservation of the private property system (for example, factory legislation).

Thus, conservative espousal of government protection of private property is not necessarily linked to a minimalist view of government's economic functions. Alexander Hamilton, for example, extolled the benefits of manufacturing. Because of the shortage of labor and its geographic dispersal in the new American economy, Hamilton espoused urbanization, expansion in the working class through movement of labor from agriculture to industry, and an increase in the ratio of capital to labor. To foster this vision, Hamilton proposed a centralized government, with a sufficiently strong executive to provide leadership, assistance, and support for economic development, for example, through tariff support for infant industries, creation of a national bank, and construction of roads and canals. As historical evidence from mercantilism through Bismarck to twentieth-century fascism attests, conservative defense of propertied interests often goes hand in hand with an economically active government.

LIBERAL LOCKE

What is here called "Liberal Locke" is partly a blend and partly an extension beyond Radical and Conservative Locke. In effect, Locke implies a blend between overlapping but divergent class needs. The propertied need organized political society to protect their property. All classes need government to protect life and liberty. Hence, a government that protects "life, liberty, and estate" is supportive of fundamental needs and enhances the freedom of all classes. It is thus rational for individuals, regardless of class, to consent to the institution of political society. If government truly restricts itself to the basic end of protection of all subjects within its domain, it thereby functions as a impartial umpire among individuals and classes.

But some subjects (the propertied) have the franchise and participate actively in governance, and others (the propertyless) do not. How is this fundamental inequality made concordant with a liberal perspective? Locke's response contains several arguments, which have profoundly influenced liberal thinking about government down to the present day. Everyone benefits from protection of life and liberty. Because capital accumulation increases labor productivity, all classes likewise benefit from the protection of property. Moreover, government is limited in its powers and is presumed to do no more than to protect the property system; it does not side with property owners to oppress or exploit nonowners. The dependency of workers on the authority of their employers is only temporary and is based on free consent. In any event, because all subjects are formally equal in the eyes of the law, there are no formal impediments to upward economic mobility.

Liberal Locke's vision of government was thus one of limited economic functions as well as limited powers. Everything other than protection of life, liberty, and estate could be attained, he believed, by "men living in neighborhood without the bounds of a commonwealth" (cited in Parry, 1978, p. 87). Such a limited government, however, need not necessarily be small. First, although a Lockean government would not redistribute property, it would regulate it. In principle, this includes such functions as prohibition of racial discrimination, provision of health and safety legislation, and protection of the environment. Second, protection can be expensive; thus, even Liberal Locke envisages the possibility of significant taxation, albeit monitored by a representative legislature. Third, Locke suggests that where pursuit of property interests would result in famine, the property owner has a duty to assist the starving person, who has a right to support from the property owner's surplus. In principle. this argument could be extended to support a much more interventionist state than Locke expressly identifies (Seliger, 1968, pp. 172–79).

Liberal Locke presupposes that the propertyless are content to remain second-class citizens and that the propertied (and the politicians) are content to use government in a strictly neutral manner and solely to protect lives, liberty, and estates. But these presuppositions are discordant with historical experience. With industrialization, as John Stuart Mill observed in the mid-nineteenth century, the working class increasingly came to believe that its interests diverged from those of employers and that restriction of the franchise and political influence on the basis of property could not be sustained indefinitely (Mill, 1926, pp. 756–61). As the franchise was extended and liberalism was gradually transformed into liberal democracy, the primary economic function of government changed from adjudication among the propertied class to adjudication between the propertied and the nonpropertied. As many radical thinkers, notably Karl Marx, have observed, this social relationship is inherently unstable because it presupposes workers will be content with what is attainable through the franchise and not press for radical social change, while the owning class will be content with economic suzereignty and will not press for restoration of political oligarchy cum plutocracy. Liberals, from John Stuart Mill to the present, have contended that a viable middle ground is feasible, indeed necessary, for the successful pursuit of both economic growth and social welfare.

So Liberal Locke's vision of government and its functions was challenged by the "democratic revolution." It was also unrealistic from the opposing perspective. Propertied classes and political leaders, together or independently, have often failed to provide systems of governance that were impartial among individuals and classes. On the one hand, propertied classes have turned to government to obtain a more favorable distribution of wealth, not merely to protect existing wealth. Tax and expenditure policies of the Reagan Administration, for example, contributed significantly to a redistribution of wealth from poor to rich. On the other hand, governments are at least partly independent from social-class relationships and economic circumstances, and do what they do partly on behalf of political leaders, ranging from personal aggrandizement to competition for world power leadership. In closing, it is instructive to recall Mill's practical commentary that in

the particular circumstances of a given age or nation, there is scarcely anything really important to the general interest, which it may not be desirable, or even necessary, that the government should take upon itself, not because private individuals cannot effectually perform it, but because they will not (Mill, 1926, p. 978).

One is tempted to say, with Aristotle and in critique of Locke, that the individual is a political, as well as social and economic, creature, and that government is integral, rather than external, to economy.

REFERENCES

Commager, Henry Steele (ed.), *Living Ideas in America*. New York: Harper & Row, 1964.
Draper, Hal. *Karl Marx's Theory of Revolution*, Vol. 1: *State and Bureaucracy*. New York: Monthly Review, 1977.
Farrand, M. (ed.). *The Records of the Federal Convention, 1787*. Vol. 1. New Haven, Conn: Yale University Press, 1937.
Locke, John. *Second Treatise on Government*. New York: Arts & Sciences Press, 1952.
Macpherson, C. B. *The Rise and Fall of Economic Justice*. New York: Oxford University Press, 1985.
———. *The Life and Times of Liberal Democracy*. New York: Oxford University Press, 1977.
———. *Democratic Theory*. New York: Oxford University Press, 1973.
———. *Possessive Individualism*. New York: Oxford University Press, 1964.
Marx, Karl, and Frederick Engels. *Manifesto of the Communist Party*. New York: International Publishers, 1948.
Mill, John Stuart. *Principles of Political Economy*. New York: Longmans, 1926.
Nisbet, Robert A. *The Sociological Tradition*. New York: Basic Books, 1966.
Parry, Geraint. *John Locke*. London: George Allen & Unwin, 1978.
Randall, John Herman. *Making of the Modern Mind*. New York: Columbia University Press, 1976.
Rousseau, John Jacques. *The Social Contract and Discourses*. New York: Jean E. P. Dutton, 1950.
Seliger, Martin. *The Liberal Politics of John Locke*. London: George Allen & Unwin, 1968.
Smith, Adam. *Lectures on Jurisprudence*. R. L. Meek, D. D. Raphael, and P. G. Stein (eds.). New York: Oxford University Press, 1978.

————. *An Inquiry into the Nature and Causes of the Wealth of Nations*. E. Cannan (ed.). 2 vols., combined edition. Chicago: University of Chicago Press, 1976.

Sweezy, Paul M. *The Theory of Capitalist Development*. New York: Monthly Review Press, 1942.

9

The Chicken and the Egg

John J. Flynn

Economic thought and the theories it generates depend on a background regime of law—the establishment of rules defining fundamental relationships within a society and mechanisms for their enforcement. The rules and the means for implementing them must be consistent with underlying moral beliefs concerning justice, individualism, and community and with the use of collective power in the hands of the state and other collectives recognized by law. It is, after all, a basic function and responsibility of government to serve as the vehicle through and by which fundamental relationships may be defined and implemented in light of the moral values of society. Among the most fundamental definitions are those establishing the basic units of society on which legal rights and re- sponsibilities are premised, the scope and enforceability of the rights selected in relation to the state and to other individuals and institutions, and the means by which rights and responsibilities are to be implemented. These definitions, in turn, reflect the selection of basic values to be implemented among and between members of a society and the system of government chosen—values defined by the moral beliefs of a culture in light of its history, experience, and commitment to a theory of justice.

The basic values defining the functions of government and the rules it adopts are dependent on underlying economic, social, and political beliefs about human nature and the world about us. The liberal arts of history, politics, economics, sociology, psychology, and philosophy provide us with normative and empirical insights for developing theories of government and for exploring the conse- quences of adopting one or another role for government in striking a just balance between individualism and community (Sandel, 1984). Governments formed or functioning without paying attention to the well-founded normative insights of the liberal arts are doomed to economic, political, and social failure because they are detached from the moral roots granting government legitimacy. Some schools of economic and political thought (and many lawyers) simply assume the existence of a background legal and economic regime establishing these basic premises without investigation of their deeper moral origins, the circumstances in which they were chosen, or their implications and consequences for the system of government chosen and its function in contemporary reality.

Obviously, there is a chicken and egg problem of which came first—government or economics. What are the fundamental assumptions of the role of government in establishing background roles and rights from which economic analysis proceeds? What is the role of economics (and the other liberal arts) in defining background roles and rights from which the determination of governmental institutions and responsibilities proceed? The resolution of these questions lies in abandoning linear thinking and recognizing that the answer is neither and both. Government is the product of a long-standing dialogue within society—a dialogue between all of society's intellectual disciplines and other sources of moral and factual insights—reflecting the enduring difficulty of understanding and reconciling the centrifugal forces of individualism and the centripetal forces of community in accord with the underlying cultural values of society. Government and its laws are the basic tools for imposing order on what would otherwise be chaos. If there be a motto for the institution of government it may be: In the beginning God looked out on the chaos and said, "let there be a government committed to justice, and therefore, some order in the midst of all this chaos."

Lesser beings than God have also grappled with establishing basic normative premises usually based on factual assumptions about human nature on which to organize and order a just society. Existentialists, for example, have argued for the basic view that there is no common human nature; each person is a unique human being, and each is responsible for all of humanity. It is the agony of the existentialist to be condemned to make choices as if making them for all of humanity (Sartre, 1948, pp. 28–32). It is a position in which the role of government and its laws are to recognize and protect the freedom of each member of society to carry out their responsibility to decide as if each individual is deciding every question for all humanity.

A second view, stemming from the political assumptions of Locke and the economic assumptions of Adam Smith, acknowledges or attributes common traits to all human beings. Among them are "the natural predominance of self-assertiveness, egoism and the desire to realize oneself through the attainment of personal happiness" (Bodenheimer, 1986, p. 209). The role of government and its laws in such a system is to control and prevent the tendencies of some to invade the rights of others in their life, liberty, and pursuit of happiness and to enable each to realize as fully as possible the maximum freedom to pursue one's self-interest. Hobbes saw human nature in similar but more pessimistic terms—as a combination of fear, hatred, and mistrust. For Hobbes it was essential that the individual enter into a compact to turn the sovereign power of the many over to the state, "Leviathan," if peace and safety were to prevail. Hobbes did not see Leviathan as an absolute dictatorship, but rather as a strong government using its powers to enable individuals to realize their own potential without interference by others. In this regard, Hobbes saw as necessary the creation and protection of property and contract rights and free exchange as essential to the good society. In its more modern manifestations of the New Right in both politics and economics, the untrammeled right of materialistic self-gratification by the majority or those with power is held in highest esteem and is to be given the right of way by government through noninterference by law, except where a majority demand otherwise or the aid of the state is necessary to enforce contract or property rights (Macedo, 1987, pp. 42–43).

A third view emphasizing the social nature of human beings and the desire and necessity to live in communities has persisted ever since Aristotle. Noting that altruism and mutual aid have long been attributes associated with human nature, this approach assumes that the desire for community and order are far stronger than the demand for individualism. Indeed, it has been observed that a human being would likely starve to death if left solely to individual devices to survive in this world (Fuller, 1968, p. 103). Marx and others have emphasized the social nature of human beings and the basic need for engaging in collective action in order to develop individually. Freed of the oppression of economic systems that denied collective ownership and control of the means of production, human beings and society would flower to such a point that the state would simply wither away as the social nature of human beings took over in organizing life (Fromm, 1966).

Each of these approaches to the enduring problem of striking a balance between individualism and community begins with narrow and fixed assumptions about human nature—assumptions influenced in turn by history, religious beliefs, the circumstances of their time, and commonly accepted political, psychological, economic, and philosophical beliefs. Each also depends to some extent on the existence of government and a functioning legal system to define and enforce values believed fundamental or in accord with the demands of a particular view of human nature. Significant legal and economic consequences follow when those assumptions define the basic legal units on which rights and remedies are to be imposed. It makes a difference when the basic entity recognized by law is primarily the family, the individual, a collective like the church or the corporation, or some combination of these "persons." The availability of one or another economic system of belief is also dependent on assumptions about what kind of basic entities will be legally recognized and the scope of the rights and responsibilities attached to them and vice versa.

The predominant Western economic and political ideology of today assumes that the individual human being is the basic organizing unit of society. This background assumption, however, has not been free from doubt and controversy, nor has it been followed consistently. Indeed, Western society has not been organized solely, or even predominantly, on such a principle. In the long term, institutions like the family, the church, the corporation, and feudal tenure have played a far more significant role as the basic organizing institutions of government on which legal rights and remedies are premised. In modern times, significant areas of law developed since the New Deal concerning economic relationships are premised on status rather than individualism. By this is meant that the individual's rights and responsibilities are determined by their status within an organization like a corporation or a union or by a status like that of a holder of pension or health insurance rights, rather than on individual merit or by virtue of individual bargaining. It is the collective or group characteristics that are recognized as the basic unit having rights and responsibilities. The rights and responsibilities of the individual are derivative of the collective or the group classification and are determined by one's status within the collective or classification. It is a system more like the feudalism of medieval times than the current popular belief that our society is organized on principles of individualism and economic liberalism.

In this the age of the corporate and welfare state, society's most significant economic laws are directed toward defining status relationships and the scope of rights and responsibilities attaching to the status defined, rather than basing rights and responsibilities on human individualism. It is a reality of great significance for defining the economic foundations of government and the government foundations of economics. For example, one's status as an investor in the stock market entitles an investor to certain predefined rights without regard for the individual's personal bargaining, knowledge, or ability to protect him- or herself. Buyers of products are entitled to guarantees of safety and warranties determined by law rather than by individual fault. One's employment status and right to Social Security or place in a pension trust is of far more legal and economic significance than one's status as an independent and unique individual. Members of a union have statutorily defined rights against employers and their union by virtue of their status as a union member. Most of our economic rights are determined by one's status in a large organization or by virtue of classifications of employment, age, or other indicia of status and not by individual bargaining, consent, or fault. The nineteenth-century concept of contract in the sense of a freely bargained consensual arrangement between individuals of relatively equal bargaining power is indeed dead as the primary conceptual legal device for allocating rights and responsibilities in most legal and economic transactions of significance (Gilmore, 1974).

Although the ideology of economic and legal individualism remains pervasive in prevailing economic and political theorizing, it is largely a myth in the reality of the law and economic life of late twentieth-century America. Sir Henry Maine's famous dictum stating that "the movement of the progressive societies has hitherto been a movement *from status to contract*," written on the eve of the Industrial Revolution and the rise of the welfare state, the advent of the modern corporation, and the legal recognition of unions, pension trusts, and the other collectives and classifications of modern life, must be reversed (Maine, 1986, p. 165). Today, Maine's dictum should read: "the whole movement of the law in progressive twentieth-century societies has been from *contract to status*." Although the expansion of individual civil liberties during this same time period may lead one to believe individualism rather than status is still the basic organizing principle of economic and governmental reality, it is misleading to view that expansion of civil rights in a vacuum. Indeed, a major part of that expansion has also been based on status—one's status as a racial, sexual, or other minority. When compared to the vast growth of status over contract as the basic organizing principle for defining economic rights, the movement from community to individualism in some areas of civil rights is more likely an unarticulated felt need for protecting some realm of individualism and personal autonomy in the face of the spread of status-defining economic rights rather than individualism doing so. The often unnoticed drift toward status is an ongoing example of the enduring need to balance reflectively the moral demands of individualism and community in light of history and unvarnished contemporary reality lest the one becomes submerged by the other. It is not, but should be, a matter of considerable debate in a contemporary America drifting in the direction of a political and economic oligarchy, rather than the fuller realization of a government of, by, and for the people. It is a debate which economics and the other liberal arts should be exploring at its most basic level of moral philosophy, rather than simply assuming that the mythical "is" of individualism defines the "ought" of the goals of legal rules, contemporary reality, and the functions of economics and government.

The basic understanding of the source, nature, and scope of contract and property rights in American constitutional law has also been under controversy since at least the New Deal, as well as in nineteenth-century America (Michelman, 1987). Originally, James Madison recognized property as having two meanings: "that dominion which one man claims and exercises over the external things of the world, in exclusion of every other individual" and in a "larger and juster meaning" as "embracing everything to which a man may attach a value and have a right, and *which leaves to everyone else a like advantage*" (Madison, 1884, p. 478). In the latter and Hohfeldian sense (Gjerdingen, 1986, p. 881; Grey, 1980) of property consisting of a system of rights that exist *between* persons with respect to things, rather than a right *in* things,—a means to an end, not an end in itself (Macpherson, 1987)—Madison included within the concept of property one's rights in theirs: "opinions and the free communication of them"; "religious opinions and in the profession and practice of them"; "safety and liberty of . . . person"; and "free use of . . . faculties, and the free choice of objects on which to employ them" (Madison, 1884, p. 468). "Property" was viewed as an essential dimension of individualism and as a means to the end of insuring the privacy and civil liberties of the individual vis-à-vis government and others. This concept of property as a relational right is a moral proposition that was lost sight of in later times when a materialistic concept of individual property rights *in* things began to dominate.

In the nineteenth century, the legal and economic concept of property gradually became reified to mean exclusive rights *in* things to be protected by the judiciary from intrusion by the other branches of government through the doctrine of "substantive due process." Substantive due process viewed property and contract rights as ends unto themselves rather than as means by which government balanced individualism and community in light of the long-term moral commitments of the culture. The reign of substantive due process in the courts produced the governmental and economic paralysis in the Great Depression as the inflexible, reified, and fixed concepts of property and contract applied by the courts and assumed by many economists and leaders of government handcuffed constructive government response to economic chaos. It was an economic chaos caused by an excess of economic individualism and doctrinaire views concerning the economic role of government and the government foundations of economics in a time of substantial change in our economic institutions and our economic reality.

In 1937, with its dramatic shift in view concerning "substantive due process" and the authority of courts to review state and federal legislation on economic grounds, the U.S. Supreme Court generally withdrew from the role of protecting inherent and preexisting property and contract rights in things. In what has been described as the "transactional justice vision" (Gjerdingen, 1986, pp. 876–78; Sandel, 1984, p. 5), the pre–1937 Court assumed that property and contract rights predated the state and that persons had certain spheres of personal autonomy as features of their existence as human beings. Individuals were assumed to be autonomous and free from the control of others and of government. The individual was viewed as having rights in things and was assumed to be free to bargain with others under the regime of a free market and a neutral government umpire. When disputes broke out, it was the role of the state to arbitrate the dispute without changing existing boundaries of property and contract rights or interfering with the exercise of individual autonomy. The status quo was assumed to be just, and the "is" determined the "ought." But it was a status quo that ignored the deeper moral responsibilities of government and the moral roots of economics. It was an ideologically frozen status quo that ignored the deeper moral roots of government and economics. Consequently, it was an ideology that could not deal with the crises of a massive depression and the modern realities of an industrial and postindustrial society.

A second view, one that has been called a "Distributive Justice view" (Gjerdingen, 1986), emphasized the validity of existing distributions of power, wealth, and position in society without regard for past claims of fixed rights. Under this view, existing patterns of rights distributions are measured against the overall goals of society and idealized patterns of distributions in light of modern circumstances. State intervention or nonintervention in relationships is not determined by some preexisting definition of who or what are legal entities in which rights are vested or by some preexisting core of property and contract rights, but by an agreed upon set of end goals. Such goals are "ought" criteria determined by majority rule in the democratic state subject to some constraint by a written constitution limiting the scope of majority rule in sensitive areas of individual rights and requiring procedural fairness in their determination and implementation. Neoclassical economists may see those goals as the "efficiency" criterion of their model without regard for the existing distribution of rights or wealth or as the protection of property and contract rights exercised under a market regime. A populist may see the goals that government ought to implement mandating a redistribution of wealth for social or political ends, without regard for existing contract or property rights or neoclassical efficiency concerns. Either approach would be "right" since no objective benchmark of fundamental moral values underlying both government and economics would exist—aside from majority rule—for determining the validity of the course chosen, except procedural fairness in taking the vote.

In this approach to rights it is obviously crucial to determine end goals—both the process for determining end goals and the content and source of the content of those goals. For example, utilitarian proponents of neoclassical thought who emphasize the "efficiency" objective for defining the role of government in economic affairs ignore the debate over the normative roots and current reality of rights in property and contract and the shift from contract to status as the basic means for defining legal entities entitled to such rights. In its more extreme utilitarian form, all else is made subservient to the end goal of permitting any conduct maximizing individual self-gratification, save that which results in a reduction of output. In view of the narrow rationality assumption about consumer behavior (Harrison, 1986) and the unrealistic assumption of perfect competition, a wide range of individual and collective behavior becomes presumptively lawful and entitled to governmental protection in the name of fulfilling the narrow utilitarian objectives of the model. Associated simplistic claims of being a "science" in the mechanistic sense of a value-free and neutral mathematical methodology for observing and predicting human behavior are relied on to detach the entire exercise from deeper normative questions that might muddy or upset the smooth functioning of the analysis and its two-dimensional model in providing the scientifically "right" answer. Economics and the other social "sciences," however, are disciplines that cannot avoid performing on the much higher and more demanding level of an art deeply concerned with the underlying moral values of society and evolving understandings of reality in the process of providing a part of the intellectual foundations of government. Detaching such disciplines from their deeper normative roots and cultural circumstances in the name of "science" is a form of discredited logical positivism, rather than rational intellectual and empirical inquiry aware of its own assumptions and the moral roots of the society in which it functions.

In economics, for example, one's ingoing assumptions and the tools selected for analysis will determine what it is that is to be measured as the "reality" with which government must deal. Like the Ptolemaic version of the nature of the universe, one's ingoing assumptions will dictate "output," or output in the sense that the assumptions underlying the model determine what will be allowed to be considered fact and value to be measured by the model and, therefore, dictate what will be allowed to be considered the output considered "scientifically" true. One can be caught in a superficial two-dimensional and circular form of reasoning detached from the normative roots that must be explored and honored to answer the riddle of the economic foundations of government and the governmental foundation of economics. The chicken and the egg can easily become an endless circle—a rebirth of the discredited tautology of logical positivism in economic and political thought—detached from reality and the moral roots of the culture by reliance on a closed model of the ''is'' to determine the ''ought'' (McCloskey, 1985).

It should be apparent that both government and economics must search elsewhere, and do so reflectively, to discover the foundation of each and of both. Like all other areas of intellectual inquiry, the search must be for identifying and understanding the underlying moral and normative roots to which a society is committed and by which reality must be understood and evaluated. Just as it is inescapable for every legal decision to be a moral decision (Cohen, 1959, pp. 3–7), every economic and governmental decision is a moral decision premised on ''ought'' propositions concerning what we are as a culture and as a society. Central to both economic and government definitions of the roots of what we are as a culture are our concepts of individualism, property, and contract in light of our broader consensus on what justice means (Griffen, 1987). These are central and basic propositions around which most of our economic, political, and legal thinking revolve. Their meaning draws from a common pool of moral beliefs confronted by every society when it determines to establish a government to resolve the dilemma of making order out of chaos and to reconcile peacefully and justly the moral demands of individualism and those of community.

The American Declaration of Independence and the Preamble to the United States Constitution are devoted to setting forth the justification and basis for forming our government; and to defining the proper balance between individualism and community. Both evidence underlying moral assumptions concerning individualism, property, contract, and justice defining the economic foundations of government and governmental foundations of economics. The Preamble to the Constitution states that the purposes of the document are ''to establish a more perfect Union, establish Justice, insure domestic tranquility, provide for the common welfare, and secure the blessings of liberty to ourselves and our posterity.'' The long list of complaints in the Declaration of Independence and the normative assumptions underlying them are directly related to and give meaning to the Preamble and other provisions of the Constitution. It is submitted that the protection of individualism and the freedom of individuals to relate one with the other with respect to their political, economic, and social activity in the context of a peaceful and just society were of central concern to those who framed our system of government. It was recognized that there is an unending tension between individualism and community with individualism recognizing deep philosophical and religious beliefs in the integrity, independence and personal responsibility of the individual and community recognizing the need for a just community and a method for sorting out peacefully conflicts of individual rights and protecting the individual from the collective and the collective from the individual. Both the transactional and distributive views of justice must be accommodated in establishing the governmental foundations of economics and in reconciling the conflict between individualism and community. The significance of property and contract rights as a means of protecting individualism and community, not ends in themselves, cannot be ignored in the calculus, nor can they be made subservient to narrow utilitarian or libertarian political ends of the model builders (Michelman, 1987).

The function of economic analysis in establishing foundations of government must also be to study and explicate a system of economics accommodating both a transactional and distributive view of justice, a system compatible with moral values that insure domestic tranquility, provide for the common welfare, and secure the blessings of liberty within the limits of the moral constraints of our commitment to individualism and community. Economic and government models inconsistent with these underlying moral objectives and contemporary reality— like the absolutism of libertarian systems premised on immutable property rights in things and absolutist rights and purely utilitarian systems that make individualism and the rights of property and contract completely subservient to tautological concepts of rationality and efficiency—repudiate the common moral roots of both government and economics. By the same token, governmental systems that refuse to accord individual economic decisions respect and provide stability and justice in standards for why, when, and how such rights are to be enforced or not enforced deny the relevance of economic insights to government and the subtle relationship between protecting economic rights and the vitality of the civil rights of individuals. Such simplistic efforts are akin to finger painting in circumstances where the hand of a great artist immersed in the history, traditions, and values of our society is needed. In this day of an increasing drift to political and economic oligarchies threatening both individualism and community, we are in need of the hands of great artists in both government and economics to understand and deal with contemporary reality in light of our moral traditions.

In the end, it is not a case of either economics determining the role of government or of government determining the role of economics. Each serves to define the other in light of our cultural heritage, the insights of other disciplines, and the moral values that a reflective awareness of our history and experience defines for us. It is a case of incorporating insights from both economic and political thought, in light of the moral reasons common to both, to explain why we as a culture have collected the many into the one in the name of protecting the liberty and freedom of the one and of the all in matters of government and in matters of economics. The economic foundations of government and the governmental foundations of economics are to be found in the deeper moral reasons for why our forebears chose to form a government and the moral reasons for why we choose to keep the commitment in light of contemporary reality (Griffen, 1987)—or at least keep the commitment as long as our underlying moral beliefs are held in common and are honored in the name and spirit of our collective sense of justice. Like the riddle of the chicken and the egg, the economic foundations of government and the government foundations of economics are to be found in the deeper insights of moral philosophy. These insights are illuminated by an awareness of our history and experience, and not in the axiomatic definition of the foundation of one to the other.

REFERENCES

Ackerman, Bruce. *Reconstructing American Law*. Cambridge, Mass.: Harvard University Press, 1984.

Atiyah, P. S. *The Rise and Fall of Freedom of Contract*. Oxford: Oxford University Press, 1979.

Bodenheimer, Edgar. *"Individual and Organized Society from the Perspective of a Philosophical Anthropology."* *Journal of Social and Biological Structure* 207 (1986).

Cohen, Felix. *Ethical Systems and Legal Ideals: An Essay on the Foundations of Legal Criticism*. Ithaca, N.Y.: Great Seal Books, 1959.

Fromm, Eric. *Marx's Concept of Man*. New York: Frederick Unger, 1966.

Fuller, Lon. "Freedom as a Problem of Allocating Choice." 112 *Proceedings of the American Philosophical Society* 101 (1968).

Gilmore, Grant. *The Death of Contract*. Columbus: Ohio State University Press, 1974.

Gjerdingen, Donald. "The Politics of the Coase Theorem and Its Relationship to Modern Legal Thought." *Buffalo Law Review* 35 (1986): 871.

Grey, Thomas. "The Disintegration of Property," in *Property*, *Nomos* 22 (1980): 69.

Griffen, Stephen M. "Reconstructing Rawl's Theory of Justice: Developing a Public Values Theory of the Constitution." *New York University Law Review* 62 (1987): 715.

Harrison, Jeffrey. "Egoism, Altruism and Market Illusions: The Limits of Law and Economics." *UCLA Law Review* 33, 1986, p. 1309.

Hicks, Sir John. *Causality in Economics*. New York: Basic Books, 1979).

Hobbes, Thomas. *Leviathan*. London: J. M. Dent and Sons, Ltd.; New York: E. P. Dutton and Co., 1914. Part II, Ch. 17, 18.

Kaireys, David, (ed.). *The Politics of Law: A Progressive Critique*. New York: Pantheon Books, 1982.

Macedo, Stephen. *The New Right v. the Constitution*. Washington, D. C.: Cato Institute, 1987.

McCloskey, Donald N. *The Rhetoric of Economics*. Madison: University of Wisconsin Press, 1985.

Macpherson, C. B. "Property as Means or End." In *The Rise and Fall of Economic Justice and Other Essays*, 86, Oxford: Oxford University Press, 1987.

Madison, James. *Letters and Other Writings of James Madison*. Vol. VI. New York: R. Worthington, 1884.

Maine, Henry. *Ancient Law: Its Connection with the Early History of Society, and Its Relation to Modern Ideas*. Classics of Anthropology Edition, A. Montague (ed.), 1869; Tempe: University of Arizona Press, 1986.

Michelman, Frank I. "Possession vs. Distribution in the Constitutional Idea of Property." *Iowa Law Review* 72 (1987): 1319.

Peller, Gary. "The Metaphysics of American Law." *California Law Review* 73 (1985): 1152.

Sandel, M. (ed.). *Liberalism and Its Critics*. New York: New York University Press, 1984.

Sartre, J. *Existentialism and Humanism*. P. Mairet, trans. London: Methuen, 1948.

10

True Fundamentals of the Economic Role of Government

C. Lowell Harriss

Governance of individual and group life involves a variety of factors. The concern of this volume centers on elements identified with political processes. Such predominantly nonpolitical forces as tradition, culture, religion, custom, convention, myth, and acceptance of institutions exert influences that have significance for economic life. They have some consequence for what would seem to be an ideal role for political processes. Their effects will differ somewhat from time to time and place to place.

My conclusions reflect, of course, my education over the years—something that I hope will continue. The frame of reference is Western civilization, chiefly in the Anglo-American tradition. Some core generalizations receive apparently universal agreement. One must then move from such generalities to specific elements required to convert them into workable realities. Doing so enlarges the area of probable, and then certain, disagreement.

One soon faces choices of the difference between essentials and degrees of desirability. No sharp, clear lines separate fundamentals of essentiality from aspects of goodness. Who will be satisfied with government alone as distinguished from qualities of good government, of the better and the search for the best? I will try to recognize the inevitability of imprecision. Many economies have functioned and progressed where government has been poor according to standards that most of us (and many of the people being governed) would consider worse than just poor.

GOVERNMENTS AS GROUPS OF ACTING HUMAN BEINGS

Governments (in the United States there were 83,217 in 1987) are means that human beings use to achieve objectives. Governments are human institutions. It is common, but very misleading, to personify "government" and to speak as if some entity has power to act as an agency independent of the people who make choices.

American governments differ enormously—from the national government to single-purpose special districts. They contrast in many ways with market-type units (businesses), families, religious groupings, labor unions, and many other types of voluntary associations. Individuals group together to work and play, to worship and study, to explore and to invest. We can distinguish among our associations according to the degree of freedom of choice—whether to associate at all, in what ways, for what purposes, and for how long, making certain contributions of effort and funds. One crucial difference between government and other forms of association is the power of coercion by those in charge—the extent of compulsion and the ways human beings exert it.

One constructive use of coercion through government is to protect humans against other coercion.

PROTECTION OF PERSON AND PROPERTY

Human life, including but not by any means limited to the economic aspects, depends on law and order. A classic, fundamental function of government is the protection of person and of those things outside oneself with which one is involved, one's property. Protection has profound significance for what we know as economic life. Production equipment outside the self—including housing (recall the disincentives of rack-rents in Ireland for house improvement!)— depends on a legal system and the enforcement of rules.

The reality of possible danger and of threats to personal security can hardly be judged by persons who have always lived in civilized societies where governments provide policing and protection. Yet muggings and other private uses of force do threaten and affect economic life. Governments, notably local, fall short of former standards in providing the basic function of protection.

The threats to property are also more evident than we would like—the holdup on the street, the theft from home or by the shoplifter, the embezzlement of investments. Government failure appears too often. But economic life continues.

Not all protection of person and property must be done by governmental organizations. Private security agencies both in this country and elsewhere operate within a legal system under which businesses and individuals are protected against certain private uses of coercion. This system permits others to count on our doing what we have agreed to by contract. Most issues never go to court. Some get to formal arbitration, under law.

Questions about the protection of property justify more discussion than is possible here. A modern economy requires commitments of funds and real resources for long periods. Government can provide some kinds of protection, as can insurance. Owners may seek governmental protection, for example, from imports and against other threats. Government itself can create risks that are not ordinarily insurable—those of new health or environmental regulations, deregulation, zoning change, added powers to labor unions, and so on. "Protection of property" is not a simple, clearcut matter.

DEFENSE AGAINST OUTSIDE ENEMIES

Protection against outside enemies is a fundamental responsibility of government. History has many examples of aggression. Perhaps human nature will change, but the evidence to date gives no support to a dream of economic or other safety and security without national defense.

Serious and continuing debate does affect our economic life—not about the need for protection but about the means to secure the proper amount. The needs of Singapore differ from those of Israel and the United States.

In a world of large and growing internationalization of economic life, collective agreements and obligations to be respected have economic significance.

FRAMEWORK

The word "framework" suggests a fundamentally basic role of government. It may convey more of a sense of a deliberately constructed edifice than is correct. The central idea is the set of rules by which individuals and businesses carry on their affairs. The coercive power of the state stands ready to enforce these rules when necessary. They provide stability and certainty and general conditions by which potentials of action can be judged.

Much of economic life involves commitments for the future. The framework of rules eliminates or reduces some uncertainties, permitting the making of more decisions with a greater sense of security than if the rules did not exist.

Economists almost without exception agree on the need for a rule-setting and contract-enforcing agency—one with the power of government to compel compliance. But what about the *content* of rules? At this point economists are likely to express differences. Many of us probably know rather little about the details of the legal framework of our economy. Specifically, some of us may need to know about the structure of the tax system or antitrust rules or labor law but not much about contract, property, tort, and other law.

Much of America's legal structure evolved as the common law over centuries. It was definitely not constructed as the framework of a factory is built. The Napoleonic Code had a different origin. Economic life goes on under each and every system. What is truly essential is that there be some framework, some set of rules and provisions for enforcement.

The structure should include mechanisms for its own revision. Market forces will produce change. Institutions develop and some wither away. The natural processes of economic life modify our ways of doing things without necessarily altering what government does. Yet one of the great challenges of organized life is for human beings using government to preserve, on the one hand, and to modify, on the other, elements of the framework. Recognizing the possibility of change, of altering "the rules of the game," we should see that it can create temptations.

The power of government can be used not merely to compel men and women and businesses to obey the rules, but also to convey benefits and impose losses. Results reflect not the *quid pro quo* of outcomes of free, voluntary decisions, but the "takings" and "windfalls."

The power of government to alter the framework with profoundly significant results, economic and other, can be restricted by written constitution, by checks and balances, and by other means. But pursuing this branch of the assigned topic is not possible in this short chapter.

MONEY

Money as the medium of exchange is crucial to effective cooperation in economic life. Privately created media of exchange might serve adequately in some circumstances, but for practical purposes we will conclude that authority over money goes along with sovereignty (with potential for delegation). The power to create media of exchange has enormous economic significance.

The medium of exchange is used as a store of value as well as a unit of account and as a standard of deferred payment. The historical record of the role of government includes much variety among nations over time and from one country to another at the same time. No one type of governmental policy can be cited as inherently fundamental in the sense of always being followed. Nor will economists who have studied money in some depth agree on what would be the results over time of alternative monetary policies in the years ahead. Doubts about the definition of "money," uncertainties about velocity changes, and the internationalization of finance in a world of floating exchange rates combine to create uncertainty.

Although tempted to comment on the challenge to government officials—and to the public they represent—to improve the management of monetary policy, I recognize the limits of our assignment. Except: Over the long sweep of history, and in many periods of only a few years, people have been subject to, or subjected themselves, to loss of purchasing power of the unit of money.

"PUBLIC" FACILITIES: INFRASTRUCTURE

People who act through governmental institutions—using coercion—can make various arrangements for facilities for common or collective use. Streets, parks, fire stations, prisons, courthouses, water and electric supply systems, schools, and so on—all are part of economic life. What is the fundamental role of government in their provision? The answers to this question today (1988) will reflect less certainty, I expect, than would the answers half a generation or more ago. Privatization and variations on relations of government and market participation are evidently affecting thought and practice.

One set of issues involves eminent domain. Coercive power can be used to great advantage—for example, in getting efficient and workable electricity or telephone or sewer systems. Economic life as we know it requires general public compulsion to take certain rights and real resources, paying compensation. Use of the power does not, however, imply that the activity involved is conducted by a governmental agency. Many electric utilities in this country are called public but are owned privately. Conditions may be attached to the granting of use of eminent domain. We should also note the possibility that actual use of this coercive power can be associated with extortion and corruption as well as with constructive wisdom.

The mention of infrastructure tempts one to comment on a variety of issues relevant to the role of government, both in theory and in practice. But once again space limits must be recognized, and so only one more topic will be raised in this section.

Are there not potentials for substantial economic benefit from arranging for a larger as against a smaller use of fixed capital—the declining-unit-cost condition? In some cases, a pricing system that covers full costs will curtail usage when the benefits exceed the variable cost. Might it not be possible to obtain the funds necessary to cover total expense while permitting the more complete use of resources that would be unused with full-cost pricing? In principle, the answer is "yes." (Some of us were taught that general benefits would result from taxing output produced under increasing cost to subsidize decreasing-cost output. Oversimplified but tempting as an objective!) The coercive power of government might be used to enlarge human welfare, but dreams can become nightmares. Experience with government subsidies and pricing shows very much indeed that economic analysis would not applaud.

ENCOURAGING COMPETITION: CURBING AND CONTROLLING MONOPOLY

The earlier discussion of the "framework" role of government can be amplified by an explicit reference to the economic as well as the other fruits of human freedom and of problems arising from monopoly-monopsony. In the market people can benefit by doing what others want. Decisions and choices made freely and with alternatives must be expected to go farther in satisfying human beings than decisions imposed. Decisions about what is to be produced, and how, will be better in human terms if the conditions of free markets (as economic analysis pictures) do prevail. The temptations to limit the other person's freedom can be expected from potentials for "extra" gain from restrictive forces.

This line of reasoning, and the faith embodied in the normative elements of the discussion, cannot be pursued here. Suffice it to say that people can influence the conditions for competitive market freedom and the nature and degrees of monopolistic restraints. The issues are enormously complex. A "basic fundamental'' role for collective action (government) cannot be defined here with enough precision to guide the operations of the political processes.

The proper role of patents and copyrights, the secrecy needed for national defense, the value of economies of scale, and so on create real issues of public policy. The ''common man'' cannot possibly know the details needed to make the many decisions that get into the governmental arena. Nor can the ''common man'' be sure whom to trust among the possible experts. At times we are told that such matters or the counterparts are handled better elsewhere—Japan, Sweden, France, and so on. Who can say, really?

Where people grant an exclusive franchise and monopoly power, governmental regulation is the rule in this country. Such association seems logical. The results, however, receive and often deserve criticism. The historical record of two of the more regulated activities, banking and railroading, can be instructive. The degree of exclusive monopoly power differed and changed with changes in conditions. Governmental response lagged.

HELPING THE POOR

One can look at the past and see many cases in which people failed to use government to alleviate misery. Helping the poor may thus seem less than a fundamental function of government. Today, however, our elected officials have overwhelming public support in reducing avoidable misery. Forcing everyone to pay taxes for help to the poor does not exclude voluntary aid, of which quite a bit remains, but the role of government is large.

It is also controversial—not that government should act but concerning the best methods of action. Which of the various programs have had what results? How should they be evaluated? What alternatives are available? How do immediate results contribute to desirable and to deplorable longer run consequences? And so on.

Here one faces inherently difficult problems. Today millions of children in the formative stages of life are growing up in conditions most of us can scarcely imagine. The challenges should get high priority among those things to which we as voters give attention. We, and *our* children, will be influenced by infants and youngsters now growing up in poverty, with a close exposure to crime and drugs, inadequate parenting, and so on.

EDUCATION

Public schooling and governmental universities are relatively new in human history. Even today a considerable amount of schooling is conducted by private, profit-seeking organizations and church groups. Many colleges and universities are nongovernmental. Yet federal financing of students and research, and various forms of state and local help plus tax exemption influence ''private sector'' education.

A general, collective interest in education grows out of the values of living with educated as against ignorant neighbors. Principles of common interest, positive externalities, and cumulative benefit, among others, provide convincing reasons for the use of power of coercion in the advance of education. But how?

THE ADVANCE OF KNOWLEDGE

The changing times may bring changing concepts of what ought to be considered a fundamental function of government. Today, do we not generally believe that the collective interest in research and the advance of knowledge are great enough to create a convincing reason for governmental responsibility? The most that can be hoped for from private activity—nonprofit (university) and industry—will fall short of what would serve us well. Of course, there is national defense. But there is more.

The principle, the goal, appeals. The conversion to reality of government performance presents problems, more than could be noted here if I had not run out of space.

AND SO ON

Externalities, regulation, environmentalism, immigration control, prevention of domestic balkanization, bankruptcy, the conduct of foreign affairs, air safety, and so on—there are so many things for which a case can be, and is, made favoring governmental action. The Founding Fathers and their intellectual models could not have known about much of modern life. They knew about human nature and had much of value to tell. We can hope to see farther because we can stand on their shoulders. In doing so, however, we should try to keep our feet on the ground of reality—confusing the figure of speech. We should look at how human beings do act through politics. The Public Choice materials can help in guiding decisions to avoid a romantic dreamworld without renouncing aspiration.

11

Economists' Role in Government at Risk

Werner Z. Hirsch

In "The Fire of Truth: A Remembrance of Law and Economics at Chicago, 1932–1970," Edmund W. Kitch (1983) (a lawyer by profession) wrote: "There is great legitimacy given to the idea that the government is going to be doing these things [make public policy] and we in the law schools should try to help the government do it right." Likewise, economists should try to help government do it right. With this objective in mind, I will seek to examine the condition in which economics today finds itself, specifically, to explore why its present status may impede it in effectively assisting government decision making.

For the economic role of government to be effectively carried out, it is important that decision makers have knowledge of reality and be aware of values. This condition is in part a matter of the information which economists provide decision makers. Undue mathematization and ideological biases can impede the role of economists. In recent years the work of economists and the language they use have moved the discipline into a corner. Perhaps few economists realize that this has been happening; even fewer had intended it to happen. Two prevailing phenomena are responsible for this state of affairs—an excessive reliance on mathematics, and politicization of economic research. These common practices and trends, some originally designed to advance economics as a social science, have had the undesirable effect of exposing economics to the risk of being of little use to decision makers in and out of government.

Unfortunately, examining the dangers facing economics in the late 1980s involves, to some extent, criticism of economics and its practitioners. While I am not attracted to the role of a critic, I am following an admonition by Jacques Barzun (1978): "What all the professions need today is critics from inside, men who know what the conditions are, and also the arguments and excuses, and in a full sweep over the field can offer their fellow practitioners a new vision of the profession as an institution." I do not presume to be able to take "a full sweep over the field," but I hope to offer some insight.

First, however, I would like to offer a historical review of how philosophers and social thinkers have viewed the development of political philosophy and social and economic policies as well as their implementation.

BRIEF HISTORICAL REVIEW

Plato thought that a group of sages could discover correct solutions to the transcending social problems of the day; he even wanted to give an elite of sages the responsibility to implement the solutions. Philosophers who followed him have been less ambitious. Still they have been pondering how best to advance the systematic examination of the relations of human beings with each other. They have engaged in the moral inquiry of how life should be lived and have offered beliefs of how groups and nations should interact. In so doing, they have sought to develop what we have come to call political philosophy. In this endeavor they cannot discover the single truth about human, national, and societal relations because any social philosophy is rooted in values about which disagreements abound.

Frustrated that they could not arrive at a single political philosophy and therefore a solution to a given problem area, they sought to become more scientific and objective in the manner in which they conducted intellectual inquiries. Duly impressed by the rapid strides made by the natural sciences and the success of their methods, often based on mathematical techniques, they began to emulate them. Their hope was to establish similar irrefutable laws in the realm of human affairs. They thought to introduce the methods developed by natural science into the social sciences with the objective of formulating hypotheses, testing them (perhaps even by experiments), and deducing universal principles and insights from them. In this manner, it was hoped, intellectual confusion could be ended, prejudice eliminated, and great progress toward the solution of social problems made.

For a while the world was seen through rose-colored glasses. As in the natural sciences, all significant social questions must have one true answer; there exists a dependable path toward the discovery of these truths; and these true answers are compatible with one another and form a single whole.

In the nineteenth century, some thinkers including Hegel and Marx questioned the power of research methods and the individual's ability to derive a single, timeless truth. They realized the importance of ever-changing conditions, with human horizons altering over time and people, even the best intentioned ones, espousing different values and objectives.

Economists in the twentieth century, and especially since World War II, recognized these problems. In North America, the United Kingdom, and Scandinavia in particular, they worked diligently to make economics a rigorous science. They reached agreement on a number of fundamental axioms from which major economic propositions could be derived. The four major axioms of economics are:

Axiom 1: Individuals' wants are limitless whereas resources are scarce.

Axiom 2: Individuals are rational in the sense that their decision-making process is consistent with their aims.

Axiom 3: Individuals seek to maximize self-interest.

Axiom 4. It is possible to separate conceptually the individual from his environment.

Using these axioms, economics as a science seeks to derive propositions about the optimal actions of individuals and their coalitions in their concern with efficiency and equity, as they respond to the environment in which they operate. With the aid of these propositions, it has become possible to explain economic phenomena, point to existing deficiencies in social regulations, and offer alternatives with the possibility of evaluating their merits. Empirical methods, especially econometric ones, have helped test the propositions thus derived.

Altogether, economists have worked hard at developing deductive economic theories as well as econometric methods for their empirical testing in the hope of perfecting a powerful and systematic body of intellectual inquiry. One purpose, and in my view a major one, has been to assist decision makers in and out of government to carry out their role in the economic sphere. Economists have done so for quite some time, perhaps more in the United States than in many other Western countries, and on all three levels of government. On the federal level, for example, the creation of the Bureau of the Budget (later renamed the Office of Management and Budget) and of the President's Council of Economic Advisors in the executive branch, and of the Joint Economic Committee of Congress in the legislative branch, are indicative of interest in economic expertise.

It would be wrong, however, to consider the role of economists in government only in terms of their actual service in government on a full-time or consultative basis. Although Lord Maynard Keynes, for example, served in the British government, his ideas and theories more than his physical presence probably affected governments. The same holds for many economists, particularly the Nobel Laureates.

THE ROLE OF ECONOMISTS

Economists and economics play a variety of roles in assisting governments. They cover the spectrum from mundane, routine operations to high-level advice to those who make major economic decisions. In connection with major decisions, which is the concern of this chapter, one of the most powerful models is for economists to help improve the manner in which decision makers first think about fundamental goals and then make informed choices among the more attractive alternatives. In relation to government, this means that economists should (1) provide systematic information with regard to possible goals, (2) identify the more attractive alternative steps to achieve them, and (3) attempt to quantify their likely gains and losses, as well as distribution of these gains and losses among relevant segments of the population and economy. Having produced this information in a rigorous and comprehensive manner as well as in generally comprehensible language, economists should step back and leave it up to elected policymakers to choose what they consider to be the best, politically acceptable, alternative.

This model for the economist's role in government decision making requires that they act qua as scientists and not as ideologues or advocates. The ideological role is open to them as citizens and voters. Mixing up these two roles can be damaging. As scientists, however, they must also guard against using methodologies and assumptions that are very far removed from reality, and against speaking in a language, for example, mathematics, which leaves a wide gulf between them and their patrons, be they government officials or the public.

THE PRESENT RECORD

Monitoring and evaluating the state of economics is not an exact science. Nevertheless, fully aware of the magnitude of the task, we will attempt a first cut. We find significant evidence that the credibility of economists and their usefulness to their patrons are imperilled by two developments in the profession: its emphasis on mathematics and its compromises with scholarly objectivity.

Overly Mathematical

The recent trend of economics has been to place great stock in the mathematical treatment of economic issues. This focus has all too frequently forced economists to incorporate into their work restrictive assumptions that are highly unrealistic. As a consequence, their work has been far removed from the real economic world which is so very complex and ever changing. This fact has reduced the applicability of research results and the usefulness of economists to decision makers.

It is very demanding to examine masses of economic articles in terms of the extent to which they use mathematics and realism in their assumptions. We can benefit from work done by Herbert G. Grubel and Lawrence A. Boland (1986), who reviewed 15 economic journals of great diversity for the period 1950–1983. They found in the most venerable and highly regarded *American Economic Review*, the *Journal of Political Economy*, and the *Quarterly Journal of Economics*, as well as the more recently founded *Journal of Monetary Economics* and the *Canadian Journal of Economics*, that about 50 percent of all articles in the early 1980s were mathematical treatises. As was to be expected, the percentage was even higher, that is, 85 to 100 percent, in such specialized journals as the *Journal of Economic Theory* and the *Review of Economic Studies*.

Separately, we have surveyed the 1983–1987 volumes of the *American Economic Review*, focusing on it as the official publication of the main professional association in the United States and the most widely cited and prestigious economics publication in the world. Our concern was not only with the use of equations in general and mathematical economics in particular, but also with the econometric testing of mathematical models. Our findings of the 263 articles published in the *American Economic Review* during 1983–1987 (we did not cover shorter papers and proceedings volumes) can be summarized as follows:

All but 16, that is, a total of 94 percent of the articles, had some mathematical equations. (The 16 nonmathematical articles included most of the annual presidential addresses.) More significantly, 129 articles, or about half, were in the nature of mathematical economics, that is, they presented mathematical models without any empirical testing. Eighty-nine articles, or about a third, were econometric. In conclusion, there is little doubt that articles recently published in the lead journal of the American Economic Association have been highly mathematical.

We are not the first to worry about economists' heavy reliance on mathematics. A strong admonition to mend their ways came from John Maynard Keynes (1936):

Too large a proportion of recent "mathematical" economics are mere concoctions, as imprecise as the initial assumptions they rest on, which allow the author to lose sight of the complexities and interdependencies of the real world in a maze of pretensions and unhelpful symbols.

More recently, Wassily Leontief (1971) warned economists in his 1970 presidential address that economics has taken a wrong turn:

. . . an uneasy feeling about the present state of our discipline has been growing. . . . anyone capable of learning elementary, or preferably advanced calculus and algebra, and acquiring acquaintance with the specialized terminology of economics can set himself up as a theorist. Uncritical enthusiasm for mathematical formulation tends often to conceal the ephemeral substantive content of the arguments behind the formidable front of algebraic signs.

Leontief (1982) continued this theme in a letter to *Science*,

. . . professional economic journals are filled with mathematical formulas leading the reader from sets of more or less plausible but entirely arbitrary assumptions to precisely stated but irrevelant theoretical conclusions. . . .

Year after year economic theorists continue to produce scores of mathemetical models and to explore in great detail their formal properties; and the econometricians fit algebraic functions of all possible shapes to essentially the same sets of data without being able to advance in any perceptible way, a systematic understanding of the structure and the operations of a real economic system.

An equally critical concern has been expressed by Frank H. Hahn (1984), a former president of the Econometric Society and himself a highly respected mathematical economist:

The achievements of economic theory in the last two decades are both impressive and in many ways beautiful. But it cannot be denied that there is something scandalous in the spectacle of so many people refining the analysis of economic states which they give no reason to suppose will ever, or have ever, come about. . . . It is an unsatisfactory and slightly dishonest state of affairs.

Although these critical views on economics in general are expressed by thoughtful insiders, policymakers too have begun to express concern, for example, in relation to such specialized fields as urban economics. In conversations I have heard a secretary of the U.S. Department of Housing and Urban Development express great dissatisfaction with what economists have contributed to effective policy formulation. The minister for Housing and Construction of the United Kingdom has expressed similar misgivings to me.

Wanting Scholarly Objectivity

We would hope that carefully crafted economic theories and models as well as their implementation with the aid of econometric methods would meet the most stringent test of intellectual integrity. This requirement is stipulated by the unique circumstances of social science research which can never be totally insulated from the values of investigators. It is a fact that many scholars have deep-seated, often unconsciously held, beliefs that can affect the outcome of their research. This can happen by influencing their choice of questions to be researched and the angle of the approach used. Even the most objective researcher is faced by these circumstances in the form of unexamined beliefs. These widely recognized circumstances make it essential that economists make an all-out effort to conduct their research with the greatest possible objectivity.

Since the 1960s, however, ideology-driven economic research appears to have gained in importance in the United States. It has been accompanied by ideological polarization. Such polarization of economists is relatively new for the United States, though it has existed in the United Kingdom for many years. For example, the Faculty of Economics and Political Science as well as the Department of Applied Economics at Cambridge University have long been known to favor strong government intervention. Some of its members, for example, the late Nicholas Kaldor, worked closely with the Labor party and significantly influenced its economic policies. At the same time, the Economics Department of York University has been known as laissez-faire champions, as has the Institute of Economic Affairs, with its Arthur Seldon seeking to shape economic policymaking of the Conservative party.

In the United States since the 1960s, ideological influences have also become more pervasive. Although it is difficult to pinpoint the date when this trend began, the role of research institutes, often referred to as think tanks, is a good indication. Thus, in the mid–1960s, with the active support of the Johnson Administration, the Urban Institute was established, with a liberal orientation.

During the Nixon Administration such existing research institutions as the American Enterprise Institute and the Hoover Institution were revitalized and given significantly larger resources, and their research results began to be widely disseminated in such major publications as the *Wall Street Journal*. Later, some new conservative think tanks were established, with the Heritage Foundation perhaps being the most important. Members of these think tanks played a particularly important role in the economic policy formulation of the Reagan Administration, which some of their leaders not only admitted, but also boasted about.

University departments also appear to have become more divided along ideological lines. The Chicago school, with the subfield of law and economics at Chicago, is an excellent example. Its evolution and ideas are well documented in the Proceedings of a 1981 conference summarized in a 70-page article called "The Fire of Truth: A Remembrance of Law and Economics at Chicago, 1932–1970" (Edmund Kitch, 1983) and my review in the JAI Research Annual on *Law and Policy Studies* (Werner Hirsch and Unghwan Choi, forthcoming).

It is difficult, though not impossible, to quantify the tendency of ideology to affect economic research. Particularly demanding and hazardous is the attempt to identify scholars with a liberal or conservative philosophy and to correlate this fact with the nature of their research findings.

In recognition of the difficulty of testing individuals for ideological bias, our inquiry concentrates on whether select scholarly journals publish mainly articles on a specific policy issue written from a particular angle and consistent with the journal's ideological bent. We have selected an economic policy issue that continues to be the subject of much intellectual interest and economic research, that is, government regulation. Moreover, it is one of the policy issues which, in part, have been subjected to a survey of the attitude of economists in five countries, including the United States.

In the early 1980s, Bruno S. Frey et al. (1984) surveyed more than 2,000 economists as to whether, in their views (1) antitrust laws should be used vigorously to reduce monopoly power from its current level and (2) "consumer protection" laws generally reduce economic efficiency. The survey found a high level of consensus in favor of regulation. Specifically, in the five countries 48.9 percent generally favored vigorous use of monopoly laws, 37.3 percent did so with some provisions, and only 12.5 percent generally opposed it. The numbers in relation to the inefficienty of regulation were 13.6, 23.6, and 61.4 percent, respectively. For the United States the monopoly numbers were 47.8, 35.1, and 14.7 percent, and the regulation inefficiency numbers were 23.2,, 27.0, and 46.0 percent.

For our review, we have selected two journals. One is the *Journal of Law and Economics*, which for many years has been edited by a distinguished economist and published by the University of Chicago. It is very closely associated with the Chicago School of Law and Economics which has pronounced views on government regulation of industry. Thus, its disciples believe in the efficiency of free market exchange and call for removal of constraints to free trade. Toward this end they oppose regulations, particularly since, in their view, parties will attempt to circumvent legal restrictions that are inconsistent with the perceived self-interest.

The second journal surveyed is the prestigious *Economic Journal*, published for many years at Cambridge University and alleged to favor strong government intervention, including regulation of the workings of the economy.

There can be little doubt that the Chicago School has a clearcut position opposing regulation. But should the *Journal* only publish articles whose conclusions, particularly empirically derived ones, are supportive of this position? We reviewed all articles published in the *Journal of Law and Economics* between 1982 and 1987 and found that a very large percentage of its articles addressed regulation. Although it is not always easy to classify such articles, we made a sincere effort to do so fairly. Of these 45 articles, 30, or 67 percent, reached conclusions inimical to regulation, 3, or 7 percent, were favorable to regulation, and 12, or 27 percent, were neutral.

When we made a similar analysis of the 1980–1986 articles in the *Economic Journal*, whose editors appear to have a more positive attitude toward government regulation, quite different results were obtained: 16 of its articles were related to regulation, with 6, or 38 percent, reaching conclusions favorable; 4, or 25 percent, unfavorable; and, 6, or 38 percent, neutral to regulation. Although the tenor of the *Economic Journal* articles is somewhat more balanced than that of the *Journal of Law and Economics*, the thrust of the two appear to be in opposing directions.

SOME CONCLUDING THOUGHTS

In the past economics has been credited with being one of the more rigorous, powerful ''scientific'' social sciences. The reasons, no doubt, are that its concerns are more readily quantified than those of other social sciences and that able investigators have excelled in effectively advancing the field. However, we have detected two trends of recent vintage that can spell trouble. Economists appear more and more to engage in research that tends (1) to be overly mathematical, producing results far removed from real life and presented in a manner all too often inaccessible to most public decision makers, and (2) to suffer from a lack of scholarly objectivity, with the result that much economic research tends to be ideology-driven.

Under these circumstances, government decision makers who should be thinking about fundamental goals and who need to make difficult choices may not get the help from economists which they need to raise the quality of their decisions. In the presence of ideological polarization, liberal officials tend to hire liberal economists and conservative officials to hire conservative economists. Under these conditions, economists will often merely reconfirm their patrons' biases or be used as window dressing. Flora Lewis (1987) was right when she wrote, ''Politicians will be politicians. But that's not a reason why scientists shouldn't have to be scientists, during working hours. Off duty, they've a right to personal views like anybody else, but they owe it to their professionalism to make the distinction."

Matters are exacerbated by the fact that today economics is too mathematical and, as Simon Kuznets is reported to have said on the occasion of his eightieth birthday, "too formal, too divorced from the real world" (Fogel, 1987). Moreover, Kuznets had become

impatient with economists who become infatuated with elegance and forget that the aim of theory was to promote the search for tested knowledge about economic behavior. There was a limit to how far theory in economics could become separated from the product which the patrons of economics—the policymakers—demand of the discipline (Fogel, 1987).

Should these two trends continue, economists will increasingly be forced into a position in which they can rightly be accused of lacking scholarly integrity, of being of little use to serious-minded government officials bent on raising the level of their decision-making capability, and of possibly becoming altogether irrelevant. I would hope that we could begin to reverse this unfortunate trend which threatens to put economics at risk.

NOTE

The author would like to thank Unghwan Choi who assisted in reviewing the *American Economic Review*, the *Journal of Law and Economics*, and the *Economic Journal*, and to Professor Luc Weber for critical comments.

REFERENCES

Barzun, Jacques. "The Professions Under Siege." *Harpers*, October 1978, p. 68.

Fogel, Robert. *Some Notes on the Scientific Methods of Simon Kuznets.* Working Paper No. 2461. Cambridge, Mass.: National Bureau of Economic Research, 1987.

Frey, Bruno S., et al. "Consensus and Dissention Among Economists." *American Economic Review* (December 1984): 986–94.

Grubel, Herbert G., and Lawrence A. Boland. "On the Efficient Use of Mathematics in Economics." *Kyklos* 39, (1986): 427–30.

Hahn, Frank. *Equilibrium and Macroeconomics.* Cambridge, Mass.: MIT Press, 1984, p. 88.

Hirsch, Werner Z., and Unghwan Choi. "Law and Economics: An Overview and Analysis." *Law and Policy Studies* (forthcoming).

Keynes, John Maynard. *The General Theory of Employment, Interest and Money.* London: Macmillan, 1936, p. 298.

Kitch, Edmund W. "The Fire of Truth: A Remembrance of Law and Economics at Chicago, 1932–1970." *Journal of Law and Economics*, (April 1983): 26, 175–76.

Leontief, Wassily. "Theoretical Assumptions and Nonobserved Facts." *American Economic Review* 41 (March 1971): 1–2.
———. "Academic Economics." *Science* 217 (1982): 104–107.
Lewis, Flora. *New York Times*, November 13, 1987, Y.27.

12

The Public Costs of Private Blessings

Irving Louis Horowitz

There are as many pitfalls as there are portholes in addressing this topic. To start with, what one considers to be "fundamental" in contrast to that which is "specific" or "routine" with respect to government intervention in the affairs of the economy rests heavily on certain nameless metaphysical dispositions. Historically, in the earliest stages of the United States, the issue is one that dates back to the struggle between Jeffersonian Republicanism and Madisonian Federalism. Furthermore, from an analytical perspective, what constitutes government apart from state and society is by no means readily apparent. Operationally, we may denote government as the art of satisfying the wants and needs of a citizenry, whereas the state represents the legal structure that provides a monopoly of force and authority to insure the continuance and extension of national sovereignty. Thus, in the act of trying to address what is presumably a straightforward and "objective" issue, one rather quickly moves into the realm of moral sentiment and philosophical subjectivity. So we are not too much further along in vision at least than the legacy bequeathed to us by the dual forces of Anglo-American constitutionalism and European institutionalism.

It is worthwhile, albeit risky, to state what is common to all social systems with respect to the economic role of government. Historically and currently, the economic role of government in an open market system is less active than in a planned market system. At the same time, within nominally free enterprise systems such as Japan, the amount of government intervention is far higher than Western conventions allowed for in past epochs. Certainly, the litmus test of a social system in the twentieth century is its capacity to provide basic needs for human survival and to do so in a context in which egalitarian inputs (if not outcomes) can be assured (if not guaranteed).

This ever-expanding role of governance results from the infinite regress of equity demands. As a single example, what the Marxists of the late nineteenth century contemptuously referred to as the lumpenproletariat, the raw cannon fodder of bourgeois assaults on proletarian virtue, by the late twentieth century has become the virtuous homeless. Once the larger goals of racial and gender equality have been realized, at least in the main, attention turns toward refinements of all sorts: the aged, the infirm, the handicapped, the street people, the sexually different, and so on. In short, since equity demands are infinite, so too are government obligations to raise the capital, or better, the supplies, necessary to resolve such special interest needs. Deficit spending as a way of life is not a normal outcome of any equilibrium model but rather the moral consequence of an equity model.

The economic role of government in the twentieth century is without precedent because the size and structure of government has been so radically enlarged in this century from all previous centuries. In the past, the government, or if you will, the state, had as its primary purpose guaranteeing the survival of its citizens from foreign invasion, threat, or intimidation. If in the act of so doing, the state felt at liberty to also threaten and intimidate a sector of its population, this behavior could readily be justified in the name of *Staatsrason*. This was well understood from Thomas Hobbes to Friedrich Meinecke. In this way, the Machiavellian and the Hobbesian premises of the relationship between ruler and ruled held sway (Meinecke, 1957). Questions about a standing army and how to provide for the maintenance of the realm were central to the study of government. The only time the issue of the economic role of government entered public discussion in centuries past, or more precisely underwent select elite scrutiny, was precisely when the national or dynastic structure, that is, the social order itself, came under immediate danger of extinction and extermination.

Defense of the realm is clearly no longer the exclusive or even the major function of governance in the late twentieth century. Indeed, as warfare between nations becomes more remote, made so by technological instruments of total devastation and mutual destruction, the role of government has increasingly shifted from a foreign to a domestic venue. The state, far from being the praetorian guard of the ruling class, as Marx claimed for it in *The German Ideology*, becomes the great benefactor of the working masses. The appeals of equity are not made on the basis of individual assistance of the fortunate to the needy, or mediated through claims of a philanthropic sort, but rather are directly expressed through the political system and addressed to the federal government from the bottom up as it were. The government becomes the fulcrum of demand, as well as the source of economic well-being and potential succor. Regulating inflation and unemployment becomes the critical feature of macroeconomic policies, as well as the defining characteristic of partisan politics in advanced governments (Hibbs, 1987).

For what we have witnessed, and what Max Weber earlier in the century pinpointed, is the relative decline of older social classes—the peasantry in the nineteenth century and the proletariat in the twentieth century. This is coupled with the growing importance and influence of a new class of administrators and bureaucrats called the government. In point of fact, this class sector has become the most rapidly rising economic entity in the present century. Thus, to address the question of the economic role of government one must never ignore the parallel fact that government as such is a system of economy, and hence the issues are not so much two forces facing off: economy versus government, but the interlocking nature of the two in the fabric of an advanced civilization—whatever its political system.

All social systems in our time claim that they uniquely can provide a superior set of equities for all citizens, or at least that class of citizens deemed meritorious. Even dictatorial regimes do not lack a rhetoric to express such equity considerations. In exchange for loyalty, citizens claim, and most often receive, a survival floor in staples beyond which such citizens in ordinary circumstances are not allowed to fall. Thus, to properly evaluate the issue of the economic role of government is to take seriously the budgetary claims that governments make to solicit and elicit the support of its citizenry. For as Aaron Wildavsky has often and properly reminded us, the budget is the lifeblood of governments, democratic and totalitarian, and hence is the financial reflection of the political intentions of government as such (Wildavsky, 1986).

In any earlier epoch, when the libertarian aspects of society prevailed, the hue and cry of the dominant social sectors was "that government governs best that governs least." The judicial function of government was translated into minimizing its allocational features at the economic level (Nozick, 1974). Even at the turn of the twentieth century, a capital city like Washington, D.C., was a rather provincial affair. By the end of the same century, it has grown tenfold—from 250,000 to 2.5 million in the greater District of Columbia area. This growth parallels the claims of government to administer those laws that presumably guarantee equity and justice, and reflects change not only in the economic role of government, but no less, in what the philosophers of the people mean by government, namely, the prevention of discrimination and the exercise of justice (Rawls, 1971). As envisioned in a charter such as the United States Constitution, government was comprised of three branches: executive, legislative, and judicial. But the administration of equity has changed the parameters of all this, so that a fourth branch, what might be termed the policy sector, determines what economic roles a government will play and perform. It does so in the context of an intensified pluralist style of politics in which demands of the self often merge with demands of self-interest (Laumann and Knoke, 1987). What this means, of course, is that the normal rationality of the marketplace becomes increasingly distorted and then discarded. Economic supplies and demands are displaced by the rationality of social requirements.

The question might be raised as to what are the specific grounds on which private sector supply and demand is to be given privileged status versus public expenditure decisions. To be sure, no categorical response to such a line of reasoning is possible. But on specific moral grounds the advantages of the marketplace are clear. In cases of specific choice—for example, the right to know versus the right to copyright protection—the marketplace can better adjudicate differences of such ultimate choices with far greater ease than mandates of political economy on behalf of one or the other approach to evaluating the costs of ideas. Can decisions that tilt toward public expenditures over free market expressions be made? Of course they can. But then the issue shifts dramatically to the efficacy of dictatorship over the presumed inefficiency of democracy. Here the economic history of top-down planning regimes holds few joys over bottom-up free market systems. Even the socialist sector in the Soviet Union and China has come to recognize as much.

Along with this recognition of the role of "public choice" in all advanced economies is a parallel awareness that the role of government in insuring such choice is very great indeed. The cutting edge, the fine line distinction, is between a government role that enhances market choice in contrast to a role that usurps such choices for itself. But the old nineteenth-century idea that the state is the running dog of ruling-class interests has been abandoned by all save the hard-bitten Leninists. It is more nearly the case that economic classes and political elites do not so much arrive at tradeoffs as they melt into one another at the functional, bureaucratic level.

The United States' experience demonstrates a perfect ideological scale in which the balance has shifted from the pure Madisonian federalist ideology of bare minimal treading on citizen activities, to Jeffersonian republican values emphasizing the social responsibility of government to its citizens. This is not merely a concept of rich versus poor. Bailing out such corporations as Lockheed and Chrysler represented successful attempts not just to salvage losing firms, but to maintain the jobs and careers of the working people connected with such troubled firms. It might well be that the support of corporations at the economic top of the ladder is greater and more successful than support of mothers on welfare with dependent children. But the critical factor is that government takes its task of satisfying equity demands most seriously across class lines, as long as the bonds of the economy and society as such are not sapped and severed.

In short, in the twentieth century, the choices are within the parameters of system survival and equity claims, and not between an all-powerful economic role of government and a nonexistent role. Thus, the bitter, partisan struggles on the appropriate economic role of government essentially take for granted that such a role is legitimate to start with, a presumption that was not transparently self-evident in earlier centuries. What is most extraordinary is the consensus across political systems that this is the case. States do not "wither away" in the socialist bloc, nor do they become "command posts for the bourgeoisie" in the capitalist West. Such talk among social scientists is scarce indeed, a reminder of an analytically naive past.

The effectiveness of government is measured by how well its economic allocations are carried forth, not by whether it has an entitlement to perform such a role. In that context, the issues shift from meeting equity requirements as such to meeting such requirements without destroying the social compact (not contract) as a whole. Thus, every regime must ask what portion of income should be redistributed to insure an equity outcome without parallel destruction of the economic system as a whole, that is, the willingness of people to work and save, the capacity of scientists to innovate and take risks, and the ability of a citizenry to accept a doctrine of obligations as well as one of rights. Furthermore, every regime must also be willing to control national monetary policies and consumption patterns so that its currency will serve nonnationals, or in more utopian parlance, the international economy, as a store of wealth. In this way enlightened self-interest becomes a notion extended to relations between sovereigns no less than relations between classes (Gilpin, 1988). This new application of the doctrine of enlightened self-interest becomes a notion underwritten by government.

In this sense, minimalist, pragmatic, and maximalist perspectives are less principles of government and more practices and policies of everyday decision making. Conservatives, liberals, and socialists, or if one prefers, technocratic regimes without clear ideological masks, are faced with a set of choices and tradeoffs that each of these policies entails. Again, system survival rather than class domination becomes the hallmark of modern government.

The minimalist perspective argues that government should step in and try to make repairs only when there is a break in the system. In this sense, antitrust legislation is acceptable because monopolization of industry does away with unimpeded competition and thus with the free market as such. "Trustbusting" became a way of insuring the proper operation of the free market. The Soviets and Chinese face the same set of options in reverse: they must stimulate private initiatives to prevent economic stagnation. This is done to prevent a hardening of the economic arteries and to stimulate new forms of socialist construction. But there are enough problems in these parallels to make one cautious in drawing such analogies.

The pragmatic perspective argues that, even if there is no break in the seam of the system, government intervention can take place, and that the state has an economic role to play. For example, an economic system may work relatively well by having a racial or religious minority perform certain menial tasks and hence provide a reasonable balance of supply and demand of unskilled labor. Yet, higher considerations of a moral or political sort make government intervention necessary. Thus, all sorts of fair employment practice legislation is enacted, not necessarily to make the economy work smoother, but to make the society more politically viable and morally worthy.

Finally, there are maximalist positions in which the issues are not framed so much in terms of systemic survival as ideological rightness. These too possess strong doses of the moral and the political, but they advance principles, that is, the principle that private acquisition of capital is evil, and the principle of the social ownership of the means of production as an unmitigated blessing. Such maximalist systems—one can refer to them as Robespierrist or Leninist—are premised on the belief that the issue is not the economic role of government as a public choice, but the essence of the polity as an elite requirement. Enshrined in many such systemic concerns is a near-perfect symmetry between party and bureaucracy to ensure such maximalist outcomes.

In short, the most fundamental aspect of the economic role of government is precisely the legitimacy of government, that is, taking for granted that equity concerns should prevail. Differences arise basically over strategies and techniques for getting such results. As a result, it is probably easier to describe the economic role of government than its noneconomic role. But in fact, the question of government, the very word "government," disguises two quite disparate realms of activity: society and state.

Let me illustrate this point by noting that in the United States we have roughly 25,000 voluntary associations, whereas in the Soviet Union, with the exception of the church groups, there are *none*. The assumption is, of course, that one needs voluntary associations in societies in which there is a private acquisition of wealth, but no such similar needs exist in societies in which all property and possessions are owned in common, that is, in which the whole system is voluntary. We know that this notion is largely chimerical, even absurd. In point of fact, the restraints on the ability of government to impede such associations, beyond taxing privileges, serves to guarantee a noneconomic core to the democratic system. Indeed, the existence of a noneconomic core is exactly what one means by a democratic system (Horowitz, 1977).

The difficulty in defining a strictly economic role of government is the supposition of the legitimacy of such roles in every instance. It is the core notion of the political society that economic roles produce potentials for political abuse, for control of the very plant or person who is presumably being helped. Thus, it is that the question of the economic role of government must be prefaced by a study of the constraints on such roles built into the fabric of the political process. That is why the subject of political economy must share the stage with analogies from political sociology and political psychology, that is, of the place of political parties, voluntary associations, personality differences, ascribed features of a system. Only in this way can scholarship move beyond the conventional range of discourse which comes under the rubric of political economy.

What is at stake is less the shifting boundaries of research than the admission that the play of social forces extends beyond the theme of the economic role of government itself. That role is now secured, but it is hardly unlimited. Allocation is not production; regulation is not consumption. The entire panoply of social and economic forces is what constitutes equilibrium, and not just a specific model of balanced economic exchanges. As the century wears to a close, certain forces are at work to maintain free market societies, with an apportionment for welfare and support systems. At the other end, the planned market systems begin to build in nongovernmental units, free farmers markets, and petty-bourgeois operations such as restaurants and taxi services for tourists, which make possible an expanding economic role for nongovernmental forces.

Prediction in this area is risky. My own feeling is that forces are at work to establish a new social or institutional equilibrium among government and private sectors (or at least nongovernment sectors), and this permits societies to maintain their fabric. That is, they can be capitalist, socialist, or welfare varieties, and at the same time they can accommodate to the realities of a new mix, one in which equity concerns are still high-priority items, but only in contexts that permit economic growth, technological innovation, and political pluralism.

This may be a more optimistic reading than is warranted by the evidence. To be sure, the points of reference herein identified are the United States, Western Europe, Southeast Asia, and parts of the world in advanced industrial situations. For the rest, for vast stretches of Africa and parts of Asia, and select portions of Latin America, the economic role of government continues to be very high, and certainly much more weighted on the side of administrative and bureaucratic domination and expenditure than elsewhere. But this very imbalance, this very absence of a new equilibrium of economic, political, and social forces, tells us much about the differences between the advanced and backward segments of modern societies.

The conclusions are clear: (1) the increasing economic role of government is a response to a long-run secular demand for equity relations between people at all levels of ascribed and achieved equilibrium; (2) this role is reinforced by the stagnation of traditional classes and the expansion of administrative and service sectors; (3) the economic role of the government is managed by a huge bureaucratic and appointed class, whose interests as a class are in the maintenance of the system intact; (4) this in turn makes possible a new impulse toward change, one predicated on a mix of social, political, and economic factors, and not simply on the economics of supply and demand as such; (5) such tendencies are likely to continue, but only within the context of advanced industrialized states; (6) and, finally, to break out of the bottleneck of backwardness means to create new forms of public-private, rights-obligations, tradition-innovation linkages that permit change within the context of established relations and that also permit the maintenance of social order.

As a final caveat, it must be said that the commentary provided herein represents a certain ideal-typification of actual structures. It is not intended as a description of any one society or of a belief that any one economy is necessarily a model for all other societies. That sort of broad assumption, common to the literature on development in even the recent past, presumes a unitary character to growth which we have repeatedly seen more breached than observed.

Societies have the capacity to survive, even if they exhibit strong disparities in rates of growth or quality of life. Indeed, a great deal must go wrong before any advanced society is toppled—and going wrong is hardly the same as doing right. Survival is likely to be even more the case as the costs of war escalate to impossible degrees. This escalation has the double effect of eliminating foreign intervention as a prime source of nation-state instability, while redirecting the energies of governments of advanced societies toward internal security and survival.

To be sure, this new emphasis on the nation-state as the prime source of all goods great and small is a mixed blessing. There may yet be a longing after the good old days when governments came and went, rather than the present dedication to overcoming all challenges and threats to its survival starting with the total management of the national economy. The impulses of totalitarian regimes toward survival in the present century betoken widespread concern, no less than academic reflection.

REFERENCES

Gilpin, Robert. *The Political Economy of International Relations*. Princeton, N.J.: Princeton University Press, 1988.

Hibbs, Douglas A. *The American Political Economy: Macroeconomics and Electoral Politics in the United States*. Cambridge, Mass.: Harvard University Press, 1987.

Horowitz, Irving Louis. *Ideology and Utopia in the United States: 1956–1976*. New York and Oxford: Oxford University Press, 1977.

Laumann, Edward O., and David Knoke. *The Organizational State: Social Choice in National Policy Domains*. Madison: University of Wisconsin Press, 1987.

Meinecke, Friedrich. *Machiavellism: The Doctrine of Raison d'Etat and Its Place in Modern History*. New Haven, Conn.: Yale University Press, 1957.

Nozick, Robert. *Anarchy, State, and Utopia*. New York: Basic Books/Harper & Row, 1974.

Rawls, John. *A Theory of Justice*. Cambridge, Mass.: Harvard University Press, 1971.

Wildavsky, Aaron. *Budgeting: A Comparative Theory of Budgetary Processes*. New Brunswick and Oxford: Transaction Publishers, 1986.

13

The Boundaries of the Public Domain

P. M. Jackson

Once there was a sense that government was part of the answer to social and economic problems. Today it is frequently seen as the problem. During the immediate post–1945 years, a new social democratic consensus emerged in the Western democracies built on the newfound economic powers given to the state by Keynesian economic policies that emphasized corporatist solutions and offered hope that economic depressions might be a thing of the past. One of the state's economic functions was to be the maintenance of full employment.

The slowdown in economic growth and prosperity during the stagflationary years of the 1970s destroyed many of these earlier hopes and visions. Not only did the Keynesian approach to policymaking break down, but also a new political authority emerging from the right of the ideological spectrum challenged many of the beliefs about the appropriate economic role of the state. The 1980s reaction against modernism and secularism has turned the tide against the wave of liberalism of the swinging 1960s.

The fiscal crisis of the "tax state" which had occupied Joseph Schumpeter's (1918) attention so many years ago seemed to come of age during the 1970s. Fears were expressed about the rapid growth of government, the all-consuming Leviathan hunger for resources; the crowding out of private sector activity by the public sector as the ratio of public spending to GNP rose in all Organization for Economic Cooperation and Development (OECD) countries; the destruction of incentives caused by high marginal tax rates, too much regulation, inappropriate subsidies, and mimimum wage legislation. Alongside these arguments which expressed concern for the economic health of the nation were others of a more fundamental type: Was the public sector (the state) unaccountable to the electorate? Were liberties and freedoms being eroded? Are the revenues raised by government filling a bloated bureaucracy of individuals who are much better off than those whom they seek to serve?

Much of the increase in public spending had been a rational response to market failures and social problems such as the alleviation of poverty, but equally much had not. Too much public spending, some claimed, had been brought about by power- and rent-seeking politicians engaged in the politics of envy. There was also a sense of frustration and disappointment among the electorate. Growing public sector problems had on many occasions failed to change anything: social problems, such as those found in the inner cities, remained despite the public resources directed at them; there were catalogues of planning disasters and while absolute poverty had improved in the sense that life is not so short, nasty, and brutish for the poor, nevertheless, relative poverty had changed little despite a progressive system of taxation and welfare payments.

This chapter reassesses the fundamental questions and issues about the economic role of the public sector in a modern mixed economy. Where are the boundaries of the public domain? Are they clearly defined? Are they changing, and if so, where are they moving to? While attention is given to the functions of the state, nothing will be said about how these functions should be financed. Throughout this chapter it will be assumed that the financing of the public spending which reflects the economic role of the state should impose the least amount of distortion on relative prices (commodity prices, interest rates, and exchange rates) elsewhere within the economy.

THE ORDERLY ANARCHY OF THE MARKET

One means of defining the economic functions of the state is to consider the role and limitations of markets as a social institution for the allocation and distribution of resources. Down through the ages of time, the debate has been conducted in terms of the relative effectiveness of the market as an allocative mechanism compared to nonmarket systems such as a planning/administrative organization. Is the market as a means of resource allocation superior to nonmarket public sector bureaucracies? Under what conditions is it superior, and when is it not?

The unfettered market solution advocated by many neo-liberals, such as Friederich von Hayek, depends crucially on a specific but frequently inadequately stated conception of the market process. Elementary economics textbooks present the invisible hand theorems of contestable markets. A competitive market requires a large number of buyers and sellers, and each potential entrant into a market should have the ability to duplicate the costs and product of existing incumbents. Consumers and producers have equal access to all relevant information and decision, or transactions costs are zero. Given these assumptions, it can be demonstrated that there are significant efficiency gains to be obtained from the price mechanism compared to most other alternatives. The reason is straightforward. Market exchanges coordinate the decisions of many buyers and sellers within the minimum amount of information being transmitted/communicated between market agents. All the necessary and significant information is embodied in the price signals at which trading takes place. It is not necessary to know the utility function of each consumer or the production function of each producer as in a nonmarket planning exercise. Nor is it necessary to know the constraints that each faces.

Thus to Hayek, and the Austrian economists generally, the market economizes on information because all relevant information for decision making is embodied in prices. Competition, like natural selection, gets rid of inefficiency. This system is compared with a planning system that demands more information about consumer demands, production functions, and the set of constraints facing producers and consumers. Without this information the plan cannot be computed. Once the plan has evolved, there are additional costs in implementing it and coordinating all of the various actions of producers and consumers. Coordination through market interactions is less onerous, however, as the references to the "invisible hand" make clear. Another feature of competitive markets which is attractive to neo-libertarians is that not only will they produce Pareto-efficient allocations, which is regarded to be a desirable feature, but also market exchanges do not interfere with individual liberties and freedoms.

The case for unfettered markets is not an argument for no government intervention. Rather, it is a prescription for a particular form of government and economic growth and development. It is realized that development requires a system of property rights—a means of defending property and a tax system that does not destroy the link betwen effort and reward or reduce it to tolerable levels. This is the essence of the "nightwatchman" theory of the state. That is, it is the role of government to define and enforce property rights; to enact and implement a system of laws; to maintain a system of external defense and to maintain the value of the currency. Without laws, efficient markets will not come into existence. The law is an antecedent to market coordination (Buchanan, 1975).

The public sector as nightwatchman is, therefore, the minimal role of government consistent with the neo-libertarian advocacy of free markets. Even this, however, is too much government for the so-called modern libertarian anarchists or property rights anarchists. For M. Rothbard (1973) and Milton Friedman (1973) there is no logical foundation for public collective action.

BEYOND NEOCLASSICAL THEORY: THE INCOMPLETENESS OF THE MARKET SOLUTION

The price system of elementary textbooks and the heuristic fiction of the Walrasian general competitive equilibrium is not without severe limitations as a description of modern monetary/market economies.

Postindustrial society is not Walrasian. It is not like the Middle Eastern bazaar which approximates the barter exchange model that characterizes the classical Walrasian model of perfect competition. Instead, the outcomes in modern monetary/market economies are the products of

1. *Increasing returns to scale in production functions*. Under these conditions, rational decision makers will not set price equal to long-run marginal cost. Barriers to entry will enable them to set price above marginal costs and to enjoy economic rents that enter into the overall distribution of income. A wedge is driven between producer and consumer prices, with income being transferred from consumers to producers (managers and shareholders).

2. *Inappropriability*. That is, the existence of externalities, such as pollution and congestion, in production and consumption, and the existence of indivisible public goods bring about a divergence between private and social costs (benefits).

3. *Uncertainty*. Today's consumption decisions are made in spot markets, but many decisions such as those relating to savings and investment are made intertemporally (across time). If futures markets do not exist or if they are thin and imperfect, then not only will the price system fail to allocate intertemporal resources efficiently, but also the absence of futures markets can feed back onto spot markets causing inefficiencies in current period decisions. In the absence of sufficient futures markets, the allocative function of market prices is weakened. Furthermore, the failure of the price system to adequately handle risk bearing reduces the role of prices. In these instances, information other than that contained in prices is sought.

4. *Competition is limited in intensity*. The modern economy is a ''supermarket economy;'' consumers do not haggle over prices. They take them or leave them. Consumers face a bewildering array of brand names and differentiated products. Extended choice improves the public welfare, but it presents the consumer with the problem of how to be informed. Differentiated products are generally sold at prices that exceed marginal cost.

5. *Information is not perfect nor is it acquired without cost*. In reality, information is poor, unequally distributed, and poorly communicated. The level of ignorance is high. In these conditions, producers can set price above marginal cost. Asymmetry in the distribution of information arises from complex principal/agent relationships. Such a relationship offers the potential for the violation of trust between principal and agent.

6. *Monetary economies differ from pure barter economies*. The existence of the social institution of money is a means of minimizing transactions costs, but the existence of money markets presents problems for the definition of a competitive equilibrium.

7. *Modern market economies suffer from coordination failures*. In the Walrasian neo-classical model decisions are made simultaneously: trading does not take place until equilibrium prices have been established. Decisions are made sequentially in real time. If futures markets do not exist or if they are imperfect, then decision makers must form expectations about future prices. Trading can, therefore, take place at disequilibrium (or false) prices. Market prices will fail to coordinate the multitude of decisions by consumers and producers. This insight lay at the heart of Keynes' *General Theory*. In the absence of perfect futures market, there is no guarantee that savings (*ex ante*) will equal investment (*ex ante*). If coordination failures exist, disequilibrium shows up as unused resources (Keynesian unemployment).

Taking the limitations of the market system together, what does it add up to in terms of the economic role of government? In addition to the nightwatchman role to enforce the law of contract; trademark laws; copyrights and patents, and so on, government has, in R. A. Musgrave's (1958) terminology, an allocative function and a stabilization role.

Government's allocative function is to improve the efficient allocation of resources (in a Paretian sense.) It can do so by regulating markets; reducing the deadweight loss of monopoly through antitrust legislation; introducing pollution taxes; and providing public goods. The stabilization role is effected through fiscal and monetary policies and income policies.

When discussing the desirable limits of the state, identifying the acceptable boundaries between the public and private domains, economists are frequently interested primarily in the efficiency of the resource allocation mechanism. This is essential to the preceding discussion. However, it sets economists in a relation of tension with other disciplines which assign to the state an ethical role. In addition to his allocative and stabilization branches of government, Musgrave considered the distribution function. While a competitive market might generate a Pareto-efficient allocation of resources, the resulting distribution of resources (welfare) need not be socially just. A change in the initial endowments between economic agents (producers and consumers) will produce a different Pareto efficient allocation. Thus, a set of Pareto efficient allocations exist, each with a different distribution of welfares. The problem is to decide which Pareto-efficient allocation conforms to society's notions of distributive justice. What rule is to be used in this decision?

The problem of social justice, which lies at the heart of modern welfare economics, is not the sole province of economists. It must, however, be pointed out that it has been economists who have recently made the most significant contributions to this debate. (The works of Arrow, 1984, and Sen, 1982, are important in this respect.) Some economists, such as Knut Wicksell, ignored the distributional problem by assuming that economic and political power had been equalized between political parties. The problem that then faced government was to search for the Pareto-efficient budget.

Establishing the economic functions for government is relatively trivial once the limitations of the competitive market model have been identified. The problem is choosing the instruments of policy. Much of the output of economic analysis has been a contribution to the design of policy. What is the appropriate mix of monetary and fiscal policies? How do monetary and fiscal policy instruments interact? What are the consequences of pollution taxes? In the absence of non-distortionary lump-sum taxes, how should a tax system be designed which will redistribute incomes while minimizing distortions to relative prices; and, finally, what form should regulatory policies take? The economic analysis of public policy is a search for answers to these questions. But it would be a mistake to assume that once and for all answers can be provided. Economic policies are made in uncertain environments. There is, therefore, only a probability that they will be effective; no two time periods are identical in all respects; and economic agents learn about the outcomes of previous policy regimes, which then causes them to modify their behavior.

GOVERNMENT FAILURE

Transactions costs, which are the major source of market failures, drive a wedge between producer and consumer prices, which results in welfare losses. One frequently noted response is to reduce these welfare costs by introducing an alternative resource allocation system: in particular, public sector interventions into the marketplace and the direct provision of services through public sector budgets using planning systems that employ surrogates for market decisions, such as cost-benefit analysis. Government, nonmarket, decision making, however, also involves transactions costs. There are the costs of acquiring information via demand studies about consumer voters' preferences for public services; information processing costs; the welfare costs of imposing a single "median voter" solution on nonmedian voters; the costs of satisfying the interests of monopoly professional suppliers of public services rather than the preferences of consumer/voters; the distortions to relative prices (and hence the allocation and distribution of resources) brought about by government policy instruments.

These costs result in government or bureaucratic failures—a failure to achieve an efficient allocation of resources; a failure to satisfy consumer/voter preferences; a failure to eliminate bureaucratic waste and x-inefficiency; and a failure to check the growth of the juggernaut of government.

In the presence of government failure, public provision of services is not a straightforward substitute for the market system. The imperfections of two alternative allocative systems need to be compared. The choice is not between an imperfect market system and a perfect public sector. Instead, the choice is between imperfect public sector bureaucratic resource allocation mechanisms and that of imperfect market; or between a regulated cartel and an unregulated industry with fewer firms, strong monopolistic elements, and prices in excess of long-run average costs.

Economic theory cannot provide answers to these questions. A painstaking series of empirical studies comparing the relative transactions costs and deadweight welfare losses of specific cases is the only meaningful way of resolving these issues. Economists, however, do not have reliable orders of magnitude for such costs. In the meantime, the vacuum will be filled by political rhetoric of variable quality.

THE INEFFECTIVENESS OF PUBLIC POLICY

A new set of attacks on the effectiveness of government's fiscal and monetary policies to reduce high levels of unemployment have come from the new classical economists, though Friedman (1968) and E. S. Phelps' (1967) earlier work on the natural rate of unemployment started the debate. Building on the work of R. E. Lucas (1972), where it is assumed that the real world is approximated by a Walrasian system of perfectly competitive markets and that individuals form rational expectations, a whole school of thought has emerged which argues that monetary and fiscal policy is totally ineffective in reducing unemployment which will always be at the natural rate. All that follows from government intervention is accelerating inflation, which is not neutral in terms of its effects on resource allocation and distribution. Rather than being an agent of stabilization, the state becomes a destabilizing influence.

Undoubtedly, there is something to the argument that clumsy and inappropriate interventions using inadequately coordinated monetary and fiscal policies will be destabilizing. Equally endogenous politicians can set up political business cycles, but the new-classical ineffectiveness result which concludes that the state should abandon its macroeconomic role of stabilization is once again based on strong assumptions about the underlying nature of the economic system. Real economies are not Walrasian: prices do not adjust with infinite acceleration; transactions costs, legally binding contracts, and uncertainties cause prices to adjust slowly; decisions are made sequentially in real time, not simultaneously; markets are often highly imperfect.

Individuals probably do form rational expectations in the sense that everyone uses the information available to them if it is profitable to do so. But the rational expectations hypothesis needs to be matched up with a more suitable micro-foundation which recognizes market imperfections and coordination failures across both space and time. These features of the modern capitalist system cause booms and slumps and give a role to government to manage demand in the short run. While not all unemployment is natural, this debate has forced naive Keynesians who paid too much attention to the demand side of the economy to recognize supply-side features and the effects policies might have on supply.

BETWEEN ANARCHY AND LEVIATHAN

Freedom of choice means that individuals act purposefully. It is a desirable feature of any economic system that individuals be able to predict the consequences of their acts and decisions. This ability to predict requires a degree of stability. This applies not only to markets but to governments also. If government is constantly changing the rules of the game by changing laws, then predictability is reduced and individuals face continuous surprises. While it has now been established, within the Walrasian or new-classical macroeconomics, that surprises are essential for the short-run effectiveness of macroeconomic policies when individuals form rational expectations, nevertheless, individuals facing the expectation that they will be surprised in effect face uncertainty and will devote time and resources to activities that reduce the costs of that uncertainty. Moreover, if government rules and regulations and public laws are vague, then individuals will make frequent mistakes that might be costly to themselves and to others.

It is, therefore, not sufficient to call for government intervention to correct the failures found in imperfect markets in which economic actors face instabilities and uncertainties. Questions must be asked about the stability and degree of vagueness of the rules that circumscribe government activity. J. M. Buchanan (1975) has argued this case, pointing out that political and administrative risks replace market risks. Stability calls for and demands a firm constitution that will constrain incumbent politicians and bureaucrats from changing the rules according to *their* personal preferences.

Constitutions and Bills of Rights also hold the faceless bureaucracy to account. The growth in big government has brought with it fear and distrust, a feeling that the individual citizen does not count in decision making and is powerless. There is a growing demand for administrative justice and greater accountability. It is not necessarily the case that individuals want a small public sector; rather, they want a public sector, whatever its size, to be accountable. On the one hand, there is the failure of the market and all the problems that can bring—without government intervention there is ordered anarchy. However, the other face to the problem is the Leviathan of big government. Both cause tension—which way to turn? Truly accountable government, with a firm constitutional base, increases the changes of administrative justice and minimizes the problems of the principal/agent relationships that arise from informational asymmetries. Accountable local government improves the situation even further because it is local government that allows for the variations in local tastes and preferences. Local government is inherently more efficient than a centralized system.

THE PRICE OF LIBERTY

There are those economists who value liberty for its own sake and as an objective of economic policy place it above the achievement of economic efficiency. The libertarians fall into this camp. These economists favor free market solutions because, following from Adam Smith's invisible hand theorem, Pareto efficiency and freedom can be achieved simultaneously. This, unfortunately, as was demonstrated above, is true for only the most trivial and contrived economic systems.

Real postindustrial economies do not sufficiently approximate the neat simplistic assumptions of the perfectly competitive ideal type necessary to bring about this utopia (if indeed it is utopia). Information asymmetries, costly bargaining, complexity, uncertainty, increasing returns to scale, brand names, and prisoner dilemma situations of noncooperative behavior all conspire to separate Pareto efficiency and the freedom of individuals generated through unfettered market forces.

Liberty, however, is itself a slippery concept, and many libertarian economists have taken insufficient care when using it. Hobbes recognized the dilemma facing society: to steer a course between anarchy on the one hand and the sea monster, the Leviathan of excessive government controls. Government is required to establish property rights so that voluntary exchange is feasible; it is also required to solve the prisoner dilemma games of noncooperative behavior. Limitations on freedom imposed by government in one dimension are necessary for the pursuit of other freedoms.

Isaiah Berlin (1958) distinguished between two concepts of liberty or freedom: negative freedom and positive freedom. The first concept, negative freedom (or freedom from), refers to freedom from coercion, including freedom from state intervention. Libertarians such as Hayek and Robert Nozick have concentrated on this notion. Set against negative freedom is Berlin's notion of positive freedom, the ability "to be somebody, not nobody; a doer—deciding, not being decided for, self directed . . . conceiving goals, and policies of one's own and realizing them . . . to be conscious of oneself as a thinking, willing, active being, bearing responsibility for one's own choices and able to explain them by reference to one's own ideas and purposes." Positive freedom is a freedom to do. Individual feasible sets are, however, severely constrained by race, income group, disability, and the like which prevents them from doing. This type of freedom is different from those constraints imposed by government. Indeed, government collective public action can expand positive freedoms by expanding the feasible choice set which specific groups face. This thesis underlies P. Dasgupta's (1985) notion of "positive freedom goods" such as basic food and shelter; medical care; primary education; and sanitation facilities.

Incorporation of positive freedom not only strengthens the welfarist arguments for government intervention, but also throws into debate the question of which freedom has primacy over economic efficiency. Furthermore, is positive freedom intrinsically more important than negative freedom? It means that statements such as "the restrictions on natural liberty surely constitute public bads from which it follows that their removal would be equivalent to the production of public goods" are ambiguous.

The market solution demands and concentrates on competition, but this smothers other morally good qualities such as cooperation. However, self-seeking individuals need not be corrupted by competition. They can be sympathetic to one another. Adam Smith in his *Moral Sentiments* defined sympathy and respect for other individuals in terms of forming moral judgments by being in the other person's shoes. For Smith, sympathy could result in sacrificing personal advantage for the benefit of others. In other words an altruistic motive within individuals will cause them voluntarily to distribute their incomes to others. Why, therefore, do governments pursue social security programs through redistributive taxes? Why not leave it all to private charities? As David Hume pointed out, individuals have "limited generosity." They simply might not provide enough on a voluntary basis to provide the positive freedom goods in the volume required. In addition, there are high transactions costs facing individuals in finding out about all-deserving cases; their information is severely bounded.

NEW WAYS OF PROVIDING PUBLIC SERVICES: PRIVATIZATION

Public sector economists, such as Musgrave (1958), have taken care to draw the distinction between public provision and public production. Unfortunately, the market failure argument led some economists to advocate direct public production of certain classes of goods and services that were associated with some degree of market failure or that were regarded as essential for the distribution of welfare, such as, housing, education, and health. Since 1945 there has been a growth in the public domain, with the public sector taking into its ownership and control the production of these services.

Apart from claims that public ownership and public production result in relatively higher degrees of x-inefficiency when compared to private production (claims that are difficult to substantiate empirically), there is also the argument that allocative efficiency is reduced in public production because the views of consumers are difficult to obtain in a nonmarket setting. Furthermore, consumer demands are frequently suppressed by the professional groups who act as the principal's (voter/consumer's) agent. This has led to a keener examination of the alternative ways of providing public services through means other than direct public provision. In particular, the privatization of public services has been examined.

There is nothing particularly new about the privatization debate. Much of it has lain dormant in the isthmus between the public and private domains. A case has been made for some kind of government intervention to correct market failures. Rather than taking the service into public ownership, the public sector can subcontract the production of the service to the private sector and then distribute it via the public sector on those terms that will improve efficiency and social justice. Contracting out of public services has a number of advantages: (1) competitive tendering for the contract ensures cost minimization; (2) the public sector can monitor performance in terms of the conditions set down in the contract; (3) consumer complaints and problems of administrative justice are more easily dealt with—they are not lost in a faceless bureaucracy; and (4) the public sector bureaucracy now acts on behalf of the client of the service, whereas before it had this role and that of producer.

Many public services can be and are being contracted out, and this is the way of the future. The emphasis is on specifying a clear contract and adequate regulation of the tendering and service delivery processes. These are not without severe technical problems, but they do offer an improvement on existing practice in terms of X and allocative efficiencies. Again, an appropriate regulatory regime has to be found.

Improvements in the efficiency of that part of the public sector that remains to produce services directly can be achieved through the greater use of "internal markets" and performance reviews. An internal market in a public sector bureaucracy is nothing other than a decentralized information system (financial and nonfinancial) that provides decision makers with devolved budgets and an information set that mimics the prices in the marketplace. It is supplemented by a system which, through a series of indicators and measures, monitors the performance of the public sector. By relating the pay of public servants to their performance, public sector productivity and efficiency can be improved.

The public sector of the future will differ in structure and process from that which exists today. More services will be contracted out; greater explicit use will be made of prices; public servants will act more as regulators than as producers; the consumer of public services will again become sovereign. Rather than being a provider, the state will become a facilitator that enables individuals to satisfy their own preferences more fully. The enabling state will also expand choices by offering a greater variety of public services.

CONCLUSIONS

The strength of the mixed economy is that it is mixed. Under certain conditions, markets will work efficiently relative to systems of fiat and command. This, however, is not always so. There is a role for nonmarket bureaucracies and hierarachies. The economist cannot provide a definitive answer to where the boundaries of the state should lie. An answer depends on deep-seated value judgments as expressed in political ideologies. It does not, however, automatically follow that "government failure" is always more severe than "market failure." Not only is a perceived failure to one citizen regarded as a success to another, but the question is essentially an empirical one and to date there is insufficient evidence to make a judgment either way.

The public sector economist is faced with many exciting challenges for the future. As the design of the new public sector is considered with a greater propensity to contract out public services, so the boundaries of the public domain will be redrawn. These boundaries will not necessarily be smooth or neat. Joint ventures between the public and private domains will make for a greater dovetailing and an obscuring of the edges. Greater attention has to be given, in the future, to internal systems of public sector management (internal markets and performance reviews) and to consumer demand. The design of regulatory systems and procedures of accountability also present difficulties. However, no matter how successful the economist is in responding to these challenges the perennial question will remain: where does the limit to the public domain lie?

REFERENCES

Arrow, K. J. *Social Choice and Justice.* Oxford: Basil Blackwell, 1984.

Berlin, I. *Two Concepts of Liberty*, Inaugural lecture. Oxford: Clarendon Press, 1958. Reprinted in *Four Essays on Liberty*, Oxford: Oxford University Press, 1969.

Buchanan, J. M. *The Limits of Liberty.* Chicago: University of Chicago Press, 1975.

Dasgupta, P. "Positive Freedom, Markets and the Welfare State." *Oxford Review of Economic Policy* 2, No. 2, (1985).

Friedman, D. *The Machinery of Freedom.* New York: Harper & Row, 1973.

Friedman, M. "The Role of Monetary Policy." *American Economic Review* 58 (March 1968): 1–17.

Lucas, R. E. "Expectations and the Neutrality of Money." *Journal of Economic Theory* 4 (1972): 103–24.

Musgrave, R. A. *The Theory of Public Finance*. New York: McGraw-Hill, 1958.

Phelps, E. S. "Phillips Curves, Expectations of Inflation and Optimal Unemployment Over Time." *Economica* 34 (1967).

Rothbard, M. *For a New Liberty*. New York: Macmillan, 1973.

Schumpeter, J. *The Crisis of the Tax State*. Originally published in 1918 as "Die Krise des Steuerstaates." In *Zeitfragen aus dem Gebiete der Soziologie* (Graz). English translation in *International Economic Papers 5* (London, 1954).

Sen, A. K. *Choice, Welfare and Measurement*. Oxford: Basil Blackwell, 1982.

14

Strategic Behavior and the Role of Government

Alexis Jacquemin

Economists traditionally recognize efficiency and distributive equity as two main goals of economic policy. Although broader views can be defended, there is a large consensus for considering that the concept of economic efficiency derives from the Pareto principle: in a Pareto optimal allocation of resources, it is not possible to make anyone better off without simultaneously making someone else worse off. As is well known, under certain assumptions about the technology of production and the preferences of individuals, the allocation of resources resulting from the operation of competitive markets under laissez-faire conditions will be Pareto optimal. This results from a formalization of Adam Smith's "invisible hand" argument, according to which the invisible hand of self-interest is apt to correct any inefficiency and to promote the collective welfare of the society.

There is much less consensus about the equity concept. One central aspect concerns the determination of an equitable distribution of income and wealth. Two of the many possible criteria on which equity might be based are utilitarianism and the Rawlsian maximin principle. Whatever is the criterion, however, it always involves strong philosophical premises and assumes an ability to make explicit value judgments about interpersonal comparisons of utility.

It must also be stressed that efficiency and equity are far from being separable: Most of the time they interact either to reinforce each other or to conflict. Some welfare programs simultaneously improve equity and efficiency. For example, policy actions to mitigate destitution among groups of citizens who would otherwise live in poverty and to increase social mobility may create new opportunities and have net positive efficiency implications. On the other hand, government intervention via fiscal redistribution could lead to inefficiency because it could reduce the total amount of income available for redistribution.

Finally, it can be argued that governmental intervention cannot be evaluated only on the basis of its consequences for economic efficiency in production and consumption or for redistribution. An optimal allocation created by dictatorial decisions would probably be rejected by many who prefer a relatively less efficient allocation arrived at in the spirit of voluntary actions. The individual may be interested in the process by which a certain bundle of products is achieved and "values the act of choosing as such, which means that freedom of choice also has an intrinsic value" (Lindbeck, 1988, p. 314).

Within the limits of this chapter, we will not cover the whole area of these complex issues. Instead, the focus will be on one main reason why, in our modern decentralized economies, the "invisible hand" theorem and the freedom of bargaining and choosing could provide insufficient arguments against active government policy. The main reason is based on the existence of strategic actions designed to influence the behavior of others. In a world characterized by various forms of imperfect competition, economic agents are not passive and do not view market structure and behavior of others as given. They try to influence other agents' expected payoffs, either by irreversible commitment having lasting effects on cost and demand conditions, or by exploiting asymmetric information and influencing the beliefs of others, even if actual cost and demand conditions are not affected.

Two views of the market system can be contrasted (Jacquemin, 1987). The first one considers that productive structures, existing market forms, and organizational methods adopted by enterprises are a good approximation of the efficient adaptation that should result from some external order dictated by the existing technology.

Given the output vector in a specific market as well as the monetary value of the required physical and organizational inputs, the natural market structure will emerge, that is, the one in which the corresponding monetary value of inputs is lower than the monetary value of inputs required for any other possible allocation of outputs. Minimization of both production and transaction costs is then obtained. What exists is reasonably efficient, so that all observed industrial configurations—competitive, oligopolistic, or monopolistic—are assumed to correspond to a stationary equilibrium realizing an optimum. For example, according to this logic, the development of faithfulness to a brand through specific advertising investment is not a barrier to entry, despite its largely irreversible and sunk nature. These activities are at the service of the consumers who wish to be tied to the incumbent because information is scarce and costly. More fundamentally, this alleged barrier would be a characteristic of an optimal allocation when incomplete information has been incorporated.

Existing firms have an advantage only insofar as their existence commands loyalty. Existence commands loyalty only if it reflects lower real cost of transacting, industry specific investments, or a reputable history, as, in general, it will. . . . A reputable history is an asset to the firm possessing it and to the buyer who relies on it because information is not free (Demsetz, 1982a, pp. 50–51).

The second viewpoint stresses the role of economic agents modifying their environment instead of being subjected to the predetermined conditions. These are innovators of combinations and of new forms; they can manipulate their environment and to some extent can determine market conditions. In this perspective, the configuration of industrial structures and organizational forms is as much the outcome of deliberate strategies as of initial conditions and predetermined rules of the game. The evolution over time of market structure is determined by a transformation that depends not only on structure at a given moment of time and on time, but also on conducts. Corporations respond in a strategic manner to environmental pressures, partly by amplifying the imperfections of their environment at the expense of rivals and consumers. In a dynamic framework, with incomplete information, they manipulate information by investing in "disinformation," and they alter the rules of the game, organizational forms, and institutions to their own advantage. There is then no presumption that such strategic behavior is socially efficient, even as a second best solution.

Theses two approaches can be put in a wider intellectual framework in which ideological presuppositions are increasingly evident. In fact, one can envisage the evolution of our industrial societies as a selection process in which the fittest economic agents, social groups, nations, and institutions emerge. Hierarchies and the dominance of certain forms would then be the outcome of a selective filtering process and of a diffused competition that tend to maximize efficiency even if it is not perfect.

Economic and social institutions, the distribution of income, and the international division of labor are expressions of the adaptation to a "natural" order dictated by technology, factor endowments, qualifications, and productivity of individuals. Today this Darwinist vision finds a new dimension in the application of sociobiology to economics.

In contrast, other analyses portray the economic agent as striving to orient its evolution, to use innovation in order to provoke ruptures, and to impose new norms and new forms of equilibrium rather than to submit to the environment. Some economic agents alter the institutions and the rules of the game; the comparative advantages between nations are partly fabricated or imposed; income inequalities are partly the outcome of actions of groups defending their interests. The main driving force behind the undeniable process of evolution is therefore not a mechanical selection, and its logic is not merely the requirements of the environment.

The implications of these two views for the economic role of governments are straightforward. For those who have full confidence in market mechanisms, the only real requirement is the existence of a healthy macroeconomic environment. All governmental actions for improving efficiency must be either excluded or simply a general label for all measures aimed at facilitating an automatic process of adjustment. A good infrastructure, a professionally adapted labor force, easy access to capital and credit, and a fiscal policy unopposed to economic rationality are all conditions that must be satisfied in order for the price system to send out the correct signals and for economic agents to react to them correctly. In such a context it is then assumed that the market's selective game and the spontaneous forces of competition are sufficient to ensure a Pareto-efficient equilibrium. For example, according to Demsetz (1982b) those who were active in the founding of the American Economic Association did not find it difficult to justify industrial concentration.

They were swept along by the tide of Darwinian thought. Combinations and trusts were regarded as evolutionary social advances, as the outcome of natural laws calling for social cooperation to replace personal actions (p. 17).

And Demsetz concludes:

The United States is now almost two-centuries into its unique experiment to strengthen economic competition, however silly that may seem to sociobiologists (p. 18).

For his part, Jack Hirschleifer (1982), in reply to a criticism by Kenneth Arrow, deems that the sociobiological approach, in economics as in other fields, leads to a deterministic view of social phenomena. To the extent that the juridico-economic universe is largely determined by the evolutionary process, policy, be it individual or social, is no longer relevant. On the contrary, spontaneous competitive mechanisms and laissez-faire are inevitable channels.

In contrast, there is a whole tide of research questioning whether the market alone can efficiently accomplish selections. Two levels of arguments can be distinguished.

First, we can refer to the long list of so-called market failures: the existence of important externalities and of product differentiation valued by the consumers and the fact that many products and resources have the character of public goods, the role of strong indivisibilities linked with nonconvexities in production and organization, and consequences of uncertainty in an economy in which all in-tertemporal and all contingent markets do not exist so that some mutually ad-vantageous exchanges between agents are prevented. Governments could then favor organizational forms and design cooperative behavior (Axelrod, 1984; d'Aspremont and Jacquemin, 1988) that internalize the external effects of im-portant technological choices and so promote social welfare. Through financial aids and specific public programs, they would be required to stimulate investment in human capital and to support research and development in high-technology industries affected by important fixed and sunk costs. They could ensure a minimum socialization of risks in activities characterized by high levels of risks and incomplete information. Macroeconomic policy alone is insufficient to deal with this kind of problem and may even create perverse effects despite its apparent "neutrality." If it is accepted that inter- and intra-industrial variations are sig-nificant and that the degree of price flexibility depends in particular on structural characteristics of each industry, then macroeconomic measures without microeconomic foundations are likely to be incompatible with the adjustment process occurring in real markets.

A second level of argument in favor of active government policy in the promotion of efficiency goes beyond the consideration of failures inherent in certain markets. It concerns strategies that deliberately exploit natural imperfections lying in the exogeneous characteristics of the demand and cost functions, and that extend the initial degree of imperfection. The main point is that once the neoclassical paradigm is abandoned, there is no longer the kind of general welfare theorem about the Pareto optimality of the methods of strategic competition that we have for perfect competition.

Even when each individual is maximizing through unilateral action, the outcome is often inefficient. Improvements then demand regulation and joint actions, which require negotiation and coordination. Similarly, modern analysis of bargaining under incomplete information shows that contrary to the Coase theorem, free bargaining does not lead to Pareto-efficient outcomes. ''When people don't know one another's tastes or opportunities, then experience, theory and experimental evidence all confirm that negotiations may be protracted, costly and unsuccessful'' (Farell, 1987, p. 115). On the contrary, some form of mechanism design will be necessary to get private information revealed and to avoid strategic manipulations. Given that finding simple automatic schemes to solve these problems is not generally possible (for example, Gibbard-Satterthwaite theorem), active government policies are again relevant.

These policies do not imply a growing and paralyzing interventionism on the part of public authorities. The abuses of the welfare state and the dangers of a growing government bureaucracy are known. They are on the contrary compatible with a severe limitation of the sphere of control of the state. To start with, one must recognize the role of the many actors and new forms of social organization that ensure, at the local, regional, and international levels, that options are safeguarded, that changes of suppliers are workable, and that abuses of economic power are checked. As clearly shown by Walter Adams and James Brock (1986), the best remedy to the dangers of public as well as private power is to promote and organize structural decentralization. The problem therefore does not boil down to a radical and irreversible choice between public initiative versus private initiative, thus freezing the abilities of each. Rather, it should raise the issue of the difficulty of implementing mobility in respective spheres according to appropriate modalities. For instance, deregulation of some spheres mismanaged by the state is undoubtedly desirable. This, however, does not imply the return to a utopian free and efficient market but a change of regulation: deregulation of functions, grants for public services, or transfer of assets to the private sector must be matched with institutional rules and alternative forms of social control. It could be recommended that the state renounce the monopoly of determining social welfare. It would nevertheless remain a privileged player among the participants in the games of social and economic relations. In the successive disequilibria that characterize our evolution, it would safeguard pluralism, avoid replacement of public monopolies by private cartels, provide nonexcludable public goods, enforce cooperative behavior when socially desirable, and ensure effective redistributive transfers.

If productive and organizational structures are no longer the outcome of some sort of natural necessity and if relations of power, in a context of scarcity, become a central issue, then one has to provide within our decentralized economies instruments likely to ensure a better compatibility between individual interest and public interest. This is particularly the role of competition and nonprotectionist industrial policies. Moreover, legal aspects of the intervention of public authorities in economic life find their full meaning. Contrary to common practice, rules of law should be used less as a deterring constraint, acting as an obstacle to efficiency, and more as a decision variable likely to promote the functioning of the system. Alternative forms of institutions, judicial organizations, and regulations should be compared in order to chose those that are best capable of regulating the economic situation in question. Legal analysis and its logic are thus at one with economic analysis in the concern to develop a blueprint for society.

REFERENCES

Adams, Walter, and James Brock. *The Bigness Complex*. New York: Pantheon Books, 1986.

Axelrod, Robert. *The Evolution of Cooperation*. New York: Basic Books, 1984.

d'Aspremont, Claude, and Alexis Jacquemin. "Cooperative and Non-Cooperative Behavior in Duopoly with External Effects." *American Economic Review* 78, No. 3 (September 1988).

Demsetz, Harold. "Barriers to Entry." *American Economic Review* 72, No. 1 (1982a): 47–57.

———. *Economic, Legal and Political Dimensions of Competition*. Amsterdam: North Holland, 1982b.

Farrel, Joseph. "Information and the Coase Theorem." *Journal of Economic Perspectives* 1 (1987): 113–29.

Hirschleifer, Jack. In R. Zerbe (ed.) *Research in Law and Economics: Evolutionary Models in Economics and Law*. London: JAI Press, 1982.

Jacquemin, Alexis. *The New Industrial Organization*. Cambridge, Mass.: MIT Press, 1987.

Lindbeck, Assar. "Individual Freedom and Welfare State Policy." *European Economic Review* 32 (1988): 221–25.

15

Ideology and the Economic Role of Government

Dwight R. Lee

The proper performance of all but the most primitive economies requires an important role for government. There is no serious debate over this straightforward proposition. There is, of course, serious debate over what it is that constitutes government's proper economic role. Even when attention is focused on economies based on private property and voluntary exchange, which will be the case throughout this chapter, one finds a broad range of ideological convictions as to government's proper role. There are those who believe that government should do little more than enforce the free market rules of the game with a referee's indifference to the particular outcomes that emerge. At the other end of the ideological spectrum are those who believe that government should engage in detailed regulation of a host of economic activities for the purpose of promoting particular outcomes. Ideological convictions concerning the proper economic role of government are obviously based on some understanding, either explicit or implicit, of how government performs. Less obvious, but equally important, is the fact that government performance is influenced in important ways by the prevailing ideology regarding government's proper economic role. Here it will be argued that the role of ideology in political decision making creates doubt as to the feasibility of limiting the economic role of government and raises concern over the consequences of not limiting that role.

CLASSICAL LIBERAL VERSUS MODERN LIBERAL

The disagreement between those who want to tightly limit the economic role of government (referred to here as classical liberals) and those who favor an actively discretionary economic role for government (modern liberals) is partly explained by perceived differences in how the market works. Classical liberals are more sanguine about the potential of unfettered market forces to generate desirable outcomes than are modern liberals. Real world markets are, of course, far from perfect, and responsible classical liberals along with modern liberals (whether responsible or not), accept the conceptual possibility that market outcomes can be improved by discretionary government policy. But how likely is it that this conceptual possibility will be converted into concrete reality? The dividing line between classical liberals and modern liberals that is relevant to the present chapter centers on this question.

Although classical liberals may believe that enormous economic benefits flow from government, they believe that these benefits are primarily the indirect rather than the direct result of government action. From the perspective of classical liberals, the performance of all economies depends on how well self-seeking individuals interact with each other in ways that expand the opportunities of all. The information and incentives necessary for this interaction requires a stable social setting characterized by well-defined and enforced rules and the existence of a few basic public goods. The establishment of such a setting is seen as the only legitimate economic role for government. When the rules are those that protect private rights to property and facilitate voluntary exchange, classical liberals believe that a pattern of economic outcomes will emerge which, over the long run, are more advantageous to the general well-being than that which results from the intentional direction of government.

If government could be depended on to be a dutiful agent of the public interest, then government could surely generate positive net social benefits by going beyond the referee's role and becoming actively concerned with distributional and allocative outcomes. Granting government the discretionary power necessary to play such an active economic role, however, creates a power that classical liberals believe will be abused by politically active groups organized around narrow economic interests. It is the concentrated concerns of the special interests that will be communicated to politicians, not the diffused desires of the general public. The strong tendency then is for discretionary political power over economic outcomes to be used to promote special interest advantages at the expense of the common good.

Modern liberals are less concerned about the influence of narrow economic interests on political decisions than are classical liberals, and more sanguine about the likelihood of promoting the public interest through discretionary political decisions. No one argues that people completely ignore their narrowly defined self-interest when making political decisions, but modern liberals believe that genuine concern for the general community is more likely to motivate people in their political roles than in their market roles. By its very nature, politics invites people to look beyond their immediate personal interests by developing and expressing ideological visions of the good society. As expressed by Steven Kelman (1987, p. 22), "there is the elementary fact that political decisions apply to an entire community. That they do so encourages people to think about others when taking a stand. This is in contrast to making personal decisions, when people think mainly of themselves." This willingness of people to put the public interest ahead of private interests when making political decisions is seen as an important reason for believing that an active economic role for government is consistent with good policy. Again quoting Kelman (1987, pp. 208–209), "My contention is simple: when people try to achieve good public policy, the result tends to *be* good public policy" (emphasis in original).

Both the classical liberal and modern liberal views, at least in the simplified form presented here, leave a feeling of incompleteness. It is hard to deny that most people, most of the time, make market choices on the basis of narrow private interests, and it is equally hard to argue that some fundamental motivational transformation occurs when people move from a market role to a politcal role. At the same time, however, there can be no doubt that people are capable of, and commonly exhibit, genuine concern for others. It is simply impossible to explain the richness of human behavior, particularly political behavior, without recognizing the satisfaction people receive from promoting interests that transcend their own private advantages. But what logically consistent ground is there for accepting the modern liberal view that political behavior is less self-seeking than market behavior?

IDEOLOGY IN POLITICAL DECISION MAKING

As opposed to an individual's preferences, or tastes, with regard to what is in his or her narrowly defined private interest, an individual's ideology is concerned with his or her view of what is in the interest of the broader community of which the individual is a member. Accommodating one's preferences may be satisfying, but it is seldom uplifting. On the other hand, an uplifting feeling of virtue is the companion of efforts to promote one's ideological view of the good society. The feeling of uplift, indeed of moral virtue, that comes from ideological commitment and expression serves to make ideology essential to effective political action. By its very nature, political decision making exaggerates the influence of ideological commitment and expression.

A pervasive feature of political action is a tenuous relationship between an individual's actions and the outcome that results. Whether the action being considered is joining a group whose objective is to achieve a political outcome, or simply voting in favor of a particular outcome, the individual realizes that his or her participation is unlikely to be decisive. That this indecisiveness creates a tendency for individuals to be "rationally apathetic" politically, to free ride on the participation of others, has long been recognized.[1] This tendency toward rational apathy makes ideological commitment so important in motivating individuals to contribute to political outcomes. Few will become involved in a political quest if the objective is to secure incremental increases in some commonplace advantage. Noble objectives tied to shared ideological beliefs inspire mass support to a political cause, and those who are best able to foster and appeal to such beliefs will be the most successful politically. This point was recognized by Douglass North (1981, p. 53), when he argued that "any successful ideology must overcome the free rider problem. Its fundamental aim is to energize groups to behave contrary to a simple, hedonistic, individual calculus of costs and benefits.''

There is no reason to question the proposition that, once inspired with a sense of ideological mission, people will take political actions in support of their ideological objectives with little regard to costs. Certainly one explanation of this fact is that dwelling on the cost of engaging in an ideological quest is inconsistent with, indeed demeaning to, the spirit of mission which is so essential to the experience. It is useful, however, to consider an explanation for the diminished importance of cost in ideologically motivated political participation that remains disciplined by the cost-benefit considerations of economic logic.

The tenuous relationship between an individual's political choices and the outcomes that emerge from the political process lowers the cost, as perceived by the individual, of the choices he or she makes. Assume, for example, that an individual feels an ideological commitment to greater income equality and receives satisfaction from contributing to this goal. Making this contribution politically, by voting for poverty programs or for politicians who support these programs, will be far less costly to the individual than making a direct contribution of an amount equal to his tax share of the poverty programs. The difference between a direct contribution of, say, $700 per year to help the poor and voting for a government poverty program that, if passed, will cost the voter $700 per year is that the direct contribution decisively determines the contribution whereas the voting decision is indecisive in determining the contribution. Because the individual's vote, with a probability close to zero, will have no effect on the outcome of the election, his anticipated tax contribution to the proposed poverty program is the same whether he votes yea or nay. So if one receives ideological satisfaction at the polls from expressing herself in favor of helping the poor, she will certainly do so since this expression will not cost her a dime more than will expressing herself in opposition to helping the poor.[2] Having voted in favor of a poverty program, however, few voters will attempt to monitor the performance of the program in order to insure that it is actually helping the poor as advertised. To do so would be a far more costly form of ideological expression than voting. There is no reason to believe that the demand for ideological satisfaction is less likely to be downward sloping than the demand for anything else.

More generally, when an individual's ideological perspective favors an active role for government as a means of solving particular problems and promoting a more just society, he or she will tend to vote for government programs that appear to promote desirable social goals without being actively concerned about the effectiveness of these programs. This explains why organized special interests, no matter how politically powerful they may be, invariably package their programs with the rhetoric of public interest. It has often been pointed out that beneficiaries of special interest programs, farm programs, for example, could be served more efficiently through direct cash transfers than through indirect subsidies. These beneficiary groups resist direct transfers, however, because they correctly recognize that such transfers would undermine the public interest justification for the programs. Without that public interest justification, public support vanishes and the programs cease to be politically viable.

The suggestion here is that, although ideological objectives are essential in generating political support for an active economic role for government, ideological objectives often have little influence on how government carries out this role. Ideological considerations are important in establishing the extent and general direction of government action, but nonideological, special interest considerations are dominant in determining the details of government action. The crucial factor here is that the ideological content of political decisions diminishes as the decision maker becomes more politically organized and influential. There are two explanations for this diminishing ideological content; one well known and the other an outgrowth of our previous discussion.

It is well known that it is easier for a group to organize effectively for political action (overcome the free-rider problem) if its members are motivated by focused objectives common to all.[3] Although these focused objectivess can be, and sometimes are, primarily of an ideological nature, typically they are more narrowly economic in nature. Certainly, few would deny that groups motivated by focused economic concerns have an advantage in organizing for political action. Narrowly focused, nonideological concerns facilitate the exercise of political influence. But it is important to recognize that the reverse is also true. Being in a position to exercise political influence motivates an emphasis on narrowly focused, nonideological concerns. In terms of decisiveness, the politically influential group is somewhere between the voter, who lacks decisiveness and therefore is strongly influenced by ideology, and the shopper at a supermarket, who is completely decisive and therefore is influenced by ideology hardly at all. The fact that a politically organized group possesses a significant degree of influence over certain political decisions means that it would be genuinely costly for it to ignore the nonideological concerns of its members in exercising that influence. If an ideologically motivated group, but one without political influence, was suddenly granted a large measure of political influence, the predictable consequence is that the group would become less ideologically motivated.

This does not imply that politically organized groups will overcome the powerful ideological expression that comes from the unorganized general public. They will, however, be able to exert their political influence in ways that give the appearance of going along with popular sentiment while neutralizing, and in many cases perverting, the ideological objectives behind this sentiment. Organized groups often do little to oppose legislation that is adverse to their interests, especially when public opinion is strongly behind the legislation. Indeed, well-organized groups often "get on board" and support legislation that is intended to be inimical to their economic well-being. But, as opposed to individual citizens who vote for the legislation, or vote for the politicians who support it, and then quickly shift their concerns to other matters, the affected interest groups will be unrelenting in their attempts to determine the details of the legislation and its implementation. These attempts, despite the rhetoric behind them, will seldom be motivated by the ideological objectives that motivated the public support for the legislation. Government attempts to help the poor, to protect the environment, and to regulate business on behalf of the consumer are all examples of government's role in the economy being subverted to one degree or another by organized interest groups. The initial motivation for government involvement in the economy is generally dominated by ideological concerns, but narrow economic concerns typically lie behind the special interests that do so much to determine the results of this involvement.

IDEOLOGY AND THE CONTROL OF GOVERNMENT

The question of how extensive the economic role of government should be cannot be adequately considered in the absence of some judgment as to the degree of control the public has over the government. The more control the public has over government, the better agent the government is, and it is obvious that a good agent can profitably be entrusted with more responsibility than a poor agent. Ultimately, it is through the prevailing ideology toward government that the public exerts control over government. The proximate means of controlling government is through constitutional limits on government activities and procedures. But in the absence of a supporting ideology, constitutions lack force. As Henry Simons (1950, p. 20) pointed out long ago, "Constitutional provisions are no stronger than the consensus that they articulate. At best they can only check abuses of power until moral pressure is mobilized; and their check must become ineffectual if often overtly used."

From the discussion in the previous section it is clear that, even though it is through ideology that we ultimately control government, there is no general way of determining how effective this ideological control is. It depends on the type of activity under consideration. Ideology is very effective at controlling the general direction of government action—for example, whether or not government should oppose industrial concentration, promote equality, or encourage labor unions. But once ideology points government in a general direction, it is very ineffective at controlling the details of the actions government takes or the outcomes that result from these actions.

From our discussion, what can be concluded about the proper economic role for government and the likelihood that government economic activity will approximate this proper role? Precision in this area will always remain an elusive objective, but some general, and hopefully interesting, observations can be made. Almost surely the proper role for government requires a government whose activity goes beyond that of the impartial referee envisioned by minimal state advocates. It is hard to imagine that there exists no use of discretionary government power beyond that associated with minimal state functions which, even allowing for the imperfect control the public has over government, would generate genuine social benefits in excess of costs. But it is also almost surely the case that efficiency limits are breached rather quickly as government expands its discretionary economic role beyond minimal state functions. An expanding economic role for government quickly increases the type of government activities that require detailed public control if they are to be performed properly, but that are far more responsive to special interest influence than to public interest concerns. Ideological sympathy for an active economic role for government undermines the ideological control that the public can exert over government while increasing the need for that control.

A prevailing ideology that views discretionary government power as an appropriate means of solving a wide range of social problems is inconsistent with achieving the proper economic role for government. Such an ideology will result in politically compelling demands for government to do things that it is either incapable of doing or capable of doing only poorly and at costs that exceed benefits. Some degree, quite likely a significant degree, of ideological negativism is necessary if something approximating the proper economic role for government is to be realized. Only a pronounced public skepticism toward government can overcome the tendency for people to feel good about supporting government programs that purport to "do good" with power that will invariably be controlled, and abused, by special interests. A necessary condition for achieving a proper economic role for government is an ideology that finds a politically significant proportion of the population feeling noble about opposing government actions, no matter how noble the objectives of those actions may be.

There is little chance that general agreement will ever exist on the proper economic role of government, or that the proper role will be realized even if it were agreed upon. Our discussion does, however, suggest a reason for being cautiously optimistic that self-correcting ideological forces are operating to restrain government's economic role from moving to one extreme or another. If for example, public opinion was so skeptical of government that its role moved close to that of the minimal state, public control over government actions would improve, thus reducing skepticism toward government. Or if public opinion was so trusting of government that its role expanded far beyond desirable limits, public control over government actions would diminish, thus reducing trust in government.

How effective self-correcting ideological considerations are at preventing government from straying too far from its proper economic role is an open question. If I can be allowed a purely personal observation, there appears to be far less reason to worry about whether ideology can reverse a tendency toward too little government than about whether it can reverse special interest pressures toward too much government.

NOTES

1. The first systematic economic analysis of the tendency for individuals to avoid political involvement was provided by Anthony Downs (1957).

2. This point was first made by Gordon Tullock (1971).
3. See Mancur Olson (1968).

REFERENCES

Downs, Anthony. *The Economic Theory of Democracy*. New York: Harper & Row, 1957.

Kelman, Steven. *Making Public Policy: A Hopeful View of American Government*. New York: Basic Books, 1987.

North, Douglass C. *Structure and Change in Economic History*. New York: W. W. Norton, 1981.

Olson, Mancur, Jr. *The Logic of Collective Action: Public Goods and the Theory of Groups*. New York: Schocken Books, 1968.

Simons, Henry C. *Economic Policy for a Free Society*. Chicago: University of Chicago Press, 1950.

Tullock, Gordon. "The Charity of the Uncharitable." *Western Economic Journal* 9 (December 1971): 379–92.

16

On the Appropriate Arenas for Government Intervention in the Third World

Neva Seidman Makgetla and Robert B. Seidman

Governments in the Third World face a task more urgent and confined than that in the West: Since the majority of their peoples continue to suffer extremes of poverty and oppression, appropriate policy interventions must alleviate those ills. In this chapter we will explore the role of the state in that context.

First, we argue that a symbiosis exists between the state and the economy: The state brings about a given allocation of resources by permitting particular social groups to make decisions, while placing a range of constraints on those decisions. In effect, in more or less restricted ways, the state empowers various economic actors. In the process, it acts through the legal order. It follows that we can see the existing legal order as the cause of the peculiar pattern of resource allocation associated with underdevelopment. Its transformation then appears as a key to solving the ills of the Third World.

Next, we consider the perceptions of the legal order incorporated in the three major paradigms of development economics—supply side, basic needs, and socialist—and the associated jurisprudential schools. In effect, each development strategy ultimately blames underdevelopment on constraints which the government places on a particular social group, and calls for changes in the legal order so as to enhance that group's power.

No social inquiry can elaborate a set of prescriptions that are good for every time and place, or even for every Third World country. Rather, we present heuristic propositions to indicate what economic problems might prove useful policy targets, and how and to whom appropriate interventions would logically delegate power. In specific situations, the value of each proposition depends on the perspective of policymakers and the relevance of the underlying analysis.

OF CHICKENS AND EGGS: INSTITUTIONS, CLASS POWER, AND THE LEGAL ORDER

Governments can intervene only by invoking the normative system in which the state has a finger, that is, the legal order. That normative system consists of the *rules* promulgated by a host of lawmaking bodies (not only legislature and appellate courts, but executive and administrative officials as well), and the *behaviors* of the tribe that occupies positions in society's lawmaking and law-implementing institutions—legislators, judges, presidents and mayors, police and bureaucrats, functionaries seemingly without end.[1] To intervene in the economy, governments change rules that trigger activity by some of these officials. Because they invoke the legal order, it becomes a lens through which to examine government intervention.

Through the legal order, the government gives social groups the right to make a range of economic decisions. In capitalist economies, the state grants entrepreneurs a wide range of powers over their property but imposes various restrictions in the name of the public interest. In socialist countries, the state delegates power over property largely to its own employees, constrained by the requirements of national planning. In either case, when it modifies the legal order, the state redefines decision-making power, and a new allocation of resources results.

In contrast, some theorists hold that class power defines government policy. In this view, the state "constitutes and is bound to constitute in a class society the ultimate organizer and defender of the long-term interests of the ruling class" (Fatton, 1988, p. 253; see also Roberts, 1985). To transform the state and so the economy, we should seek, not to understand the specifics of the legal order, but to replace the ruling class.

Yet class power is one of three that are one: class power, institutions, and the law. We cannot understand class power unless we analyze its roots, not only in production itself, but also in state power (and so the legal order) and social tradition. The might of the capitalist class arises, in large part, out of institutions that allocate control: banks and corporations and agrobusiness, elections and election financing systems, and a host of others. Laws create, sustain, or restrict all these institutions. In the Third World, governments created new capitalist classes by replacing traditional tenure with capitalist property rights, often vested in new owners.

In short, class power simultaneously shapes institutions and the legal order, and results from their operation. Each explains the others. It follows that to affect class power, a government must modify the legal order formally or informally. True, such modifications generally result because a class exerts pressure on government. Nonetheless, the proponents of change can ensure appropriate measures only if they understand how the legal order affects social power.

A second group of theorists holds that the free market alone can raise productivity in the Third World. In that case, governments should act on resource allocation only in a narowly defined set of cases. "[T]he governments of market economies which have efficiently industrialized have by and large . . . established clear rules of the game, contributed judiciously to the construction of an industrial infrastructure, and otherwise intervened sparingly and carefully'' (World Bank, 1987, p. 60).

This view downplays the way in which the legal order ineluctably shapes economic activity, among others through laws on labor, property, inheritance and contracts, monetary regulations, taxation and a host of administrative decisions, even procedural rules for dispute settlement. Through these regulations, the state effectively delegates particular powers to private individuals, giving them a say in economic decisions that does not derive strictly from production requirements. Government intervention cannot remain within easily listed limits, but pervasively and unavoidably defines economic behaviors. The question becomes, not whether government should intervene, but how.

We can distinguish between theories of social inquiry that analyze how decisions come about within existing institutions, and theories that call those very institutions into question.[2] Approaches that deny the relevance of the legal order ultimately rule out discussion of how government policy can transform the existing institutions, which in the Third World ensure continued poverty and oppression for the majority. Effectively, they deny social actors the option of reshaping society to overcome its ills.

This review suggests parameters for an investigation of law and development.

Proposition 1. Every law or regulation delegates power. A key issue in government intervention, then, becomes *to whom* and *how* the legal order should delegate a particular power. Policymakers must then decide, not whether or where to intervene, but in whose favor and what form.

Proposition 2. We can treat the state's assignment of rights and duties and the associated institutional organization as determinant in the operation of every economy.

DEVELOPMENT THEORY AND THE LEGAL ORDER

Every major theory of development suggests an explanation for the continued suffering of the Third World. (See Makgetla, 1988.) Each centers on the disempowerment of the social group it considers best able to use resources to bring about development. In the process, like every theory related to the legal order, at least implicitly they address the twin questions of freedom and power. Supply-side theory stresses the constraints placed on private entrepreneurs; basic-needs theory, the deprivation of small-scale peasant and informal producers; and socialist theory, the economic and political powerlessness of workers and peasants.

Based on its analysis, each theory suggests solutions that empower a particular group. In effect, they propose different agenda for state intervention, whose usefulness in a given situation depends on the relevance of their underlying analysis. The proposals parallel schools of jurisprudence developed in the United States: supply-side views coincide with the libertarian or Chicago wing of law and economics, basic needs tenets with liberal jurisprudence, and socialist theories with an institutionalist approach.

Here we outline and briefly critique the theory of state intervention which each development strategy and its jurisprudential homologue indicates. In each case, we summarize the explanation for poverty in terms of (1) the definition of the problem; (2) the impact of government policies; (3) more specifically, the effect of the allocation of economic power through property rights; and (4) the implications for freedom.

Supply-Side Economics and Libertarian Law and Economics

Theory. In the Third World as in the industrialized West, both libertarian law and economics and supply-side theory reject a focus on poverty as the main problem for economics. After all, who can define poverty and so decide whose suffering to address? (Posner, 1986, p. 431–37; contrast Meier, 1984, p. 221). Moreover, measures to relieve poverty directly would require government intervention to redistribute resources, which in this perspective must prove highly inefficient. It follows that governments should instead seek to raise productivity. By generating more goods and services for society as a whole, that will ultimately benefit everyone to some degree.

Hypothesis 1: Economic policy should address low productivity, which harms everyone.

Prescription 1: Government should intervene in the economy only to raise productivity.

To explain low productivity, supply-side theory accepts the neoclassical perception that inefficiency results when real-world markets deviate from the conditions of perfect competition (see Stokey and Zeckhauser, 1978, pp. 297–308). In Greek legend, Procrustes had the somewhat unkindly habit of laying unsuspecting travelers in a bed and then chopping them down or stretching them to size. Similarly, this approach would use state power to make the real world conform to an ideal type. But, in contrast to more liberal neoclassicists, supply-side adherents effectively assume that no market imperfections arising out of private activity will cause severe inefficiency. It follows that "material progress is greatest if individuals have the right to pursue their own affairs unmolested by the state" (Scully, 1988, p. 653). The World Bank[3] holds that if, "to prevent abuses, to improve welfare, and to improve the pattern of investment or output," governments must intervene in resource allocation, they should exercise great caution, since "the dividing line between measures that improve and those that worsen the conditions under which the private sector operates is often fine" (1987, p. 77). By extension, nonmarket modes of resource allocation, such as the provision of free medical care and education, necessarily generate inefficiency (World Bank, 1987, Ch. 4).

Hypothesis 2. Virtually all free markets mimic perfect competition adequately to ensure high productivity. Therefore, government constraints on entrepreneurial decision making cause low productivity.

Prescription 2. The state should avoid interfering in entrepreneurial decision making.

Corollary 1: To solve undeniable market failures, reorganize property rights so as to minimize externalities, and then restore the free market.

Corollary 2: Where inefficient resource allocation arises in the absence of a market, use state power to develop free market sales of the goods at issue.

From this perspective, the market cannot function efficiently if the state limits entrepreneurial power, which derives in large part from private property rights. If the state limits private control of resources or, by reallocating rights, makes bargains difficult or impossible, productivity must suffer. For the World Bank, development requires that economic actors know "clearly who owns what and how goods and services can be used, bought and sold." By extension, the Third World suffers from a "perceived insecurity of economic rights" that derives from political pressure, bureaucracy, corruption, "uncertainty over whether legal and contractual rights would be upheld by the courts," and frequent changes in the law (World Bank, 1987, p. 62; see also Scully, 1988, p. 653).

It follows that to ensure efficient development, governments should protect existing property rights, however inequitable, ensuring the power of the private entrepreneur against the claims of the community or workers.

Hypothesis 3. In the name of equity or efficiency, Third World governments all too often limit or reallocate the rights of private entrepreneurs, or at least threaten to do so. Inefficiency must ensue.

Prescription 3: Governments should neither restrain entrepreneurs' control over their resources nor redistribute property.

Both supply-side theory and Chicago law and economics consider bureaucratic decree the main remediable threat to freedom. (See Makgetla and Seidman, 1989.) In this view, "Life, liberty and property are not additively separable attributes; the diminution of one diminishes all" (Scully, 1988, p. 653; see also von Hayek, 1967 [1966]). The market may restrict choice, particularly for the poor, but its strictures cannot be overruled without cutting productivity and so the range of choice for society as a whole. By contrast, governments often give officials more power than is required to meet social goals, letting them restrict the choices of others at whim. Governments maximize freedom, then, by permitting all individuals to dispose freely of their resources.[4] This analysis coincides with Arthur Venn Dicey's assertion that, when the legal order permits bureaucratic or even judicial discretion, it falls short of the Rule of Law.

Hypothesis 4: The principal restrictions on individual choice are state regulation and market conditions. Society cannot efficiently eliminate economic strictures, but it need not suffer unnecessary government interference.

Prescription 4: To maximize freedom, lawmakers should permit individuals to use their resources as they see fit.

Corollary 1: Ideally, government intervention should always be expressed in terms of general, bright-line rules of law that leave officials no discretion.

Combined, these prescriptions imply an explanation for poverty and oppression: the owners of productive property have too little power over economic decisions. Raising productivity thus requires that the state enhance the power of the minority that currently controls the bulk of the Third World's productive resources. In the short run, that solution may mean further impoverishing and politically disempowering the majority. This analysis informs the International Monetary Fund's "austerity" programs, which sought to "increase the relative share of profits in national income and reduce the relative share of wages" (Nashishibi, 1983; see also IMF, 1985, pp. 183–87).

Critique. In the Third World, the analysis underlying supply-side theory came under attack for refusing to address poverty directly; for ignoring the gulf between real markets and perfect competition; and, ultimately, for demanding uncritical acceptance of the very institutions that led to poverty and oppression for the majority.

Socialist and basic-needs theorists agree that the Third World's massive inequalities in wealth and income represent an obstacle to efficiency, not a necessary stimulant. In that case, Third World states need not choose between equity and growth, but can pursue them simultaneously.

Furthermore, most Third World markets, no matter how free, diverge dramatically from the perfectly competitive ideal. Income inequalities mean that market demand does not adequately reflect social need. Instead of meeting the pressing requirements of the majority, the market supplies relative luxuries for the tiny high-income group, and exports. Moreover, the Third World's small economies ineluctably generate oligopolies in the modern sector. Deficiencies in skills, transport and capital-goods industries limit factor mobility. As resources respond to changes in market price only slowly and wastefully, enduring unemployment emerges. In these conditions, to make the market resemble perfect competition, the state must intervene extensively—which in itself rules out perfect competition.

Finally, by enshrining an ideal free market as the sole viable economic path, supply-side theory prevents systematic examination and transformation of Third World institutions. A critical theory should incite examination of how social relationships of all types contribute to underdevelopment. Instead, the supply-side approach would recast policymakers as detectives intent on searching out government violations of the theory's dictates. In particular, the reluctance to question the allocation of property ignores the fact that in many Third World countries (in Africa often within living memory) those rights were forcibly and often brutally wrested from the majority of the population. In effect, by demanding that the state maintain and even enhance the power of entrepreneurs, supply-side theory supported the small group of local and foreign investors that dominated most Third World economies. It ruled out a search for more democratic alternatives.

Basic Needs and Legal Liberalism

Theory. Basic-needs theory originated in the 1970s with the perception that, although a number of Third World countries satisfied supply-side theory by achieving rapid economic expansion, the position of the poor improved little. It therefore demanded that governments address basic needs directly. Adherents defined poverty in the Third World as the position of the poorest 40 percent of the population, whom they typically identified with the peasantry and informal-sector[5] urban producers.

Hypothesis 1: Underdevelopment appears in the suffering of the poorest of the poor, typically peasants and the unemployed and underemployed of the urban informal sector.

Prescription 1: Government policy must center on meeting the basic human needs of the poorest.

Like supply-side theory, basic-needs tenets rely primarily on neoclassical economics. To explain inefficiency, however, they explore the entire range of deviations from perfect competition, not state intervention alone. In that case, inefficiency may result from the unconstrained decision making of private entrepreneurs, so that state control would prove more efficient. In these circumstances, perfect competition, and with it optimal solutions, prove a chimera, and policymakers must be content with a second-best solution. Instead of looking to general rules, they must solve each instance of inefficiency by seeking the best possible balance between the evils of government intervention in the market and the ills brought about by market imperfections and failures.

Hypothesis 2: The perfectly competitive market represents the ideal system for allocating resources, but the real world deviates from it in myriad ways. Policymakers cannot always resolve all deviations simultaneously.

Prescription 1. Policymakers must use a case-by-case approach, combining state intervention and entrepreneural decision making to achieve the best possible position.

Corollary 1: Cost-benefit analysis and project assessment become central aids in determining policies.

In the basic-needs analysis, the dualism of Third World economies decisively blocks development. The modern sector, centered on the urban areas, remains capital-intensive and import dependent, but absorbs the bulk of investment. By contrast, small-scale producers—primarily peasants, but also urban informal-sector entrepreneurs—rely on local resources. Theoretically, then, they could stimulate greater employment and output both directly and indirectly, but they have been unable to expand rapidly.

In this view, a combination of state intervention and monopolization in the modern sector condemns the small-scale sector to stagnation. First, most states in the Third World systematically impoverish smaller producers, both rural and urban, in order to benefit modern-sector entrepreneurs and their employees. They use tax revenues to build up social and economic infrastructure in the urban centers, neglecting the rural majority; depress agricultural prices to reduce food costs for urban workers; effectively ban various informal-sector activities;[6] and all too often resort to the outright expropriation of land. Second, since both local and foreign firms in the modern sector enjoy monopoly power, competition will not compel them to seek out innovative projects. They may indulge in prejudice, refusing on the grounds of ethnicity, gender, or class to buy goods and services from small-scale entrepreneurs or to lend them money.

Even if the state ends positive discrimination against small-scale enterprises, their past impoverishment and the consequent market imperfections initiate two vicious cycles. On the one hand, small-scale producers could historically acquire only primitive technologies, and so can neither finance investment themselves nor attract outside capital. On the other, low incomes for the majority dampen demand for the simple goods and services which smaller producers provide.

In short, the current allocation of property rights causes low productivity as well as inequity. To break the vicious cycle of poverty, the state must step in to reallocate resources to small-scale entrepreneurs. To that end, for instance, it might provide them with subsidized credit, training, and improved infrastructure, initiate land reform, and eliminate price controls on food products. If it subsequently permits producers to use their resources as they wish, a dynamic but equitable economy should result.

Hypothesis 3. Existing laws and institutions divert resources to modern-sector producers and employers from peasants and small-scale informal-sector producers. In the process, they cause poverty, limit economic growth, and hinder job creation.

Prescription 3: Government should gradually divert an increasing share of resources to small-scale producers.

Like liberal jurisprudents, basic-needs adherents imply that severe poverty constrains personal freedom as much as state intervention in market choices. Redistributing wealth to the poorest, then, enhances freedom, even if it requires some restrictions on the property rights of the wealthy—the local elites and foreign investors. Typically, however, basic-needs studies focus on ways to use resources to improve the lot of the poorest, rather than exploring new or greater sources of government revenue. In effect, instead of fundamentally reallocating economic power, basic-needs programs would focus on ensuring the poorest a greater share in new wealth, essentially by redirecting government services. Agriculture provided the only exception, because many basic-needs adherents favor a land reform. Even then, however, they would prefer to compensate the original owners and to reallocate only underutilized or inefficiently farmed land to smallholders (Adelman, 1988 [1986], pp. 500–502).

To reallocate resources, the state must replace impersonal allocation through the market with a degree of official discretion. Where that might permit bias and corruption, basic-needs adherents offer four countermeasures. First, at the local level, community control over resources should both ensure that programs meet local needs and encourage the contribution of local resources, especially labor. Second, for central agencies, cost-benefit analysis provides a systematic and apparently objective set of criteria similar to the market but more responsive to social needs. Third, profit-maximizing public corporations seemingly harness to government's purposes the feral competencies of the entrepreneur. To that end, they rested on laws that permitted government control only through corporate law and ministerial directions "of a general nature."[7] Finally, legal liberals place considerable faith in the incorruptibility of well-trained technocrats.

Hypothesis 4: Poverty may impair individual choice more than state intervention.

Prescription 4: To give meaningful freedom to the poorest of the poor, the state must provide them with resources. That may compel it to replace the impersonal market with enhanced official discretion and, at the local level, heightened community control.

In sum, basic-needs adherents blame underdevelopment on the diversion of resources from potentially dynamic small-scale entrepreneurs. The solution becomes the gradual strengthening of peasant and informal-sector producers as the government uses more of its expenditures to meet their needs.

Critique. By the early 1980s, basic-needs theory faced a crisis. Governments that had attempted to provide more resources to the poor withouut interfering radically in the control of modern-sector wealth typically found themselves heavily in debt, with little or no economic expansion to show for their pains.

Criticism of the basic-needs approach centered on the failure to face up to the political and economic requirements of a significant redistribution of wealth. To reallocate resources at the national level, basic-needs adherents look not to the mobilization of the poor themselves, but to benevolent bureaucrats. Despite the initial basic-needs focus on the disempowerment of small-scale producers, in the end they imply rather that the local technocratic (i.e., Westernized) elite is not powerful enough.

Politically, discussion of the need for popular participation remains limited to local projects, rather than central economic and government institutions. Basic-needs research, which is typically addressed to foreign aid agencies and existing governments, considers only cursorily the need for fundamental changes in central political institutions to bring about a redistribution of resources. (See Streeten and World Bank, 1984, pp. 34–36.) The stress on the poorest of the poor, defined as a minority of the population, works against consideration of a mass political base for redistributing wealth. Yet in most Third World countries, absent organized political pressure, central government officials remained remote from the lives, much less the political will, of the poorest. Peasants had no place in their waiting rooms or neighborhoods. Willy-nilly, most top officials came to empathize more with other members of the high-income group than with the mass of the population. Short of famine (and not always even then), decisions to distribute resources to the poorest became notable more by their absence than their presence.

On the economic side, basic-needs proposals generally downplay discussion of where states should find the resources to give the poorest, focusing instead on finding desirable objects for government expenditure. (See, for instance, ILO, 1983, passim.) This approach implies that redistribution need not affect the wealth of modern companies, whether local or foreign, private or state-owned. In almost every Third World country, however, comparatively few firms control the bulk of productive resources. If their ecoonomic and political might persists, only an insignificant reallocation of resources and power seems possible.

The basic-needs stress on small-scale producers cripples analysis of economic power. Both supply-side and socialist theorists argue that in central sectors of the economy, and particularly in industry, small-scale enterprise cannot utilize adequately productive technologies. In this view, at least in the long term, smallholdings, smithies, or miners with picks cannot replace estate farming, steel mills, and power drills. Limiting popular participation to small-scale production, then, ensures democracy only in poor, peripheral projects.

Socialist Theories and Institutionalist Jurisprudence

Theory. For socialists, the principal object of government policy became the elimination of alienation—the economic and political disempowerment of the majority of the population. In the Third World, this approach usually translates into a focus on the poverty, unemployment, and political vulnerability of workers and poor peasants.

Hypothesis 1. In the Third World, the majority face economic and political power-lessness, which need not exist.

Prescription 1: Government policy should seek to give workers and peasants greater control over both economic and political decision making.

Socialist explanations for the Third World's difficulties reject the neoclassical methodology. Instead, they hold that the economic ills of the Third World arise because a minority of the population—local and foreign capital in the private and state sector—controls the lion's share of productive resources. Because the real world cannot achieve the utopia of perfect competition, the capitalists' profit-maximizing activities will not benefit the majority. Above all, monopoly shackles the invisible hand. Despite its negative economic and social impact, the minority persists for three reasons: reliance on highly complex technologies that require managerial control; state support through the legal order, and ultimately open force; and the perpetration of an ideological hegemony fostered by the educational system, social tradition, and, in many countries, the mass media.

This analysis leads socialists to unique prescriptions for legal intervention. As a central cause of the Third World's difficulties, they identify the existing legal order and its protection of the rich minority.[8] Therefore, to enhance the power of the majority, the first task becomes to change existing political and economic institutions and the laws, regulations, and norms that sustain them. Thus, socialists place the burden of proof, not on the advocate of change, but on the advocate of stasis.

Hypothesis 2: The existing economic institutions and the legal order that supports them permit the owners of productive property to maximize, not the public good, but private profit.

Prescription 1: To empower the majority, governments must massively change the existing economic and political institutions, and to that end the state's allocation of rights and duties. Over time, therefore, governments must transform the legal order.

Socialists argue that in the Third World, in order to raise living standards while providing employment on a broad scale, the state must initiate enormous changes in economic structure. To that end, it must step in to guide investment into relatively unprofitable sectors producing consumer and producer necessities. To empower workers, however, the state must give them a greater say in management. Clearly, the objectives of heightened state control over investment and greater worker power may conflict. (See, e.g., Davies, 1987.)

In any case, the state cannot intervene at will. Third World governments suffer a severe shortage of skilled labor. Market-oriented theories largely avoid this problem by assuming that, to maximize profits, private individuals will nonetheless find efficient ways to combine factors. By contrast, socialists require that people initiate a social transformation to enrich the community or country, not primarily themselves. In effect, the strategy requires not simply qualified personnel, but cadre. Furthermore, severe limits on investable surpluses compel governments to choose between investment projects. Finally, rapid institutional change may itself disrupt production.

It follows that governments cannot instantaneously reorganize institutions to reallocate resources. Rather, while not shirking radical change where needed, where possible they must carefully plan the restructuring of systems of economic power. The state should exert direct control only where it requires specific alterations in an enterprise's operations. That need appears to be most pressing where projects have extensive linkages with other sectors and so exert disproportionate influence over the economy as a whole, as with financial and trading institutions or capital-goods producers. Producer cooperatives or even private owners might run less strategic enterprises. In that case, the state could combine regulations and community control to protect workers and consumers, and use taxation and credit to redirect investment as desired.

Hypothesis 3: The institutions and rules of property law exclude the majority from decision-making processes with respect to the economy and their workplace, giving power to the owners of productive property. The economic ills of the Third World result.

Prescription 3: Using the legal order, the government should shape control over resources to achieve a balance between the need to restructure investment so as to develop a more integrated and dynamic national economy, and the need to empower workers and peasants. These requirements should determine the allocation of economic decision-making powers, whether formally in terms of property and contract law as traditionally defined, or otherwise.

Corollary 1: Transforming political and economic institutions as well as national production structures requires long-term planning.

Corollary 2: Given the constraints on the state, nationalization should be restricted to economic activities that promise the greatest leverage over the allocation of resources.

Corollary 3: Where the state need not intervene to dictate economic activities directly, workers or management will make decisions, giving rise to various forms of market relationship.

Finally, the socialist definition of freedom hinges not on the ability of individuals to dispose freely of their resources and selves within constraints set by the market, but on the ability of the members of a community to cooperate to control their collective destiny. In consequence, socialists demand laws that systematically empower the majority, restraining both managerial and bureaucratic might. Another of development's apparently endless deadlocks results, since the complexity of modern economic activities seems to require managerial fiat. The problem arises sharply in the Third World, where much of the population remains functionally illiterate and technically unqualified.

Socialists respond by agreeing that, although the legal order must delegate power to some administrators, it should restrain that power by strict attention to legality enforced ultimately through the organization of workers and peasants to control decision-making processes. If officials use their discretion to butter their own toast or that of others with power, the complex planned interrelationships of a socialist economy must die a-borning. A variety of means to ensure legality must evolve—often involving worker or community supervision of decision makers—although ideally minimizing red tape. Naturally, these measures work best in small communities where the population at large has enough education to understand economic and social decisions. In any case, it remains easier to prescribe the general heuristic than to develop institutions to implement it.

Hypothesis 4: Only the mass has an interest in protecting the interest of the mass; unless restrained, officials with discretionary power—whether in government or management—will use it to benefit themselves.

Prescription 4: All government interventions must ultimately empower the mass of the population, not bureaucrats or entrepreneurs.

Corollary 1: Laws and institutions must seek to foster the organization of workers and peasants to control officials and management, and thus government, without degenerating into stiffling bureaucracy.

The socialist explanation for the poverty and powerlessness of the mass lies in the institutions and legal order that disempower and impoverish them. That analysis implies not stasis but continual change. When a populist or socialist government takes power, the revolution has merely begun. Its central task becomes to transform institutions so as to empower the mass of the population.

Critique. In the Third World, attacks on socialist theory addressed its explanation for poverty and the feasibility of its central prescriptions.

First, socialists assert that mechanisms other than the market can foster rising productivity. In contrast, supply-side and basic-needs proponents agree that, in the long run, only the market can perform that function. They argue that no other social arrangement can achieve the same effects, no matter how it combines idealism and material rewards.

Second, the socialist approach implies that, particularly given massive inequalities in wealth, the political system provides for greater democracy than does the market. It suggests that workers and peasants should relinquish their power over their personal assets—essentially, their labor and perhaps a small plot of land—in order to control the commanding heights of the economy. Critics reply that no state structure can truly empower the mass. Only bureaucrats gain from the extension of state power into resource allocation. Better, then, for individuals to limit their ambitions to mastery over what resources they have.

On its own theory, socialism can empower the mass, rather than a bureaucratic elite, only to the extent that it develops genuinely democratic institutions to control, not merely elected officials, but day-to-day political and economic decision making. Its critics maintain that large-scale, modern society denies that hope, and socialism becomes mere pie-in-the-sky.

CONCLUSION

Theory generates hypotheses for testing. In this chapter, we do not attempt any detailed test of the hypotheses generated by our three theories, although the Third World's experience suggests the validity of the key hypotheses of the socialist approach.

Despite the bright promises of the 1960s and 1970s, in the mid–1980s a grazier-tribe[9] retained control over the wealth of the Third World, while the majority continued in poverty. We propose two general propositions to explain that situation. First, most Third World governments hardly changed the legal order through which they defined economic institutions. Those institutions ground out luxury for a few, but poverty and vulnerability for most. Second, the legal order always delegates power. In most of the Third World, it provided vast powers to entrepreneurs. In addition, pursuant to the prescriptions of liberal jurisprudence, development policies delegated significant power to officials. Without community control or narrow legal restrictions, many officials used their power to advance their own interests, individually and as a class.

In sum, the Third World's experience shows that, unless the legal order empowers the mass, development will not favor the mass. To empower the majority, however, requires a theory of government intervention aimed at changing both the allocation of rights and the structure of institutions. By contrast, supply-side theorists would change existing rights only to enhance the power of the already powerful. Basic-needs theorists would solve the poverty and vulnerability of the Third World with incremental changes in existing allocations of rights, effectively permitting the bureaucratic and political elite to retain or enhance its power. Only socialist approaches pointed more systematically to the need to analyze how the existing system disempowers the majority in economic and political terms. They could not provide rigid prescriptions to ensure a democratic utopia, but they did argue the need to search for systems participatory enough to ensure a reallocation of resources to benefit the majority.

NOTES

We are indebted to Professors Ann Seidman, Joseph Brodley and Alan Feld, and the participants of the Boston University School of Law Faculty Colloquium for a critique of an earlier draft.

1. A familiar aphorism expresses this expansive view of the law: "There's law in the end of a policeman's stick."
2. We are grateful to Professor Peter Dorner for this insight.
3. Although the World Bank officials adopted aspects of the basic-needs perspective, its analytical work in the 1980s accepted the tenets of supply-side theory (1987, passim).
4. In this vein, in his speech at the Republican National Convention in New Orleans in 1988, President Reagan praised the freedom of the United States as evidenced, in part, by the availability of 400 flavors of ice cream.
5. Usually defined as small-scale producers using primitive technologies, who largely operate outside the laws and regulations that define the modern market.
6. Through licensing acts, minimum-wage laws, etc.
7. This phrase, which—like the verses of Scots ballads—appears unchanged from one setting to another, first appeared in the public corporations created by the British Labour party after World War II. The British government then enthusiastically advocated similar corporations throughout the waning Empire and nascent Commonwealth.
8. That conclusion flowed from Marxist theories of the state. The state arose, they claim, to aid the economic ruling class to consolidate its power. The existing legal structure in any state represents what the political elite think necessary to consolidate its power. In most states at most times, the political elite serve as (usually subordinate) allies to the economic ruling class. Occasionally—as in some African states immediatdely after independence—a contradiction exists between new political rulers and the economic ruling

class (for example, the day after Prime Minister Mugabe's ZANU government took power in Zimbabwe). With that contradiction, the potential for revolutionary change exists. Ultimately, whether that change comes about will demonstrate itself in changed laws that in fact bring about changed behavior and therefore changed social relationships.

9. See *The Grazier Tribe*, an Irish folksong about Ireland at the end of the eighteenth century: "There's not a town from Cork to Down, / Or Dublin or Tralee, / But has a den of grazier men / To keep you in poverty. / Oh, ye men in name have ye no shame / To see this beauteous land, / Turned into one vast wilderness / By the cursed grazier band."

REFERENCES

Adelman, Irma. "A Poverty-Focused Approach to Development Policy." In Charles K. Wilber (ed.), *The Political Economy of Development and Underdevelopment*. 4th Ed. New York: Random House, 1988 [1986].

Baran, Paul. *The Political Economy of Growth*. New York: Monthly Review, 1957.

Berg, Elliot. *Accelerated Development in Sub-Saharan Africa*. Washington, D.C.: World Bank, 1982.

Davies, Rob. "Nationalisation, Socialisation and the Freedom Charter." *South African Labour Bulletin* 12, No. 1 (1987).

Fatton, Robert, Jr. "Bringing the Ruling Class Back In: Class, State and Hegemony in Africa." *Comparative Politics* 20, No. 3 (April 1988).

Hayek, F. A. "The Principles of a Liberal Social Order." *Studies in Philosophy, Politics and Economics*. Chicago: University of Chicago Press, 1967 [1966].

ILO/JASPA. *Zambia: Basic Needs in an Economy Under Pressure*. Addis Ababa: ILO/JASPA, 1983.

IMF. "Impact of External Environment and Domestic Policies on Economic Performance in Developing Countries." IMF, *World Economic Outlook, April 1985*. Oxford: Oxford University Press, 1985.

Leipziger, Danny M. (ed.). *Basic Needs and Development*. Cambridge, Mass.: Oelgeschlager, Gunn & Hain, 1981.

Makgetla, Neva. "Development Economics and Perspectives on the South African Economy." *Journal of Law and Religion* 2 (1987).

————, and Robert Seidman. "The Applicability of Law and Economics to the Third World." *Journal of Economic Issues*, forthcoming.

Meier, Gerald M. *Emerging from Poverty: The Economics That Really Matters*. New York: Oxford University Press, 1984.

Nashashibi, Karim. "Devaluation in the Developing Countries: The Difficult Choices." *Finance and Development* (March 1983).

Posner, Richard. *Economic Analysis of Law*. 3rd ed. Boston: Little, Brown, 1986.

Roberts, Kenneth. "Democracy and the Dependent Capitalist State in Latin America." *Monthly Review*, 37, No. 5 (October 1985).

Scully, Gerald W. "The Institutional Framework and Economic Development." *Journal of Political Economy* 96, No. 3 (June 1988).

Seidman, Ann. *Planning for Development in Sub-Saharan Africa*. Dar-es-Salaam: Tanzania Publishing, 1974.

Seidman, Robert. *The State, Law and Development*. New York: St. Martin's Press, 1978.

Stokey, Edith, and Richard Zechauser. *A Primer for Policy Analysis*. New York: Norton, 1978.

Streeten, Paul, et al. *First Things First: Meeting Basic Human Needs in Developing Countries*. New York: Oxford University Press, 1981.

————, and the World Bank. "The Distributive Features of a Basic Needs Approach to Development." In Pradip Ghosh (ed.) *Third World Development: A Basic Needs Approach*. Westport, Conn.: Greenwood Press, 1984.

World Bank. *World Development Report, 1987*. New York: Oxford University Press, 1987.

17

Political Economy and Public Policy: The Problem of Joint Appraisal

Richard Rose

The term *political economy* implies appraising public policies by the standards of both politics and economics. When government becomes involved in the economy, decision makers must make a political appraisal in which competing ideas are evaluated in the light of the values and goals of the elected government. But politicians cannot simply make decisions on grounds of popularity or political will; their actions must also be effective. Joint appraisal poses two different but complementary questions about a policy: Is it politically desirable? Is it likely to be effective in the economy?

A public policy approach differs from conventional political science because it addresses rather than omits substantive and sometimes awkward problems and constraints of the economy. It differs from conventional economics because it includes political institutions and values usually treated as exogenous in economic analysis (cf. Lindbeck, 1976). When economists omit the "messy" concerns of politicians, the result is what Frank H. Hahn (1985) describes as "too sparse a description of the constraints under which agents act in society."

Here the object is to consider the relation between the politician's concern with desirable policies and the economist's concern with effective economic measures. The problem is least when there is complete consensus within and between the two groups. We must also consider what happens when there is dissensus about public policy among politicians and economists, or both.

POLITICAL DESIRABILITY AND ECONOMIC EFFECTIVENESS

Although economic issues are a major concern of government, they are not the first priority. Immediately, the modern state must maintain domestic order and protect the security of its borders from foreign invasion. If it fails on either or both of these counts, the regime is overthrown by revolution or invasion. From this perspective, raising taxes and spending public money is but a means to the end of maintaining peace and domestic tranquility. Modern states existed for more than a century before they became big-spending states or accepted responsibility for managing the economy (Rose, 1976).

Today the government's impact on the economy is a major concern of politicians and of private enterprise. It is responsible for taxing and spending policies that account for a third to a half of the national product of Organization for Economic Cooperation and Development (OECD) nations. Political institutions give voice to many different and competing views about what government should do. For example, there is a Ministry of Finance to express concern about inflation, a Ministry of Defense to stress national security needs, and a Social Welfare Ministry to urge the claims of the elderly and the ill. There are always arguments about what is electorally desirable or necessary. In such a setting economic concerns cannot be the only priority.

Within government, economists are expert advisers, on tap but not on top. Knowledge is an asset, but it confers neither legitimacy nor power. The first task of economic advisers in the corridors of power is to demonstrate that their knowledge is relevant to the concerns of policymakers; this is a marketing task, not an analytic task (cf. Nelson, 1987; Hargrove and Morley, 1984). When the message is attractive, for example, that a tax cut may stimulate the economy, it is easier to get a hearing than when the news is bad. The potential market is large, for most policymakers are not economists. But the demand is low, for most have reached the top by not knowing or caring about what economists know and care about.

Desirability is the first concern of politicians, for elected officials want to do what will be popular with the electorate. While in isolation economic growth, full employment, stable prices, and a satisfactory balance of payments all appear to be desirable, collectively they can appear as competing goods, and public opinion, politicians, and government departments can disagree in ranking them in order of priority from most to least desirable. There are also disagreements about which policies are most likely to succeed in advancing toward desired goals and which group of politicians is most likely to achieve them.

A program is economically effective to the extent that it achieves a predictable impact on the economy. Effectiveness is a primitive concept by comparison with efficiency; yet a program must be effective before it can be evaluated for efficiency. The stock-in-trade of economists is expertise in determining causes of economic conditions and evaluating the consequences of economic policies. However, difficulties in national economies since the early 1970s have shown how contingent are statements about the effectiveness of policies. Yet economists can still claim far more knowledge than politicians about the effect a given policy is likely to have on the economy.

A description of the relation between politicians and economists as an arm's-length relation between customer and contractor, with politicians setting goals and economists supplying the policies necessary to achieve them, is naive. The goals of government reflect political will, but they cannot be realized indepen-

Figure 17.1
Choice about Policies with Consensus

                                        Economic Consensus

Political Consensus

                                Effective   Ineffective

Desirable   DOUBLY DESIRABLE   ECONOMICALLY

                                                        DUBIOUS

Undesirable   POLITICALLY AWKWARD   DOUBLY

                                                        UNDESIRABLE

dently of the expertise of nonelected officials. The formulation of policies, and particularly of economic policies, requires the integration of political and expert skills (Rose, 1987).

CONSENSUS AND DISSENSUS

Whether appraisal is by politicians or economists, the result of group deliberations may register consensus or dissensus. It is hardly surprising when politicians disagree, for differing political values and beliefs can lead to conflicts about priorities for economic and noneconomic concerns of government, such as national security, law and order, and social welfare. They can also stimulate disagreements about the appropriate priority for different economic objectives. There are also many grounds for disagreement about which particular policy instruments are most desirable in terms of a given government's electoral and interest group constituencies.

Economists can collectively register dissensus or consensus too. Models can differ in what they incorporate and what they externalize on to others to worry about. Within a given field, such as macroeconomic policies, different priorities may be assumed to prevail as between differing macroeconomic objectives. There are also uncertainties about effective outcomes, for social science generalizations are statements of probabilities, and there is always an error term as well as a *ceteris paribus* clause.

When political and economic appraisals are brought together, policymakers face one of four logically possible situations, depending on whether or not there is consensus among economists, or among politicians, or among both.

1. *Choice with internal consensus.* When there is consensus about a policy among politicians and among economists—and also the appraisals of both are in agreement—then a policy is doubly desirable, being attractive to politicians and effective according to economists (Figure 17.1). In a complementary manner,

if politicians agree that a policy is undesirable and economists agree that it is ineffective, it will be rejected. Doubly desirable policies are handled by routines, far from the political spotlight, since there is no controversy and effectiveness is taken for granted. Policies regarded as doubly undesirable are discarded from the political agenda, for no one considers them worth thinking about.

When politicians and economists agree among themselves but disagree with each other, then there is a test of which values prevail. A policy viewed as politically desirable but as ineffective by nearly all economists can be described as economically dubious. Alternatively, a policy may be regarded as effective by economists but as undesirable by politicians. Thus, it is politically awkward (Figure 17.1). In such circumstances, which point of view do we expect to prevail?

Endorsement of an economic policy by politicians is a necessary condition of government action. In law, the choice of public policies rests with those who hold the highest offices of state. In addition to having the legal authority to commit the government, election gives politicians popular legitimacy, which is an important consideration when the cooperation of many different groups within society is needed to make a policy work. Endorsement by economists is neither a necessary nor a sufficient condition for action. The expert opinions expressed by economists, within or outside government, simply constitute advice.

Public choice economists have a theory to predict why a government ought to endorse economically dubious but politically desirable policies and reject policies that are economically effective but politically awkward. If politicians are conceived as "egoistic, rational utility maximizers" (Mueller, 1979, p. 1), then the stronger their egoistic interest in doing what is politically desirable, the less attention will be paid to economists' doubts. A politically awkward policy will almost certainly be vetoed by politicians, notwithstanding its economic potential, for the cost of adopting the policy is certain and immediate to politicians, whereas benefits are hypothetical and diffuse.

2. *Choice without political consensus.* If politics is defined as the articulation and reconciliation of conflicting views about the activities of government, then consensus will by definition be lacking. Politicians will be expected to contest the desirability of all major policies, while economists register a scientific consensus about effectiveness (Figure 17.2).

When politicians disagree, the influence of a consensus of economists will depend on the lines of political division. In an ideal-type parliamentary system, division can be expected between a disciplined, united governing party and a disciplined, united opposition. In such circumstances, disagreement in Parliament is consistent with consensus among decision makers in the Cabinet. In such circumstances, we would expect the government of the day to proceed as in Figure 17.1.

But many governments are coalitions of parties and factions, because institutions do not require consensus or even encourage disagreement, as in the American system of checks and balances. For example, Jan Tinbergen became

Figure 17.2
Choice of Policies without Political Consensus

	Economic Consensus	
Political Appraisal		
	Effective	Ineffective
Contested	ECONOMICALLY	
Desirability	EFFECTIVE	INEFFECTIVE

Figure 17.3
Choice of Policies without Economic Consensus

	Economic Assessment
Political Consensus	
	Contested Effectiveness
Desirable	POLITICALLY DESIRABLE
Undesirable	POLITICALLY UNDESIRABLE

a Nobel laureate for his work on central economic planning, but his country, the Netherlands, is a textbook example of a political system in which there are chronic disagreements about a coalition government. Even in a system of single-party government, there can be disagreement about policies reflecting contrasting departmental interests (e.g., spending ministers versus the budget agency). Economic expertise cannot provide a solution to intense political divisions within a governing party.

When substantial divisions occur within government, there are two alternative outcomes. Divisions may be sufficiently strong to prevent any action being taken because of the political judgment that it would split the party or parties in power. In Washington, divisions within government are likely to threaten defeat in Congress, thus dooming a proposal that carries the consensus endorsement of economists, because it would only result in a vote of no confidence for the White House. In a disciplined parliamentary system, divisions within government can be overriden by party whips, and if disagreements are not strong or when there are strong pressures for action, then a consensus about economic effectiveness may even be decisive.

3. *Choice without economic consensus.* Is it reasonable to expect consensus among economists about an issue of public policy? The answer is often no (Figure 17.3). Dissensus at the theoretical level is often evident in the assumptions, the focus, and the outputs of abstract models. The extent of disagreement rises as attention is shifted to prescribing public policies for problems affected by far

more influences than are contained by the assumptions of economic theory, for example, proposals about measures that should be taken to improve the international monetary situation. Public policy requires accepting the inherent "messiness" of the political process. Economists disagree about the desirability or necessity of moving from the world of models to the world of muddles (contrast Hahn, 1985, with Leontief, 1985).

The production of economic advice for policymakers is likely to reflect dissensus in at least four ways significant to politicians. First, there is likely to be disagreement about *whether* economics has any definite guidance to offer for a given policy problem. The cautious pace of the academy and the desire to hedge any conclusion with qualifications and pleas for more research is unsuited to the world of government, where busy policymakers want conclusions. Demand is sure to call forth supply. As a realistic chairman of the American Council of Economic Advisers said to an academic economist doubting the possibility of writing anything meaningful about a large, complex topic in an hour or a weekend: "If we don't, someone else will" (quoted in Allen, 1977, p. 52).

A second source of controversy is the appropriate economic context in which to analyze a problem. A monetary economist is likely to see a recession as a problem on the supply side, whereas a Keynesian is likely to see it as a problem of inadequate demand. Unemployment may be perceived as a microeconomic problem requiring special labor market policies, or as evidence of macroeconomic shortcomings.

Third, economists can disagree about the policies they prescribe for dealing with a given problem. Sociologists of knowledge and interest group theorists would predict that an economist is likely to prescribe a solution that is consistent with his own training and specialization within a large and variegated area for study. As the Swedish Nobel Prize Committee has demonstrated, economics is a field that can accommodate views as different as those of such "progovernment" economists as Gunnar Myrdal, James Meade, and James Tobin, and such "antigovernment" economists as Friedrich von Hayek, Milton Friedman, and James M. Buchanan.

Last and not least, economists differ in the extent to which they wish to become public advocates for particular programs and politicians. Carl Kaysen (1969, p. 151), an economist with experience in the Kennedy and Johnson White House, notes: "A political decision-maker finds the ability of a technical adviser to assist in the tasks of advocacy, which are indispensable to effect changes, an important element of his usefulness." Once an economic adviser makes a public commitment to a party and to a policy, it is difficult for that individual to change his or her mind without losing face, resigning office, or both. Hence, economists with access to politicians can be forced to advance arguments on party grounds that are contested by economists outside government, who remain free to change their minds as often as they wish.

A plethora of conflicting views can be an advantage to politicians, as economists neutralize their effect by their disagreements. As long as politicians in

Figure 17.4
Choice about Policies with Complete Dissensus

                              Economic Assessment
                              _____

                              (CONTESTED DESIRABILITY

Political Appraisal   (
_____

                              (CONTESTED EFFECTIVENESS

government agree about the policy that they regard as desirable, the political course is clear. Policies (and economists) that are politically undesirable can be rejected, and measures that are politically desirable can be chosen.

4. *Pervasive dissensus*. Given that politicians can disagree with each other and that economists can also disagree, when both respond thus to a controversial issue the result is pervasive dissensus (Figure 17.4). The grounds of disagreement may be analytically quite separate, for example, sophisticated Keynesian economists find themselves the bedfellows of simple-minded politicians in favor of big-spending programs, and monetarists may find themselves the bedfellows of politicians who see themselves as practical men of affairs, not economic theorists. Alliances between politicians and economists are forged by agreement about what is to be done rather than about why an action should be taken. Politics unites what professions divide.

Given both political and economic uncertainty, there are good reasons for a politician to proceed by making serial, disjointed, and incremental decisions. The serial nature of decisions about the economy is an advantage, enabling a politician facing conflicting advice to proceed by trial and error methods, altering policies in response to changes in political pressure, intellectual fashions, or economic conditions (cf. Braybrooke and Lindblom, 1963). If a given policy does not appear to produce desired results, it can be replaced by another. However desirable disjointed policymaking is on political grounds, it may nonetheless result in economic ineffectiveness, insofar as many serial choices cumulatively cancel out. A serial policymaker remains free one day to choose a policy intended to boost employment, and the next to endorse an anti-inflationary policy that has a side effect giving a boost to unemployment.

Given that the concerns of economists and politicians are diverse, we should consider what types of issues are likely to fit each of the foregoing models. Politicians are most likely to agree and economists to disagree (Figure 17.2) about issues that can be labeled strictly academic, for the disagreement is screened out of the policymaking process by a consensus of politicians. Disagreement among politicians and agreement among economists (Figure 17.3) are likely to be greatest about choices involving values that are not considered in monetary terms, for example, laws concerning abortion, or environmental pollution. Politicians refer to nominal values in circumstances in which microeconomists would be inclined to agree to choices being structured in ways that maximize efficiency (cf. Rhoads, 1985). If there is clearcut agreement in public opinion about an issue, for example, no tax increases, then there can be, temporarily at least, a consensus among politicians, but this can be at loggerheads with the views of economists (Figure 17.1). When big issues stir up controversy, economists can find that their professional and political values lead to disagreement; this assures involvement in the policy process, not as neutral experts but as participants in a political controversy (cf. Figure 17.4).

COMBINING PERSPECTIVES?

The predisposition of any professional is to appraise problems by the standards of his or her profession—and to ignore others. Politicians ignore important issues of economic theory and many uncomfortable results of applied economic research. An economist developing a theoretically elegant model is unconcerned about the mere intervening variables of politics and institutions. It is far easier to solve a set of equations than to worry about issues of political desirability or implementation.

Although the boundaries between economists and political scientists are well maintained in universities, in government the barriers are down (Rose, 1976b). A public policy approach necessarily integrates political and economic appraisals, for the problems it deals with are both political and economic, and often have other dimensions as well.

The importance of both political values and economic analysis creates a demand for people with hybrid skills. These can be economic experts with political principles that provide clear goals to direct their choice of economic instruments, or political leaders with expertise who not only articulate goals, but also have their choices informed by the constraints of the economy. Another type of hybrid is the policy ideologue, whose commitment to a political ideology gives him or her a clear choice of goals and who can use expert knowledge to select evidence that will give a veneer of verisimilitude to views deduced by a priori ideological reasoning independent of empirical evidence (cf. Sartori, 1969; Destler et al., 1984, p. 116ff). A person with a good theoretical training is accustomed to developing arguments that are coherent and clear because they rely on simplifying assumptions and exclude inconvenient evidence outside the assumptions of a model. Politicians also cultivate the ability to argue that a policy ought to work in order to mobilize support for new proposals.

In default of a large number of policymakers with both technical expertise and realistic political criteria of desirability, joining different standards of appraisal requires exchanges between people in disparate roles, with the politicians, as the legitimate makers of public policy, in a position to determine outcomes. What politicians want from experts is not so much "neutral competence" but rather *relevant* competence that uses expertise to address problems as they concern politicians (cf. Heclo, 1975; Moe, 1985, p. 239).

An economist may enter public service with the belief that he or she is a neutral expert but quickly learns that this is not enough to be effective within the policy process. Many economists become partisan advocates of efficiency, asking questions about costs and benefits, and suggesting ways of using economic incentives and disincentives to achieve goals more easily and effectively than by administrative regulation. Efficiency partisans have "a commitment to the competitive market as an ideal, and the consequent belief that any step in the direction of the ideal is desirable" (Kaysen, 1969, p. 140). An efficiency advocate can be sure of relevance when challenging the desirability of inefficient programs. But relevance will lead to political controversy as they are defended by those who find them efficient and effective to secure their own political ends.

A politician may enter office with a belief in the power of rhetoric and will or with skill in bargaining, but in order to become a successful policymaker he or she must also learn to identify effective policies. In search of effective economic policies, politicians will start with criteria about what is and what is not desirable. But to achieve desirable economic goals they will need the advice of expert economists, and a nonexpert politician cannot choose a policy on the basis of technical arguments.

Trust is also important when a politician is confronted by conflicting views by economists. An economic adviser with a record of achievement in government has a claim to trust. An adviser who has identified successful policies in the past (or warned against disasters) is likely to be listened to again. Personal and party loyalty is a third criterion; an economist known to a politician personally or through a party network will be reckoned to be "on our side," or even better "on my side." There is tension in the relationship, for an economist may trade long-term credibility for short-term access to policymakers, designing policies that will be desirable even if they are unlikely to be effective. In such circumstances appraisals are no longer joint appraisals, for political values take over completely.

REFERENCES

Allen, William R. "Economics, Economists and Economic Policy: Modern American Experiences." *History of Political Economy* 9 (1977): 48–88.

Braybrooke, David E., and C. E. Lindblom. *A Strategy of Decision*. New York: Free Press, 1963.

Destler, I. M., L. Gelb, and A. Laker. *Our Own Worst Enemy*. New York: Simon & Shuster, 1984.

Hahn, Frank H. "Recognizing the Limits." *Times Literary Supplement*. December 2, 1985.

Hargrove, Erwin C., and Samuel A. Morley (eds.). *The President and the Council of Economic Advisers: Interviews with CEA Chairmen*. Boulder, Colo.: Westview Press, 1984.

Heclo, Hugh. "OMB and the Presidency—the Problem of 'Neutral Competence.' "
    Public Interest, No. 38 (Winter 1975).
Kaysen, Carl. "Model-Makers and Decision-Makers: Economists and the Policy Pro-
    cess." In R. L. Heilbroner (ed.), *Economic Means and Social Ends*. Englewood
    Cliffs, N.J.: Prentice-Hall, 1969, pp. 137–53.
Leontief, Wassily. *Essays in Economics: Theories, Theorizing, Facts and Policies*. New
    Brunswick, N.J.: Transaction, 1985.
Lindbeck, Assar. "Stabilization Policy in Open Economies with Endogenous Politicians."
    American Economic Review 66, No. 2 (1976).
Moe, Terry M. "The Politicized Presidency." In J. E. Chubb and P. E. Peterson (eds.),
    The New Direction in American Politics. Washington, D.C.: Brookings Institution,
    1985, pp. 235–72.
Mueller, Dennis. *Public Choice*. Cambridge: Cambridge University Press, 1979.
Nelson, Robert H. "The Economics Profession and the Making of Public Policy." *Journal
    of Economic Literature* 5 (1987): 49–91.
Rhoads, Steven E. *The Economist's View of the World*. New York: Cambridge University
    Press, 1985.
Rose, Richard. "On the Priorities of Government: A Developmental Analysis." *European
    Journal of Political Research* 4 (1976a): 247–89.
———. "Disciplined Research and Undisciplined Problems." *International Social Sci-
    ence Journal* 28 (1976b): 99–121.
———. "Steering the Ship of State: One Tiller but Two Pairs of Hands." *British Journal
    of Political Science* 17 (1987): 409–33.
Sartori, Giovanni. "Politics, Ideology and Belief Systems." *American Political Science
    Review*. 63 (1969): 398–411.

18

Assistance for Economic Development

Vernon W. Ruttan

Foreign aid as an instrument through which the government of one country transfers substantial resources to strengthen the economy or the institutions of another country is a relatively recent phenomenon. The Marshall Plan, initiated by the United States in 1948 to restore the economies of war-ravaged Western Europe, was the first major public foreign economic assistance program.

COMMITMENT TO FOREIGN ASSISTANCE

The Marshall Plan was hardly underway when the United States turned its attention to the problems of economic growth and stability in the developing world. The breakup of colonial regimes, the polarization of World War II alliances, the aspirations of people and governments in newly independent countries, and the threat of both political and economic instability focused U.S. attention on the economic and security problems of Latin America, Asia, and Africa.

Official commitment by the United States to assist in the development of poor countries dates to the fourth point in President Harry S Truman's inaugural address on January 20, 1949, and to the subsequent passage of the Act for International Development in June of 1950. Truman proposed that the United States commit itself to "a bold new program for making the benefits of our scientific advances and industrial progress available for the improvement and growth of underdeveloped areas" (Truman, 1949, p. 125).

By the end of the 1950s, the United States' assistance effort had been complemented by a large assortment of bilateral and multilateral assistance programs (OECD, 1985). Even as late as 1960, however, the United States still accounted for almost two-thirds of development assistance flows. In the early 1960s, the United States took a leading role in the formation of a donors' club, the Development Assistance Committee (DAC) of the Organization for Economic Cooperation and Development (OECD). The DAC was established to achieve more effective coordination of assistance policies and programs among donors.

In spite of expenditures of over $100 billion for foreign economic assistance, the institutionalization of the United States' commitment to foreign economic assistance and the rationale for foreign economic assistance have remained tentative and insecure. Development assistance has been under almost continuous attack from both the left and the radical left and the radical right. The right has emphasized the role of foreign aid in politicizing economic activity in less developed countries and in contributing to the expansion of public sector enterprise and employment. Furthermore, "if a country . . . cannot readily develop without external gifts, it is unlikely to develop with them" (Bauer, 1971, p. 100).

The criticisms from the left were of an opposite nature. Based on the implicit premise that assistance is effective, it has emphasized the external, rather than the internal, constraints on development. At its extreme, the left criticism tended to view development assistance as an imperialist conspiracy—as an instrument designed to reward the political, economic, and bureaucratic elites of developing countries for acquiescing in the exploitation of their resources and people (Hayter, 1971).

Aid flows from developed to developing countries have grown at a slower rate during the 1980s than during the 1970s, and the modest increases in official flows have been more than offset by reductions in other financial flows to the developing countries. Surveys of public opinion, in both the United States and in other donor countries, suggest that public attitudes toward foreign aid programs are increasingly critical. Respondents consistently show a deep concern with the plight of needy people in other countries. But the polls also reveal a deep division between "opinion leaders" and the general public. Opinion leaders indicate less concern than the general public with poverty in the developing world, but, at the same time, they are less skeptical about the economic and security benefits to donors and recipients of foreign assistance.

A combination of the slowing of economic growth and the continued evidence of differences in income and levels of living between the developed world and an emerging group of newly industrializing countries and the poor "Third" and even "Fourth World" countries has contributed to a sense of "aid fatigue" in both the development assistance bureaucracies and their domestic constituencies.

THE SELF-INTEREST ARGUMENT

Two arguments have typically been used in support of foreign economic assistance. One set of arguments is based on the economic and strategic self-interest of the donor country. The donor self-interest arguments tend to assert that development assistance promotes the economic or strategic interests of the donor country. It should be technically possible to specify the conditions under which government-to-government aid transfers could improve welfare in both donor and recipient countries. The empirical analyses needed to support such an agreement are, however, surprisingly limited. It is not sufficient simply to assert that the transfer of assistance resources may be followed by the growth of exports from the donor to the recipient country. The welfare gains and losses to donors and recipients must be calculated. As yet, the calculations have not been made.

The strategic interest argument rests on even more fragile grounds. It has been subject to even less rigorous theoretical or empirical analyses than the economic self-interest argument. The single background paper on the effectiveness of military assistance prepared for the Commission on Security and Economic Assistance (the Carlucci Commission), while asserting a positive linkage between U.S. security assistance expenditures and security assistance, noted that the evidence to support the assertion was "elusive" (West, 1983).

There is an inherent contradiction in both the economic and strategic or security self-interest arguments. There is danger that a donor country may be impelled to pursue its self-interest under the rubric of aid even if it harms the recipient country. If the donor self-interest argument is to be utilized as a primary rationale for development assistance, it imposes on donors some obligation to demonstrate that its assistance does no harm to the recipient. It is hard to avoid a conclusion that the self-interest arguments have been used more as a cynical effort to develop constituency for foreign assistance than a serious economic or political rationale. In the next section an attempt is made to offer a more serious ethical argument for foreign economic assistance.

THE ETHICAL ARGUMENT

Both the popular and official sponsors of foreign economic assistance have typically treated the ethical bases for foreign assistance as intuitively obvious. Most economists have generally felt fairly comfortable—too comfortable—with a straightforward utilitarian rationale for foreign assistance. If private rates of return to capital investment are higher in developing countries than in developed countries, investment should flow from developed to less developed countries. If, because markets are imperfect, social rates of return exceed private rates of return, then developed country governments should transfer resources to developing countries to assist in physical and institutional infrastructure development. But few economists would be willing to embrace the full implications of the utilitarian income distribution argument—that rich countries ought to give until the point is reached at which by giving more, the loss in utility in the donor country would exceed the gain in utility in the recipient country or countries.

In contrast, most political philosophers, and those economists who adhere to a Hobbesian contractarian view of the role of government, have found it difficult to discover any intellectual foundation for development assistance based on considerations of distributive justice. At the most extreme there is the argument by Hayek that in a society of free men the concept of social or distributive justice has no meaning (Hayek, 1978, p. 58). He argues, in effect, that justice is a function of the rules or processes that govern individual and group behavior and not of the outcome generated by the rules. The appropriate role of public policy is rule reform.

The Hobbesian contractarian argument with respect to foreign aid has been forcefully articulated by Edward C. Banfield:

> our political philosophy does not give our government any right to do good for foreigners. Since the seventeenth century, Western political thought has maintained that government may use force or threat of force to take the property of some and give it to others only if doing so somehow serves the common good . . . government may take from citizens and give to foreigners when doing so serves the common good of the citizens, but it may not do so if . . . all advantage will accrue to foreigners and none to citizens (Banfield, 1963, p. 24).

This argument has been vigorously restated by Robert Nozick (1974, p. ix), and it has recently reemerged with renewed force in the debate over foreign assistance in the late 1970s and early 1980s. It seems apparent that the emergence of social justice as a significant issue on the political agenda, both within nations and in international relations, is due to lack of confidence that the actual behavior of economic markets and political institutions adequately approaches the conditions specified by Hayek, Nozik, and other libertarian political philosophers (Macpherson, 1985, pp. 1–20).

Attempts have been made to develop a contractarian argument drawing on the Rawlsian "difference principle" to establish a moral obligation for foreign assistance. The central part of Rawls' theory is that in a just society departures from an equalitarian income distribution would be permitted only when differential rewards contribute to the welfare of the least advantaged members of society (Rawls, 1971, pp. 54–192). Rawls argues that this "difference principle" would be agreed to by rational individuals attempting to design a constitution— given full general knowledge of the political and economic nature of society except the positions they would occupy by virtue of social class, individual talent, or political persuasion. The Rawlsian constitution does not imply perfect equalization of incomes. If, for example, inequality calls forth economic activity that benefits the least as well as the more advantaged members of society, it would be permitted.

John Rawls (1971) made no attempt to explore the implications of the difference principle for international inequality. Charles Beitz (1979, pp. 141, 142) and C. Ford Runge (1977) have argued that an intuitively obvious extension of the difference principle to the international economic order is that justice would imply equal access by citizens of all countries to global resources except in those cases where departure from inequality could be justified on the basis of benefits to citizens of the least advantaged countries. To the extent that this argument draws on the Rawls framework, however, it remains vulnerable to the weakness of attempting to derive rules of justice from an "imagined social contract." I

would personally prefer a stronger behavioral foundation on which to rest convictions about moral responsibility for assistance to poor countries. This preference reflects my general skepticism about both the contractarian approach to
political philosophy and the public choice approach to political economy which
attempt to derive principles for the design of social and economic institutions
from primitive assumptions about human nature.

AN IMPLICIT GLOBAL CONTRACT

A contractarian argument that limits the responsibility of the rich toward the
poor to national populations has great difficulty in confronting a world where
citizens hold multiple loyalties, where national identity may be wider or more
narrow than state boundaries, and where policy interventions as well as market
forces guide the flow of labor and capital and the trade in commodities and
intellectual property across state boundaries (Keohane, 1984, pp. 120–24). In
this world, a "state-moralist" or "political realist" approach to international
relations that would limit the expression of the moral concerns of either individual
citizens or national governments about the basic political rights or subsistence
needs of people in other countries seems curiously archaic.

Increased interdependence among nations results in a rise in both political
tension and concern about lack of equity in economic transactions. The ethical
foundation for a system of development assistance rests on the premise that the
emergence of international economic and political interdependence has extended
the moral basis for social or distributive justice from the national to the international sphere. This international interdependence has resulted in an implicit
extension of Arrow's argument for redistribution to include the international
sphere: "There are significant gains to social interaction above and beyond what
individuals can achieve on their own. The owners of scarce personal assets do
not have substantial private use of these assets; it is only their value in a large
system which makes these assets valuable. Hence, there is a surplus created by
the existence of society which is available for redistribution" (Arrow, 1983,
p. 188).

The growth of global and political interdependence implies a decline in the
significance of national boundaries. Because boundaries are not coextensive with
the scope of economic and political interdependence, they do not make the limits
of social obligation in the sharing of the benefits and burdens associated with
interdependence. A functioning international economy increases the value of the
natural, human, and institutional resources of the developed countries and makes
part of this surplus available for redistribution.

SOME QUESTIONS

Acceptance of an ethical responsibility by the citizens and the governments
of rich countries for assistance to poor countries still leaves unanswered a number
of important questions.

Acceptance of an ethical responsibility for development assistance by the rich countries does not resolve the question of what level of assistance is appropriate. It was noted earlier that the utilitarian or consequentialist argument seems to be based on equating marginal utilities: the rich countries ought to give until the point is reached at which, by giving more, the loss in utility in the donor country would exceed the gain in utility in the recipient country or countries. However, the actual level of aid allocations by donor countries seems to reflect the much weaker moral premise that if it is possible to contribute to welfare in poor countries without sacrificing anything of moral or economic significance in the donor country it should be done. There seems to be an implicit moral judgment among the citizens and governments of the rich countries that the moral obligation to feed the poor in Ethiopia is stronger than a moral obligation to assure a 6 percent rather than a 5 percent rate of growth in Ethiopian GNP.

Neither the commitment to development assistance nor the commitment to a particular level of development assistance provides guidance as to who should receive aid. The acceptable ethical considerations that support the distributive justice argument imply that assistance should be directed to improving the welfare of the poorest individuals in the poorest countries. But there is also an ethical argument that aid should be directed into uses that produce the largest increments of income from each dollar of assistance—the argument that assistance resources are limited and should not be wasted.

The empirical evidence does not permit any clear inferences concerning aid impact on savings, investment, and rate of growth. There is, however, evidence that assistance resources have generated relatively high marginal rates of return— rates of return that are high relative to what the same resources would have earned in the donor countries (Peterson, 1983). What little empirical evidence we do have also suggests that donor governments are willing to trade off some efficiency for equity in their aid allocations—that recipient income levels do carry modest weight in the allocation of aid resources (Behrman and Sah, 1984). But we have little more than anecdotal evidence on the distributive impacts of development assistance in recipient countries.

Acceptance of responsibility for assistance does not resolve the question of what form of assistance to offer. The goals of assistance range from attempts to assure immediate "subsistence rights" or basic needs, to assistance designed to strengthen the capacity of a nation to meet the subsistence requirements of its own people, or to modify the institutions that influence the resources flows among nations. On some grounds it would seem obligatory to secure some minimum level of subsistence before allocating resources to the other two objectives. But this conclusion is not at all obvious if the effect is to preclude either (a) expansion of the capacity needed to assure future subsistence or (b) reform of the rules of conduct that govern economic and political relationships among nations (i.e., reforming the GATT rules on agricultural trade).

A fourth issue is the extent to which development assistance policy and admin-

istration should be directed to bringing about institutional reform in the recipient country. The extent to which development assistance directed either toward meeting basic needs or to strengthening the recipient countries' capacity for economic growth will depend on the institutions that influence relations among individual citizens, economic and social organizations, and the government.

If a donor government's ethical concern extends to an obligation to assure the citizens of the donor country that the resources devoted to assistance are used effectively, either for immediate relief of subsistence needs or to generate longer term economic growth, it can hardly avoid also entering into a dialogue with the recipient country about institutional reform when it enters into negotiations with a recipient country about resources transfers. The rationale for focusing on institutional reform is the hope that the moral concern that provided a rationale for assistance will contribute to capacity in the recipient country to more effectively provide for basic needs and generate the growth necessary to improve the quality of life. The obligation to enter into a dialogue on issues of institutional reform imposes on the donor country the requirement to build the capacity in its own cultural and social science disciplines necessary to enter into the dialogue. These capacities should be guided more by pragmatic consideration about the potential impact of policy reform in the recipient country than either ideological considerations based on the donor's internal political processes or its own economic or political self-interest.

CONCLUSION

The first conclusion that emerges from this review is the weakness of the self-interest argument for foreign assistance. The individual (or group) self-interest arguments, when examined carefully, often turn out to represent a hidden agenda for domestic rather than international resource transfers. The political "realists" have not been able, or have not thought it worthwhile, to demonstrate the presumed political and security benefits from the strategic assistance component of the aid budget. Rawlsian contractarian theory does provide a basis for ethical responsibility toward the poor countries that goes beyond the traditional religious and moral obligations of charity. It also provides a basis for making judgments about the degree of inequality that is ethically acceptable.

But the contractarian argument cannot stand by itself. The credibility of the contractarian argument is weakened if, in fact, the transfers do not achieve the desired consequences. Failures of analysis or design can produce worse consequences than if no assistance had been undertaken. There is no obligation to transfer resources that do not generate either immediate welfare gains or growth in the capacity of poor states to meet the needs of their citizens. It becomes important, therefore, to evaluate the consequences of development assistance and to consider the policy interventions that can lead to more effective development assistance programs.

Since the 1950s, our understanding of the development process has made major advances. But we can never fully know the consequences of resource transfers by one government to another or of intervention by representatives of one government into the complex and interdependent social systems of another country. Our limited knowledge about how to give and use aid to most effectively contribute to development does not, however, protect us from the responsibility to use the resources of government either (1) to fulfill the obligations inherent in the implicit global contract, or (2) to advance our capacity to understand the role of external assistance in the development process in order to better assess the consequences of either our strategic or development assistance.

It is doubtful that the answers to the questions raised in the previous section can be answered adequately by the bilateral assistance agencies of national governments or the multilateral assistance bureaucracies. At the international level we have created global institutions and global bureaucracies. We are unlikely to create a global system of governance in the foreseeable future. The political context for thinking about international cooperation and coordinations is, as Harlan Cleveland (1986, p. 80) has remarked, "a world with nobody in charge." In a world where the dividing line between "domestic" and "international" has eroded, national governments must find more effective ways of achieving cooperation in reducing global economic disparity than in the past.

The performance of the global bureaucracies has been disappointing, but there are examples of global cooperation that receive very high grades for their performance. One example is World Weather Watch, involving the cooperation of over a hundred nations, which provides the global weather forecasts on which we all rely. A second is the Consultation Group on International Agricultural Research (CGIAR), which provides funding and governance for the system of international agricultural research institutes that have been put in place over the last several decades.

The challenge to the development assistance community, and the broader society that is concerned with global disparity, is how to achieve greater equity in consumption and in opportunity in a world that demands both more effective governance and less government.

NOTE

The research on which this chapter is based was supported in part by the University of Minnesota Agricultural Experiment Station Project 14–067 and U.S. Agency for International Development Contract No. OTR–0091-G–55–4195–007. It draws on material in Krueger, Michalopoulos, and Ruttan (1989) and Ruttan (1989).

REFERENCES

Arrow, Kenneth J. *Social Choice and Justice*. Cambridge, Mass.: Harvard University Press, 1983.

Banfield, Edward C. "American Foreign Aid Doctrine." In Robert A. Goldwin (ed.). *Why Foreign Aid?* Chicago: Rand McNally, 1963.

Bauer, P. T. *Dissent on Development*. Rev. ed. London: Weidenfeld & Nicholson, 1971.

Behrman, Jere R., and Raj Kumar Sah. "What Role Does Equity Play in the International distribution of Development Aid?" In L. Taylor Syrquin, and L. E. Westphal. *Economic Structure and Performance*. New York: Academic Press, 1984.

Beitz, Charles. *Political Theory and International Relations*. Princeton, N.J.: Princeton University Press, 1979.

Cleveland, Harlan. "The Future of International Governance: Managing a Madisonian World." *Vital Speeches of the Day* 53 (November 15, 1986): 78–81.

Hayek, F. A. "The Atavism of Social Justice." *New Studies in Philosophy, Politics, Economics and the History of Ideas*. London: Routledge & Kegan Paul, 1978, pp. 57–70.

Hayter, Teresa. *Aid as Imperialism*. New York: Penguin Books, 1971.

Keohane, Robert O. *After Hegemony: Cooperation and Discord in the World Political Economy*. Princeton, N.J.: Princeton University Press, 1984.

Krueger, Anne O., Constantine Michalopoulos, and Vernon W. Ruttan. *Aid and Development*. Baltimore: Johns Hopkins University Press, 1989.

Macpherson, C. B. *The Rise and Fall of Economic Justice*. Oxford: Oxford University Press, 1985.

Nozick, Robert. *Anarchy, State and Utopia*. Oxford: Blackwell, 1974, p. ix.

Organization for Economic Cooperation and Development (OECD). *Twenty Five Years of Development Cooperation*. Paris, 1985.

Peterson, Willis. "Rates of Return on Development Assistance Capital." St. Paul: University of Minnesota, Department of Agricultural and Applied Economics, 1983.

Rawls, John. *A Theory of Justice*. Cambridge, Mass.: Harvard University Press, 1971.

Runge, C. Ford. "American Agricultural Assistance and the New International Economic Order." *World Development* 5, No. 8 (1977): 225–46.

Ruttan, Vernon W. "Why Foreign Economic Assistance?" *Economic Development and Cultural Change* 37 (January 1989): 411, 424.

Truman, Harry S. *Inaugural Address of the President*. Department of State Bulletain 33 (January 1949), p. 125.

West, Francis I. "The Effectiveness of Military Assistance as an Instrument of U.S. Foreign Policy." Paper prepared for the Commission on Security and Economic Assistance, Washington, D.C., 1983.

19

Some Fundamentals of the Economic Role of Government

Warren J. Samuels

The objective of this chapter is to answer the question, "What are the most fundamental things that can be said about the economic role of government?" The question should be understood, first, to ask what can be said of government at the truly most fundamental level and, second, to require a positive, nonnormative, answer. The chapter constitutes a precis, as it were, of my answer. The answer is subjective, but it is intended to be nonnormative.

The answer which I propose has four parts: (1) Government is deeply involved in the definition and in the creation of the economy. (2) Efforts are continually being made to obfuscate the role of government in defining and creating the economy so as to selectively channel both the definition and the re-creation—efforts that are part of the process of definition and re-creation itself. (3) The proximate critical matter is almost always the legal change of law, that is, the change by law of the interests to which government is to give its support: Government is inexorably involved in the status quo, and the question is the change of the details of that involvement. (4) Although the economy and polity are typically comprehended as essentially self-subsistent and independent—albeit interacting—spheres or processes, there is a "legal–economic nexus" in which both originate in an ongoing manner.

The economy is an artifact, very much (though not entirely) a product of human construction. The most fundamental social process is the definition and creation of socioeconomic reality. Two characteristics of this process are selective perception of and a necessity of choice between conflicting interests. Although much of the organization and performance of the economy is a matter of the unintended and unforeseen consequences of aggregated individual and subgroup activity, a key factor nonetheless is deliberative government decision making (choice) and action. Government participates in the organization and control, and therefore the ongoing social construction and reconstruction, of the economy. To the extent that government is such a participant in the social formation of the economy, economic perfomance is *pro tanto* a result of government, in any economic system.

People tend to define socioeconomic reality in terms of legal rights. Government selectively protects, as rights, certain interests and not others—and it is rights that form, structure, and operate through the market and the economy in toto. What people define as reality is thereby formed and reformed. In helping to define and create socioeconomic reality, the law also serves as a psychic balm in the face of existential and social ambiguity and uncertainty.

Government is thus an object of control by those who desire to use government to organize or reorganize the economy and redirect economic performance. This is not a matter of having government intervene in a process in which it hitherto had been absent but of (re)determining the interests to which government will lend its support.

Fundamental perennial conflicts exist between different ways of socially constructing and reconstructing the economy, between different interests that could gain from different social constructions of the economy, and between different uses to which government can be put.

Ideologies selectively and necessarily provide premises for the social (re)construction of reality and rights. Political and economic ideologies constitute belief systems that either develop (often out of wishful thinking, or rationalization, coupled with material interest) and/or are contrived and manipulated to define certain elements of social construction, certain uses of government, or certain interests, as natural and/or legitimate and others as artificial and/or illegitimate. In the context of what generally is called bounded rationality, and because the socioeconomy is not self-defining, ideology selectively defines reality to channel the use of government so as to legitimize and accommodate certain uses of government and to discredit and inhibit other uses; to promote continuity of certain uses of government and/or change of other uses; and/or to channel legal change of law. In part, certain activities and consequences of government are, through ideology, selectively perceived as governmental whereas others are not. Even ideologies that denigrate government activity comprise agendas for government (some position on continuity versus change of the interests to which government will give its support), not the least when ostensibly denying or minimizing government or affirming that government will some day wither away. Belief in limited government has the effect of seeming to limit the power of government, but it can do so only selectively, affirming much continuity of legal protection of interests while both affirming and denigrating, selectively, certain changes therein. Government in these matters is part of the myth and symbolic system of society.

Ideology so functions in part by selectively redefining reality in terms of certain privileged rights (interests) which thereby would be given further legal protection. Ideology and law render as the natural state of things what is in fact both an artifact and a matter of policy and thus subject to change. One specific way in which this is done is the denigration of government itself. On the one hand, ideology obfuscates the profound uses to which government has been and is put in the status quo, that is, how much the status quo is dependent on the use of government. On the other hand, it attempts to disengage (engage) or dissuade certain groups from attempting (to attempt) to use government to change law and rights in favor of their interests. This practice both takes advantage of and reinforces the tendency of some people to be lawtakers (treating law as given and/or assuming that they can or should have no influence on the law) and for others to be lawmakers (operating on the assumption or realization that law is an instrument that either they or someone else will control and put to use). Ideology thus helps reserve lawmaking opportunities to those who have, or are induced by ideology to have, a lawmaking mentality, excluding (or otherwise energizing) those with a lawtaking mentality. (It is ideology and the state of law *at any given time* that separates lawtakers from lawmakers. As law changes, ideology may transform from a lawtaking to a lawmaking mentality, and vice versa.)

Contrary to ideologies that pretend otherwise, government is quite fundamental with regard to the nature, structure, operation, and performance results of the economic system, even in an economic system nominally considered "market." Its involvement in economic matters is complex but no less fundamental for being so.

One entry point into the complexity is the conventional proposition that government exists to protect property. The analytical problem with this view is that government does not protect something as property because it is property, but property is property because it is protected by government. "Property" is the name given to certain already protected interests. Other protected interests are not given the name property, although they are functionally equivalent thereto insofar as they constitute government protection of interests. Designation as property, however, does give certain protected interests a privileged status insofar as property is distinguished from functional equivalents to property as a basis for further policy. Hierarchically honorific protected interests have tended to be called property, whereas others have been given less legitimizing names, such as "regulation" or the "welfare state," though these too are essentially means whereby certain interests are given the recognition and protection of government. The critical question always concerns what interests are to be protected by government whether designated "property" (or "rights") or otherwise. Historically, the category of interests protected as property has expanded, as has the range of interests understood to conflict with interests protected as property. These expansions have involved conflict over the interest protections by which the economy is defined and constructed.

Property rights are to be distinguished, moreover, not only from rights not so designated, but from interests sacrificed in favor of those protected as property rights. Where Alpha and Beta are in the same field of action, and conflict, for government to protect Alpha's interest as property (or as a right per se) is for government to deny protection to Beta's interest and to expose

Beta to the consequences of Alpha's having the right. Rights have this dual nature; moreover, externalities have a related reciprocal character. For every protected interest (right) there is another in the same field of action which is not protected but exposed. For every externality there is a reciprocal one that would be generated by suppression of the former. One function performed by government, in protecting interests and thereby defining legal–economic reality, is the specification of the interests protected as rights and thereby the interests rendered (as nonrights) exposed thereto (the recipients of the realized externality).

Government is an instrument available to whomever is in a position to control it, to put it to use. It is also an arena in which the contest for its control is fought out. The effective protection of interests by government often represents a composition of conflicting points of view in what is fundamentally a collective bargaining process, regardless of the formal structure or ideology of government. (This is not to say that all parties are equally, even similarly, situated in the collective bargaining process.) Whatever the metaphor (instrument, arena, collective bargaining process), the institutions of government are used to structure economic reality.

Government is perforce an object of control in a perpetual contest to have interests protected by government, whether as legal rights, as property or otherwise but especially as property, as immunities from the rights of others, or as beneficiaries of government programs other than the definition and assignment of rights.

Government as a protector of interests is both a dependent and an independent variable. It is a dependent variable insofar as what government does—the interests to which it gives its support—is the result of the interaction of forces acting on and through it. It is an independent variable insofar as what government does—the interests to which it gives its support—determines economic structure, operation, and performance. It is true both that the distributions of income and wealth are partly dependent on government *and* that government is partly dependent on the distributions of income and wealth. It is also true both that the working rules of law (and morals) govern the distribution and exercise of power *and* that the distribution and exercise of power govern the development of the working rules of law (and morals). It is further true both that opportunity sets are partly dependent on legal rights *and* that legal rights are partly dependent on opportunity sets, that is, that opportunity sets containing rights to seek or to effectuate change of law can change the identification and assignment (distribution) of legal rights on which opportunity sets rest.

By focusing on either the established or the exposed interest, on the realized or the reciprocal externality, and on the injury consequent to the correction of the realized externality or on the injury consequent to the externality, one exercises selective perception of rights, injuries, costs, and indeed government itself. The distribution of sacrifice is in part the result of government determining which interests will be protected as rights and which will be exposed to the externality-generating actions of others, and thus the distribution of costs (that is, the incidence or distribution of social costs as private costs). If Alpha acts so as to injure Beta, government control of Alpha can be understood to constitute either protection of Beta's rights or infringement of Alpha's rights. Ideology is selectively invoked, manipulated, and perceived by the respective parties in order to laud or to condemn government, whereas government is going to protect one interest or the other.

What is normally considered "intervention" is not the intrusion of government in an area in which government hitherto has been absent but the change of the interests to which government gives its support or which government is used to support. The question is not whether there is to be government or no government but which interests government is to support.

Government thus helps, or is used, to structure the status quo that defines reality and is used to obfuscate that very fact. Government facilitated by ideology legitimizes duly constituted authority and the status quo, and renders nugatory the fact of selective use to (re)produce the status quo. It is also true that government is both affected by and affects ideology; in part, government may strengthen and/or engage certain ideologies and restrain and/or inhibit ideologies that otherwise would be dormant.

Among the fundamental things one can say, then, about government in a positive, nonnormative way are its involvement in the social (re)definition and (re)construction of reality; its availability for and actual use as an instrument for structuring economic reality; its participation in the system of contending pretense and obfuscation in which the status quo, or some alternative set of arrangements is—however selectively—given an independent, preeminent, or otherwise privileged status; its active, if subtle, involvement in producing economic performance; its operation as a decision-making processs that both affects and is affected by the structure of nominally private power; and its inexorable involvement as a mode of change—the legal change of legal protection given to interests—at the margin of socioeconomic evolution. These being the case, the conventional distinction between government and economy, and between private and public, seems both analytically false and normatively misleading and subject to selective perception and putative abuse. For law–government is not exogenous to the economic system, and the economic system cannot exist independent of law and government. There is a legal–economic nexus in which it may appear that government and economy interact as separate social processes but in which what actually happens is that each is fundamentally involved in the (re)determination of the other and thereby of social reality. This happens at the margin of social evolution, and it is to the (re)definition and (re)construction of this margin through legal change that selective perception operates and competing ideologies are brought to bear. At that margin, the economy is an object of legal control–change in the service of economic actors and the law is an instrument of economic advantage, but through selective perception such is either passively or actively obscured.

NOTE

The author is indebted to Steven Medema and Allen Schmid for comments on an earlier draft. The present chapter represents a partial recapitulation and extension of ideas presented most recently in Samuels, 1987, 1988; and Samuels and Mercuro, 1979. The orientation of Vilfredo Pareto is also relevant (see Samuels, 1974).

REFERENCES

Samuels, Warren J. "An Essay on the Nature and Significance of the Normative Nature of Economics." *Journal of Post Keynesian Economics* 10 (Spring 1988): 347–54.

————. "The Idea of the Corporation as a Person: On the Normative Significance of Judicial Language." In Warren J. Samuels and Arthur S. Miller (eds.), *Corporations and Society: Power and Responsibility.* Westport, Conn.: Greenwood Press, 1987, pp. 113–29.

————. *Pareto on Policy.* New York: Elsevier, 1974.

————, and Nicholas Mercuro. "The Role and Resolution of the Compensation Principle in Society: Part One—The Role." *Research in Law and Economics* 1 (1979): 157–94.

20

Economy and State: An Institutionalist Theory of Process and Learning

A. Allan Schmid

The philology of the word "state" indicates its close ties to the concepts of estate, status, and standing (Fried, 1968). As related to the economy, this definition can be rephrased as a concern for the framework in which it is understood whose preferences count. The concept of the state defies concise definition. The state (or government) is the social system in which we formulate (learn) our ideas as to the expected interdependent behavior of others. These behaviors can be usefully described as fields of opportunity or rights. One perspective of the state involves territoriality or the reach of authoritative sovereignty. But authority and use of violence are scarce and costly goods and effective only at the margin and thus interactive with learned custom.

There are micro-centers of collective action defining opportunities as well as more macro-centers of authority. The state can never be simply a matter of supreme authority that integrates other conflicting power centers but is always some process of interaction among these centers. Thus, the political process is an interaction among a nation-state and its subdivisions and such collectivities as corporations and unions. The reality of the distribution of opportunities is the ongoing result of each of these being influenced by and influencing the other.

RIGHTS AS RECIPROCAL OPPORTUNITY

"Freedom for the pike is death for the minnows," says Isaiah Berlin (p. 86). In a world of scarcity it is impossible to implement freedom for everyone. One person's freedoms and opportunities are at a cost to another's. Rights defining opportunities can be understood by looking at the reciprocal relationships of people with incompatible preferences. Externalities are ubiquitous if by externalities we mean the costs for person A of B's actions. Rights then control the direction of externality.

To own is to coerce, that is, to create costs for others. It is to be able to choose without the consent of others when your acts impinge on those of others. The other person must persuade you to act otherwise. If trade is allowed, to own is to be a seller rather than a buyer. Government is a process by which some are selected to be sellers and some to be buyers with reference to a given economic action. Government may not eliminate externalities; it may only choose to shift them from one party to another. The choice of the pattern of externality is a choice of great consequence for the kind of world we live in. Government can remove an externality for person A by shifting it to B. In choosing, it weights the alternative costs and consequences.

Given the above perspective, what does it mean to describe a transaction as voluntaristic? At the most fundamental level, it can mean to have participated in government and to consent to its rights distributions. If these rights include the right to trade, then subsequent to rights distribution the parties may volunteer to exchange. The fact that a person chooses to trade does not confirm consent to what one has to trade. The nonowner is always coerced by the owner, though at a more fundamental level the parties may consent to the distribution of ownership. A market is the nexus of mutual coercion of interacting owners (Samuels, 1981, pp. 12–14). The market is the arena of solved distributional conflicts. In this sense, the market is never separate from government.

"SCOPE" OF THE STATE

The subject matter and functional boundaries of the state are coextensive with the sources of human interdependence. If there is conflict, there is a state or there is war and anarchy. Beyond anarchy, there are structural alternatives and different people may use the state, but it does not make any sense to speak of more versus less state presence. An alternative view is often referred to as the minimalist state in which the "sole functions of collective action are the establishment of the rules and the allocation of rights at the beginning and, thereafter, arbitration in any disputes that might arise from disagreements over contracts between individuals" (Whynes and Bowles, 1981, pp. 12–13). Anything more than that is regarded as interventionist.

This description of the state as nightwatchman is empirically false and not just because of market failure. It is not that markets fail after initial factor ownership is settled, but that factor ownership (endowments) is ambiguous and does not address all sources of human interdependence. The state can't be seen to intervene if it has never addressed a source of interdependence in the first place (Samuels, 1971). Furthermore, if some point in history is to be declared the initial starting place, it cannot be imbued with legitimacy as the distributive base of the social contract unless perfect knowledge is assumed. How can I agree once and for all to some initial rights distribution unless I can predict my subsequent real wealth position? As new sources of interdependence are discovered, government may have to modify rights if some original income distribution is to be maintained. The state, whether capitalist or socialist, does not come into existence to protect property rights; rather, the state is the process by which rights are learned and evolved. It is not the state that intervenes in our lives but other people who get in our hair (and I in thine). It is the state that then helps to choose whose hair gets cut.

The state is the process of choosing between continuity and change. Although there can be no presumption of a once-and-for-all agreement on rights, one can observe the consequences of different rates of change. Stability of expectations has something to do with planning horizons and investments. On the other hand, as conditions change, rights change may be necessary to maintain willing participation. The learning of what constitutes justice and fairness cannot be separated from the very existence of a state and property (Boulding, 1968; Taylor, 1966, Ch. 5).

OWNERSHIP AND REGULATION

Private ownership and regulation are instrumentally equivalent. So are regulation and liability. Both are means of opportunity. A person who wants to avoid viewing a satellite television dish (or any disagreeable activity) in the neighbor's front yard can alternatively assert that the neighbor is liable for damages or seek a regulation prohibiting this use. The suit would petition to have the offending use declared a nuisance. This would commonly be referred to as a means of defining a person's private property. The offending use is effectively defined as theft, though we usually reserve the word for those offenses that initiate criminal action. The main difference between tort law and misdemeanors or criminal offenses is that the transaction costs for redress are paid by the individual bringing the suit rather than by collective taxpayers. But in terms of obtaining one person's opportunity to be free of some neighbor's incompatible use, the result is the same.

The same result can also be obtained by a zoning law prohibiting said land use. Can this regulation be described as an attenuation of private property? It is an attenuation of neighbor B's opportunities, but it is an expansion of person A's opportunities. One important difference is that A cannot sell the right to B. Put more precisely, the right to be free of offending uses is jointly owned by A and still other neighbors. To own is to be able to participate in decisions regarding the use of a resource (either a veto power or some rule for collective choice). Since the environment is nondivisible, it is not possible for A to sell independently of owner C's utilization. The particular C with a high reservation price would reject all offers, even if the right were tradeable. This conflicts with the interests of other joint owners with lower reservation prices. The same is true for any corporate ownership. A corporate stockholder can sell her claim on profits, but not to any specific physical asset of the firm which would destroy the functioning of the whole enterprise. Such a decision is controlled by agents and collective choice rules.

The state is the process that determines who is liable, who is a lone or joint owner, who has opportunities because of prohibitions, and who bears the costs of redress. All can be designed to produce similar results. The private versus public dichotomy loses easy meaning. The nonowner who avoids a certain activity because of the anticipation of having to pay damages in a liability suit is as effectively prohibited (coerced) by the owner's options as would be the case if there were a prohibition via any regulation such as zoning or licensing.

The ambiguity of the public-private dichotomy can be further illustrated by the case of codetermination in industry versus worker damages for loss of fixed assets requiring permission to close a factory. A law requiring worker representation on corporate boards such as is found in Germany is no more or less interventionist than is the right of the workers to sue for loss of immobile assets.

Interdependence is never left to work itself out naturally by government silence and absence. The term *natural* is a matter of selective perception. Where there is capacity for interdependence, there is government. If A has the capacity to grab something (say, dump waste in the air), then it is effectively his if B is limited by capacity or right to prevent the grab. If B can't use the capacities she has (such as picketing the entrance to A's factory), then A has the right to the resource (i.e., the ability to act without interference from B) as surely as any right specifically referred to by statute or court decision. In effect, A's opportunity is defined by B's liability for interfering. Government appears nominally to be silent by specifying no rights in air. But this is instrumentally false. By limiting B's options (mutual coercions), government has defined A's rights. In this sense, no option or right is ever undefined. Opportunities are what they are as worked out by the whole system of rights interacting with capacities.

There is one sense in which rights are fundamentally undefined. Any court case or legislative proposal suggests that the expectations of the behavior of others is contested (i.e., not stable, internalized behavior). The other party's behavior is not regarded as natural, usual, and legitimate. In this sense, rights are potentially undefined and continuously evolving, both formally and in people's heads and practice.

RIGHTS AND BUDGETS

Property rights and budgets are substitutes and complements. When government wants to alter the performance of the economy, it can alter the rights of individuals to restructure incentives, behavior, and performance, or it can perform the function itself as a public enterprise via taxation and the budget. For example, if government wants to alter the flow of externality from people with communicable diseases, it could require all people to purchase vaccinations. This is often a requirement for schoolchildren. Or it could make people who transfer a disease liable for the damage to others. Alternatively, it could establish a public clinic and provide the vaccination without cost, or it could establish a hospital and treat the disease after the disease is communicated. The opportunity to be free of the disease or some of its consequences is a function of so-called private property rights and public spending.

Some get their opportunities via rights and regulations and others via the budget. No one source is more or less interventionist. The distribution of income can only be described by reference to both. It follows then that the rules of benefit-cost analysis and the budget process are instrumentally equivalent to property rights.

COST: PHYSICAL OR SOCIAL PHENOMENON?

Cost is in part a social phenomenon and institutionally dependent, and not an independent empirical fact of physics. It is not possible to contrast marginal social cost and marginal private cost as a guide to rights because cost is dependent on rights. When A utilizes an owned opportunity, she considers the costs of this opportunity in terms of what other things she could do with the opportunity, including selling it to B. If A rejects B's offer, in what sense is there an independent social value which A is not considering? What B can offer is a function of B's preferences and rights, not wishes and druthers. B might wish she were an owner listening to bids rather than making bids, but this ability is obviously a matter of rights, not physics. But what about the smoke damages which B suffers as a result of A's actions? It is factually correct to say that B would be richer if not for A and vice versa. But to say that A acts without considering social costs is only to say that you prefer B to be richer than A or vice versa.

TRANSACTION COSTS AND THE STATE

Transaction costs fundamentally affect the impact of government and rights. What if nonowner B makes an offer to A that A would have accepted, but B's total willingness to pay is reduced by transaction costs? How can government's alternatives be described? If government declares that B is the owner without paying, it is functionally equivalent and indistinguishable from a redistribution of ownership. If government wants to save the transaction cost but requires B to pay, then it will need to independently estimate willingness to pay separately from the transaction itself. This will have transaction costs of its own. Government cannot act to obtain the result without transaction costs since it itself is subject to transaction costs (Whynes and Bowles, 1981, pp. 125–27). Furthermore, the existence of transaction costs is the means of opportunity for a third party who enjoys a positive externality of A's use and does not want B to become the new owner and change use. This begs the question of whether C is really a part owner with A and thus entitled to participate in the decision to sell to B or is just another buyer.

If people are to agree on the distribution of rights, it will be useful to know how hard it will be (transaction costs) to protect those rights. Part of this involves the costs of proving damages by unauthorized users. Often it is difficult to prove just which of several unauthorized users is causing just how much damage. If the government then prohibits the de facto act that allegedly causes the damage, is it carrying out its intended distribution of rights or changing it? Is it facilitating exchange or intervening? These are matters of fundamental ambiguity requiring continuous learning and interpretation as new interdependencies evolve. No feature of a good, including transaction costs, dictates governmental choices (Schmid, p. 1987, Ch. 11).

In conclusion, the implication is that resource allocation and rights distribution are inextricably connected. The economy is not something prior to and independent of the process of government. This positive description should give no comfort to any particular party that wants the process of government to support their interests. It should, however, make the debate clearer and less presumptive.

NOTE

Thanks to James Shaffer, Eileen van Ravenswaay, and Warren Samuels for a critical review of this chapter. *Michigan Agricultural Experiment Station Publication*, No. 12665.

REFERENCES

Berlin, Isaiah. "Two Concepts of Liberty." In Robert E. Dewey and James A. Gould (eds.), *Freedom: Its History, Nature, and Varieties*. New York: Macmillan, 1970.

Boulding, Kenneth E. "The Legitimation of the Market." *Nebraska Journal of Economics and Business* 7 (1968): 3–14.

Fried, Morton. "State: The Institution." In David Sills (ed.), *International Encyclopedia of the Social Sciences*. New York: Macmillan, 1968.

Samuels, Warren J. "Welfare Economics, Power, and Property." In Warren J. Samuels and A. Allan Schmid (eds.), *Law and Economics: An Institutional Perspective*. Boston: Martinus Nijhoff, 1981.

————. "Interrelations Between Legal and Economic Processes." *Journal of Law and Economics* 14 (1971): 435–50.

Schmid, A. Allan. *Property, Power, and Public Choice*. 2d ed. New York: Praeger, 1987.

Taylor, John F. A. *The Masks of Society*. New York: Appleton-Century-Crofts, 1966.

Whynes, David K., and Roger Bowles. *The Economic Theory of the State*. Oxford: Martin Robertson, 1981.

21

On the Fundamentals of the Economic Role of Government—The Rules Governing Economic Activity

James Duncan Shaffer

This chapter starts with the proposition that what government does at the most fundamental level is to sanction the de facto rules of economic behavior. Government represents the structure of power which reinforces the code of conduct that influences what individuals take into account as participants in economic activity. Government is not simply what we refer to as the government, that is, the formal legislative, administrative, and judicial organizations. Most of the code of conduct is neither codified nor enforced directly by the government, and much of what is formally codified has little or no influence on behavior. The government that is relevant is the structure of power that shapes the opportunity sets of the participants of an economic system. Conceptually, at the base of the relationship between the formal government and government as the structure of power is the pragmatic notion that the government sanctions all behavior that is either effectively prescribed or ineffectively prohibited.

It follows that government and economy cannot be separated; they are an organic unity. The political economy exists and evolves as a system. Individual opportunity sets are always the result of interactions among individuals and with the physical environment. These interactions are always shaped by the code of conduct or rules that circumscribe behavior. The opportunity set contains the possible rewards and punishments associated with alternative courses of action. The rewards and punishments reflect the rules of behavior emanating from the structure of power and the interaction among individuals and the environment in the process of production and consumption. Participants learn from the experience and from observations of the relationship of rewards and punishments to alternative behaviors. They learn how to behave and they discover the de facto rules of economic behavior. The distribution of rewards and punishments from past periods not only shapes future individual behavior by learning (reinforcement), but also results in distributions of benefits and related capacity to influence future opportunity sets.

It follows that there are variegated combinations of rules governing economic behavior. Specific combinations of rules shape individual opportunity sets that influence individual behavior and the resultant performance of any particular political economy. A political economy is an evolving system. The opportunity sets of participants are a function of political and economic interaction. To exercise a right changes others' opportunity. Behavior is shaped by the contingencies and reinforcers in the individual opportunity sets. The behavioral rules of the system are both a product and an input. It is a system of both mutual coercion and mutual advantage.

The opportunity sets as perceived by individual participants are unknown to others. The de facto rules governing economic behavior are learned in response to a changing environment resulting from complex interactions that can never be completely understood or predicted. Because the behavioral responses to formal rules are always uncertain, capacity to predict and control the evolution of a political economy is limited. We know from observation that a small group of individuals can shape the rules of a political economy in their favor. But much less is known about the combinations of specific rules that result in the transition from poverty to an evolving political economy of sustained economic progress with equity and social integration.

It also follows that there cannot be a generic proposition dealing with government participation in the economy or the market. The economy and the market do not exist without government. Propositions to be relevant must deal with specific rules. Recognizing that it is the detailed and specific de facto rules that govern economic behavior, we will nonetheless turn to a discussion of classes of rules that are generally critical to the performance to a political economy.

At the most fundamental level the rules governing economic behavior deal with two questions: (1) By what process are preferences articulated? (Whose preferences count, how are they counted, and how are they weighted?) (2) By what process is the production possibility set searched, and how is production organized to respond to the possibility set and the articulated preferences of participants?

The process of preference articulation and the organization of production involves (1) procedures for making rules, (2) definitions of entitlements to the output of the economy, (3) rules for coordinating economic activity, and (4) rules defining jurisdictional boundaries. This is not to suggest that different sets of rules perform each of these types of functions. The functions are interdependent. All involve rules defining what is to be taken into account by economic actors. The complex set of rules collectively establish the procedures for effective preference articulation and organization of the economy. It is not possible to separate the distribution of benefits from the rules for organizing production. But entitlement is not identical with rules for economic organization, although a property right may involve both decision-making jurisdiction and a right to benefits.

RULES FOR MAKING RULES

Most fundamental for preference articulation are the rules for making rules. These rules are the effective constitution of the political economy. They determine whose preferences count in making the rules governing economic behavior. They evolve from a previous structure of power, reinforce an existing structure, and respond to changes in preferences and power. What generalizations can be made about the fundamental nature of effective constitutions and the consequences they have for the performance of political economies?

The rules for making rules reflect the fundamental distribution of power, which in turn influences the specific behavioral rules of individual opportunity sets. Again, it is not just the written constitution that controls the rule-making process. Many societies do not have meaningful written constitutions. Ideology, the general beliefs as to what is legitimate, influences both rule making and how the formal rules influence behavior.

The concentration of authority ranges from the dictator relying primarily on the terror of physical force to the accepted voting procedures of a town meeting. Government participation in the economy takes many forms under all variations in concentration of rule-making authority.

The uses of markets and political processes for preference articulation originate with the rule-making procedures, but it is in both cases the specific de facto rules defining rights and obligations which determine economic performance.

RULES OF ENTITLEMENTS

The de facto rules of economic governance include a pattern of rights to shares of outputs. These rights or entitlements specify social relationships in the form of conditions for the legitimate or accepted share of output available to participants according to functions performed or positions held.

For example, a hunter in a tribal group may have the right to kill animals that happen into particular areas. More than likely some others have the same right; and the opportunity may be conditional on the tribe excluding others from access to the resource. Once an animal is killed, the hunter may be obligated to divide it among his relatives, others who may have contributed to the hunt, and to the village chief, who in turn may distribute to others according to their status. A number of conventions and decisions by individuals vested with authority may further define hunting and distribution rights. The hunter may or may not, for example, have the right to trade portions of the animal for other goods within the tribe or with outsiders. In behavioral terms, this pattern of entitlements and the physical environment (it makes a difference what animals happen into the hunting grounds) are important contingencies of reinforcement (benefits and costs associated with alternative patterns of behavior) shaping behavior.

Entitlements are obviously necessary to the function of an economy. The

alternative is to continuously fight over the resources and the product. Entitlements reflect the power of physical force, socialization, and the more or less
rational processes of formal rule making.

Entitlements in the tribe of hunters are relatively easy to define. In the modern
industrial political economy they are much more complex. Nonetheless, they
must settle the same issues—the access to resources and the distribution of output.
The complexity arises from the nature of industrial production and the interdependencies in industrial systems. Rules are required to define inputs and outputs.
Ownership of physical factors of production becomes less important, and intan-
gible property becomes more important.

Entitlements are critical in determining costs and value of outputs. Consider,
for example, rules of liability, workers compensation, patents, copyrights, rules
for collective organization (the corporation, cooperative, union), rules protecting
(or not protecting) investments in immobile assets, rules protecting assets from
shifts in demand resulting from untruthful advertising or other things, rules on
tenure, golden parachutes, junk bonds and the sale of dangerous drugs, taxes,
rules for social security, eligibility for welfare, and on and on.

Generally, an individual is entitled to a flow of benefits as a result of a perceived
contribution to production from resources owned, including the contribution of
one's own labor, through trade of owned resources, including labor, and through
some collective decisions or customs attaching a right to share because of status.
The governance systems include many rules leading to these entitlements. That
entitlements are of great importance to economic performance is obvious. However, the relationship of the whole pattern of entitlement rules and performance
is not at all obvious. The uncertainty about the relationship is a factor influencing
the development of the rules of entitlement. Among other things expenditures
to influence rule making are more likely to be profitable given these uncertainties.

Central to the rules of entitlement are beliefs about contributions to production
and legitimate claims to shares of output. In our hunting example the contribution
of different participants was not obvious, and distribution did not follow from
a calculation of contribution. In the scientific industrial economy, individual
contribution is indeterminate, and distribution is similarly only vaguely related
to empirical calculation of contribution given already accepted definitions of
property. It is empirically obvious that the difference in productivity between
primitive economies and scientific industrial ones is not due to individual effort
or to the availability of physical resources, but the accumulated knowledge and
organization of the socio-political-economic system. It follows that the rules of
entitlement to the output resulting from the inherited knowledge are the most
important rules influencing income distribution and perhaps productivity. Yet at
least casual observation indicates that relatively little explicit attention is given
to formulating the rights to knowledge and its contributions. This is in part due
to the unique characteristics of knowledge as a productive input, the way it is
produced and stored, and the general failure to recognize its contribution to

output, which in any case is ambiguous. Thus, power and myth are particularly important in defining rights to the outputs from the contributions of knowledge.

RULES FOR COORDINATION

Another set of rules governing economic behavior are those that facilitate the coordination of economic activity. Thousands of people may contribute to the production of a single loaf of bread. Hundreds of rules may have influenced the organization of these contributions to end up with a loaf of bread with the characteristics consistent with the preferences of a consumer willing and able to buy it. Or the outcome may be a loaf of bread that goes stale for want of a buyer. By coordination here is meant the organization of activity at each successive stage of production and distribution to meet the demand for the product. Coordination is facilitated by rules that reduce conflict and improve information about the future, including expectations of the actions of other economic participants.

Traffic rules are a common example. These rules may be common-sense conventions that are essentially self-enforcing through the obvious negative consequences that follow from their violation. Others may involve little conflict and yet require enforcement to avoid cheating. Industry-developed grades and standards designed to facilitate long-distance trading are an example. Rules specifying the obligations of buyers and sellers have many possible variations and as a group can have important impacts on economic performance, in respect to both equity and productivity.

The standardization of nuts and bolts while President Herbert Hoover was secretary of commerce is said to have contributed significantly to the development of mass production in manufacturing. Coordination today would have been improved had the decision been to standardize using metric measures.

One of the most frequently mentioned functions of government is the enforcement of contracts. This is an essential function to facilitate coordination, especially in transactions with a time dimension. Credit agreements, for example, greatly facilitate transactions involved in production and depend on a high and predictable compliance with the agreement. Again, however, learned behavioral rules are likely to be more important than formal rules enforced by political authority. The consequences of losing future access to credit and peer pressures may be much more immediate and effective reinforcers than the probability of state sanctions.

Enforcement of contracts is not neutral in respect to the distribution of power, but rather reflects and reinforces the existing power structure. Most rules facilitating coordination also involve entitlements. That is, they involve rights that generate benefits and costs to participants.

RULES OF JURISDICTION

Still another set of rules of economic governance are those specifying decision-making jurisdiction. These are the rules influencing which production and consumption decisions are to be made by those in different positions in the political economy. Which decisions will be made by public officials and which by private individuals? If by public officials, which agencies have jurisdiction over which decisions? More specifically, what do they take into account in their decisions? Does the agency responsible for highway construction consider the effect of lowering the cost of transportation on the number and location of firms, for example. If private, what are the rules for collective action? What are the rules for organizing economic activity? To what extent are production and consumption decisions centralized or decentralized?

Rules of jurisdiction are pervasive and often subtle. They deal with the bounds of decision-making authority. For example, a particular court has jurisdiction over cases of a particular type in a geographic area. The judge has authority to decide a case within guidelines provided by a legislature and the norms of the community.

A school board has the authority to grant degrees within certain guidelines. Teachers have authority to give grades that qualify students for the degree. The degree may be a necessary credential to qualify for a position. If the tasks of the position are performed, the worker will be entitled to a wage. But many additional rules will influence the amount of the wage.

The management of a corporation as a group has authority to make decisions within a guideline of policy set by the directors, the law, custom, and so on. The chief accountant has authority over a special set of activities circumscribed, among other things, by the authority of the management, the code of conduct of the accounting association, and the laws of fraud.

In each of these examples the rules defining jurisdiction influence the ways preferences are articulated and the way production is organized. They influence the level, content, and distribution of output. They influence entitlements but do more than influence the shares.

Almost all economies use a mix of political and market processes for identifying and responding to participant preferences and for searching and responding to the production possibility set. Identifying the means of production as public or private, however, tells little about the decision-making jurisdictions, whose preferences count, or the effectiveness of the search of the production possibility set. It is the complex set of rules defining jurisdiction, products, inputs, and so forth, which does.

CONCLUSION

At the most fundamental level what does government do that influences the economy? It is useful to think of government not as the state but as the process of instituting the political economy. In this process the rules for economic behavior evolve. It is the de facto rules, the formal rules as implemented, and the uncodified rules of legitimate accepted behavior in economic activity, which govern. Government does what it is. It governs. Government represents power. It resolves inevitable conflicts of interests. The governance system is frequently inherited, it evolves, but the fundamental rules or the beliefs that support them are seldom examined.

What difference does it make what the rules are? The rules of governance systems profoundly influence how much of what is produced and who gets what of the output. The enormous differences in economic performance among economic systems across space and time are, to a significant but uncertain extent, due to differences in the rules of the governance systems.

What should be the rules of the economic governance system? That is a different question, which fortunately is beyond the scope of this chapter.

NOTE

I thank A. Allan Schmid and Warren Samuels for comments on this chapter and for years of interesting discussions which are reflected here.

Michigan Agricultural Experiment Station Publication, no. 12634.

22

Fundamentals Relating to the Economic Functions of Government

Richard W. Tresch

Every society wrestles with the problem of determining the proper role of the government in a nation's economy. What economic functions should the government perform? What economic decision rules should public officials follow in each area? These are the two fundamental questions of government from an economic perspective.

ANALYTICAL FOUNDATIONS

The answers to these questions turn on two deeper questions that every society must address: (1) What economic system to choose? and (2) What economic objectives to pursue?

A coherent theory of the public sector cannot exist independently from the economic system in which the government operates. The proper role of the government, and its methods of operation, quite obviously depend on whether society chooses centrally planned socialism or pure market capitalism, or some mixture of the two. In what follows we assume that pure market capitalism is the preferred choice. This is certainly the working assumption in the writings of most U.S. public sector economists.

Regarding the economic objectives of society, the humanistic tradition argues in favor of promoting the economic well-being of every individual. Since the Law of Scarcity prevents the simultaneous maximization of everyone's well-being, the humanistic ideal translates into the twin goals of efficiency and equity.

Economists have universally adopted the Pareto interpretation of efficiency: An allocation of resources is efficient if in order to make someone better off at least one person must be made worse off. Central to the acceptance of the Pareto efficiency notion is the belief in the principle of consumer sovereignty—that consumers are best able to judge their own well-being. The principle is as fundamental to the public sector as it is to the operation of the market economy.

The preferences of individuals ought to drive all economic decisions of the government, to the extent possible.

Unfortunately, Pareto efficiency is too weak to serve as the final arbiter of overall economic well-being. It admits an infinity of outcomes, including allocations in which some people enjoy lavish lifestyles while others are mired in poverty. This weakness gives rise to the second objective, equity, which refers to society's collectively determined value judgments concerning distributive justice. A society must decide what constitutes fair outcomes, either by judging the outcomes themselves (e.g., the extent of equality), or the process generating the outcomes (e.g., equality of opportunity), or both.

The twin objectives of efficiency and equity led A. Bergson (1938) and Paul Samuelson (1965) to represent society's economic objective as maximizing an individualistic social welfare function of the form

$$(W = W(U^h(X_{hi}))$$

where:

X_{hi} = good (factor) i purchased (supplied) by individual h, $h = 1, \ldots, H$; $i = 1, \ldots, N$

U^h = the utility function of individual h, and

$\delta W/\delta U^h > 0$.

The social welfare function incorporates each of the three fundamental ideas mentioned above. The form of W is determined by society's notion of distributive justice. The pursuit of individual economic well-being *as the individual perceives it* is implied by having the individual's utility functions be the arguments of the social welfare function. No group of public officials imposes its own notion of social well-being on society. Finally, the positive partial derivative, $\delta W/\delta U^h > 0$, represents the Pareto criterion. It says that social welfare increases (decreases) if any one individual's utility increases (decreases), holding constant the utility received by all other individuals.

Samuelson (1954) presented the first complete formal statement of society's fundamental economic problem as: maximize the social welfare function with respect to the goods (factors) purchased (supplied) by each individual, subject to the two fundamental economic constraints of existing production technologies and market clearance. The simplest formal representation of the Samuelson model is:

$$\text{Max } W(U^h(X_{hi}))$$
$$\{X_{hi}\}$$
$$\text{s.t. } F(\sum_h X_{hi}) = 0$$

where:

$F(X^1, X^2, \ldots, X^N) = 0$ summarizes the production possibilities of the economy in terms of the aggregate goods and factors, X^i, and
$X^i = \sum_h X_{hi}$, $i = 1, \ldots N$, are the market clearance equations for each of the N goods and factors.

This is the model which virtually all economists use to develop normative propositions about the government sector, or any other aspect of the economy.

An important property of the model is that the H*N first-order conditions (necessary conditions) for a social welfare optimum with respect to the X_{hi} can be combined into two distinct sets of conditions. The first set consists of the Pareto optimal (PO) conditions, the conditions necessary for economic efficiency. These are combinations of individuals' marginal rates of substitution (MRS) and firms' marginal rates of transformation (MRT) between any two goods and factors. They are independent of the social welfare function, W.

The second set consists of interpersonal equity (IE) conditions of the form

$$\delta W/\delta U^h \cdot \delta U^h/\delta X_{hi} = , \text{for all } h = 1, \ldots, H$$
$$\text{any } i = 1, \ldots, N$$

where:

$\delta W/\delta U^h \cdot \delta U^h/\delta X_{hi}$ is the social marginal utility of consumption (supply) of good (factor) i for individual h.

Notice that the social marginal utility is a product of the individual's private marginal utility of consumption (supply), $\delta U^h/\delta X_{hi}$, and the collectively determined marginal social welfare weight, $\delta W/\delta U^h$.

The IE conditions are meant to embody society's norms regarding distributive justice, but they do so only partially. They capture the concern for fair results but say nothing directly about the concern for fair processes.

THE APPROPRIATE FUNCTIONS OF GOVERNMENT

With the Bergson-Samuelson model in mind, let us return to the first fundamental question of government, the question of legitimacy. What economic functions should the government perform in a market economy? The answer is perfectly straightforward, in principle. Either the free market economy can satisfy the PO and IE conditions for a social welfare maximum, or it cannot. Those instances in which it fails to satisfy the first-order conditions offer a *potential* role for the government in guiding the economy back on the path toward efficiency and equity.

Public sector economists typically identify six areas of market failure.

1. *The distribution of income.* The free market system has no way of guaranteeing that the distribution of income satisfies the IE conditions because the social welfare function

is not a market construct. It must evolve from the political process.

The remaining instances of market failure all pertain to the PO efficiency conditions.

2. *Technological externalities.* The purchase or supply of a good or factor by any one individual or firm enters directly into either the utility function or production function or some other individual or firm. Markets generally fail to account for these external effects as the PO conditions require.

If all markets were perfectly competitive, addressing the first two problems would be the only legitimate economic concerns of the government. Competitive pricing absent externalities satisfies the PO conditions. Unfortunately, the conditions required for perfectly competitive markets are quite strong: large numbers of buyers and sellers of homogeneous goods and factors; free flow of information to all; and complete markets for all goods and factors. The remaining four functions of government arise because these market conditions frequently do not hold. Briefly (with the resulting governmental functions):

3. *Large-scale, decreasing cost production.* For example, regulation of natural mono-polies and large price-setting firms.

4. *Imperfect flows of information.* For example, establishing the ground rules for market exchanges, public insurance, and consumer and worker protection agencies such as Occupational Safety and Health Administration (OSHA).

5. *Incomplete markets.* For example, public insurance.

6. *Macroeconomic stabilization.* The macroeconomic problems of unemployment, price inflation, and inadequate long-run economic growth are considered to result from a combination of problems (2),(3), and (4) above.

GOVERNMENT POLICY RULES

Having identified the proper economic functions of government, what can be said about how the government should proceed? At issue here are the decision rules that should guide government policy in each of these areas.

The appropriate policy rules depend on the set of policy instruments available to the government. Economists distinguish between first-best policy rules and second-best policy rules, depending on whether the government has sufficient flexibility to bring the economy to a full social welfare optimum.

First-best Analysis

The essence of first-best analysis is that the government can do anything required to satisfy both the IE and PO conditions. In other words, the only constraints the government faces are the two natural constraints of existing production technologies and market clearance. Under these conditions, govern-ment policy dichotomizes into one set of strategies aimed at satisfying the IE conditions and another set of strategies aimed at satisfying the PO conditions.

Equity. The IE conditions are achieved by taxing and transferring resources among individuals, lump-sum, to equalize social marginal utilities. There are three important points to note about the tax-transfer policy. First, the taxes (transfers) must be lump-sum to assure that all the PO conditions continue to hold. Second, the government need only tax and transfer *one* of the goods or factors in order to achieve interpersonal equity, even though the IE conditions must hold for all goods and factors. This is so because if the PO conditions are satisfied, and social marginal utilities are equal with respect to any one good or factor, then the IE conditions automatically hold for all other goods and factors. In practical terms, the choice of the tax (transfer) base is irrelevant. Third, the lump-sum tax and transfer policy is the *only* instance of government policymaking in a first-best environment that addresses the problem of equity.

In summary, the IE conditions provide a complete theory of the optimal distribution and of optimal redistributional policy. The distribution of utilities when the IE conditions hold is the optimal distribution of economic well-being for a society. In addition, comparing the distribution of the good (factor) being taxed and transferred at an existing situation with the distribution at the optimum provides a complete description of the taxes or transfers required for each individual.

Efficiency. All other first-best policy rules are designed to satisfy the PO conditions. As such, their only concern is with efficiency. They do not depend in any way on the form of the social welfare function.

Achieving the PO conditions calls for a variety of policy strategies, depending on the nature of the problem. In a market economy the government would normally utilize one of three approaches: (1) regulation of private activity (e.g., the electric utilities); (2) taxation (transfers) (e.g., pollution externalities); and (3) government consumption or provision (e.g., defense and the postal service, respectively). All students of public sector economics are familiar with the following first-best policy rules, each being an example of one of the three approaches.

1. *Decreasing costs*: Set price equal to marginal cost for all decreasing cost services (natural monopolies) and cover the resulting deficits out of general tax revenues.

2. *Pollution externalities*: Levy taxes on polluters equal to the marginal pollution damage at the optimum.

3. *Nonexclusive public goods*: Purchase nonexclusive goods such as defense up to the point at which $\Sigma MRS = MRT$.

Taxation. Some additional comments about tax policy in a first-best policy environment are in order. The public tends to view taxes as a necessary evil, but first-best taxes are not evil at all. They only serve to promote social welfare, doing so in one of two ways. They may be the approach chosen to satisfy one of the PO conditions, as in the case of taxing polluters to correct for pollution externalities. Or, as noted above, they are levied lump-sum to satisfy the IE conditions.

Lump-sum taxes serve a third purpose as well: to finance expenditures required by the PO conditions when the policy rules themselves do not indicate how to raise the tax revenue. Examples include the deficits of decreasing cost services and defense expenditures.

For instance, the $\Sigma MRS = MRT$ policy rule for defense tells the government how much defense to buy but not how to finance it. Any *lump-sum* tax will do. But because the taxes must be lump-sum, the financing of these services is effectively subsumed within the lump-sum tax-transfer program designed to satisfy the IE conditions. The only difference is that the sum of taxes collected from individuals must exceed the sum of transfers to individuals by an amount sufficient to cover these other financial requirements.

The fact that the IE conditions play such a central role in public expenditure and tax theory is the Achilles heel of normative public sector economics. The problem is that neither economists nor anyone else have made a convincing case for any particular social welfare function. What should the relative weights, $\delta W/\delta U^h$, be for different individuals? In particular, how should the weighting scheme relate to the time-honored canons of distributive justice—desert, ability, need, and the like? All we have are a number of suggestions, ranging from John Rawls' egalitarian view that society should strive to maximize the economic well-being of those who are the worst off (in effect, all but the worst off have a zero marginal social welfare weight), to the utilitarian view that the distribution of economic well-being is irrelevant. All utilitarians care about is maximizing aggregate satisfaction, the sum of individual utilities. Most economists undoubtedly prefer some middle ground between those two extremes, but no one has ever made a convincing case for any particular social welfare function.

Given the practical difficulties associated with satisfying the IE conditions, small wonder that most public policy debate on the problem of designing equitable taxes centers around two entirely different principles, the benefits-received principle and the ability-to-pay principle. Both principles of Tax equity considerably predate the Bergson-Samuelson social welfare perspective.

The benefits-received principle states that taxes are fair if they are levied in accordance with the benefits received from the public services they finance. The principle dates from seventeenth-century England, when feudal lords paid taxes to the king in return for the state's promise to maintain law and order. The principle has obvious appeal in a capitalist society, and it no doubt explains the popularity of user-fees among state and local governments. But the benefits-received principle is also quite limited in application. It cannot be applied to finance transfer payments or any other public service whose benefits are highly diffused and difficult to measure, defense for instance.

A final point is that the benefits-received principle has no standing whatsoever as an equity principle in the Bergson–Samuelson social welfare model. The IE conditions have nothing to do with the pricing of public services. The PO conditions may call for certain prices (e.g., marginal cost pricing of decreasing cost services), but only for reasons of efficiency, not equity.

The ability-to-pay principle, commonly attributed to Adam Smith and John Stuart Mill, applies to general taxes levied to finance all expenditures for which the benefits-received principle is inapplicable. The guiding subprinciples within ability-to-pay are horizontal equity (HE) and vertical equity (VE). HE requires equal treatment of equals. VE says that unequals may be treated unequally. The only progress economists have made with the ability-to-pay principle has occurred with respect to HE. VE is none other than the problem of distributive justice discussed above, restated in different terms.

Most economists interpret HE to mean that two individuals with equal utility before tax should have equal utility after tax. The practical question, then, becomes one of determining the best possible surrogate measure of utility. That measure then serves as the tax base, so that equals pay equal taxes.

The economics profession is split between two surrogate utility measures: (1) full economic income, equal to the increase in a taxpayer's purchasing power during the year; and (2) consumption. Proponents of income as the ideal tax base adopt an annual perspective of tax policy. Proponents of a consumption tax base adopt a lifetime perspective, in which the concept of purchasing power is irrelevant. Over a person's lifetime all income is consumed, either personally or as part of a final bequest. Since consumption is the act that most directly yields utility, the pattern of lifetime consumption is seen as the best tax base.

Whether one prefers income or consumption as best satisfying HE, economists must live with the unsettling knowledge that the Smith-Mill ability-to-pay principle is generally incompatible with the social welfare, IE view of equity. The incompatibilities arise in a number of ways. First, and foremost, the IE conditions make use of social welfare weights, whereas ability-to-pay does not. Under ability-to-pay, only individual utilities matter. Beyond that, HE judges utility *levels*, both before and after tax (transfer). IE, by contrast, cares only about social *marginal* utilities, and then only at the after-tax (transfer) optimum. In addition, the ability-to-pay principle is concerned primarily with defining the fairest tax base, whereas the choice of a tax base is irrelevant under IE. Recall that any one of the goods or factors can be redistributed to satisfy the IE conditions.

In summary, these two first-best theories of equitable taxation cannot be fully reconciled. In our view, the incompatibilites render the ability-to-pay principle suspect as a fundamental principle of taxation, precisely because the Bergson-Samuelson social welfare model is the basis of all normative propositions in economics.

Second-best Analysis

First-best analysis has an obvious shortcoming. Its underlying assumptions are patently unrealistic. Government policy can never be as flexible as required to reach the full social optimum.

Second-best analysis is an attempt to add some degree of realism to the government's policy environment. It recognizes that the government is constrained in its attempts to maximize social welfare beyond the natural constraints

of production technologies and market clearance. The additional constraints make
the full social optimum unattainable. For example, a very common assumption
in second-best analysis is that the government cannot use lump-sum taxes (transfers). Instead, it must levy distorting taxes, which cause different economic
agents to face different prices for the same good (factor). This assumption
immediately rules out the attainment of the PO conditions in the taxed markets,
because markets can only be first-best efficient if everyone faces the same prices.

The desire for more realism is understandable, but one can question whether
anything truly fundamental can ever emerge from second-best analysis. Second-
best policy rules suffer a number of difficulties.

The first is that analysis in a second-best environment can never yield a set
of ''standard'' results equivalent to the classic results of first-best analysis (e.g.,
$\Sigma MRS = MRT$ for nonexclusive public goods). Adding one constraint to the
social welfare problem gives a certain policy rule. Add a second constraint and
the policy rule changes, and so on. The real world offers innumerable constraints
to choose from. There is no natural stopping point for adding constraints to the
problem in the name of realism. We may turn this point around: positing one
or two constraints is only a tiny step removed from the first-best environment.
Most second-best analysis is still not terribly realistic.

A second difficulty relates to assuming away lump-sum taxes and transfers.
Without lump-sum redistributions, the government cannot hope to satisfy the IE
conditions. If not, and society cares about equity, second-best policy analysis
is simply a mess.

The problem is that we lose the dichotomy between efficiency and equity
rules. Whereas first-best analysis yields separate PO and IE conditions, all first-
order conditions of second-best analysis contain the social welfare weights, in
general. To give just one example, the standard first-best allocational rule for
nonexclusive public goods no longer applies. In a second-best environment,
$\Sigma MRS \gtreqless MRT$ depending on the unequal social marginal utilities (as well as
other considerations). No second-best policy rules escape contamination by the
social welfare terms.

A third difficulty is that optimal second-best policy rules often imply an
inordinate (unacceptable?) amount of government intervention in the market
economy. A case in point is the famous Ramsey tax problem, which asks how
to raise a given amount of tax revenue using distorting taxes in order to minimize
efficiency loss. The answer is that, in general, *all but one* of the goods and
factors should be taxed or subsidized, so as to produce equal percentage changes
in the compensated demand (supply) of every good (factor). Intervening in all
markets when the government uses distorting taxes is a common feature of
optimal second-best policy rules.

Governments will never be that intrusive. If not, however, then government
policy may not improve social welfare. R. G. Lipsey and K. Lancaster (1956)
were the first to make this point. They proved that satisfying some but not all
of the necessary conditions for a first-best social welfare optimum may not

improve social welfare, a result they called the theorem of the second-best. Subsequent analysis by others of piecemeal policy changes has shown that the social welfare effects of such policies are often problematic.

POSITIVE ASPECTS OF POLICY ANALYSIS

The last fundamental is that the success of actual policy initiatives depends on how individuals and firms behave, in both the economic and political arenas. Economists naturally assume that economic behavior is self-motivated. Individuals maximize utility and firms maximize profit, and they respond to government policies with these objectives in mind. But how does that assumption play itself out? Normative economic modeling frequently assumes a perfectly competitive market economy. Is that a harmless assumption? Firms do behave differently in noncompetitive markets. Even if consumers and firms are *price* takers, are they *policy* takers, or do they engage in acts of gamesmanship with the government (e.g., evasion of taxes)? Is uncertainty an important consideration for a particular policy initiative? Do individuals attempt to maximize utility year by year, or over their entire lifetimes, or even across generations? Economists have shown that answers to questions such as these are crucial to the appropriate design of government policy in virtually everything governments do.

People's political behavior is, if anything, even more important, because it has such a direct impact on policy formation. Forty years ago nearly all economists assumed that political behavior was socially motivated. People devoted their political lives to promoting ''the public interest'' (i.e., maximizing social welfare). Since that time, a new theory of public choice has emerged based on the tenet that people do not change at all when they enter the political arena. They remain entirely self-motivated. The implications of self-motivated political behavior are fairly devastating, at least for democratic forms of government.

The leading example is surely the Arrow Impossibility Theorem. K. J. Arrow (1951) showed that, in general, self-interested democratic voting procedures cannot be counted on to generate a social welfare function. Yet the social welfare function is the linchpin of normative public sector theory.

Other public choice theorists have demonstrated many ways in which self-interested political behavior can undermine the quest for efficiency and equity. A brief listing would include the median voter model, special interest groups, and self-motivated public transfer programs. Quite clearly, the government might not realize its potential for improving social welfare.

If narrow self-interest truly dominates political decisions, only one fundamental economic proposition about the role of the government remains standing. Individuals (firms) simply use the public sector as a vehicle for increasing their personal utilities (profits). That is not a very uplifting proposition in a world fraught with inequities, externalities, imperfect information, and the like. But the public sector really has no other useful function to perform if people have no interest in maximizing social welfare.

SUMMARY AND CONCLUSION

The Bergson-Samuelson model of social welfare maximization provides a sound analytical framework for thinking about the economic aspects of government policy in the context of a humanistic society dedicated to free market capitalism. Yet it has not been entirely successful in answering the two fundamental economic questions of government. The model is quite helpful in establishing the proper economic functions of government, but it is far less successful in offering policymakers a set of optimal guidelines to follow with each function. In addition, the policy dictates of the model are easily undermined by self-motivated political behavior. It is fair to say that little of a truly fundamental nature emerges to guide public policy within each function of government. Be that as it may, most economists would insist that the Bergson-Samuelson model is the proper analytical framework for policy analysis.

One need not be overly discouraging, however. Much political behavior does appear to be socially motivated. Moreover, both the first- and second-best policy rule are certainly useful as policy guidelines, even though they may not be truly fundamental propositions.

For instance, taxing polluters in line with the first-best policy rule for externalities would undoubtedly be billions of dollars cheaper than the federal government's existing command approach to controlling pollution. Another example is the second-best analysis of optimal income taxation, which has underscored the substantial efficiency costs of levying high marginal tax rates on wage income. Examples such as these come easily to mind. Most economists are quite confident that economic analysis using the Bergson-Samuelson social welfare model points government policy in the right direction, the theorem of the second-best notwithstanding.

REFERENCES

Arrow, K. J. *Social Choice and Individual Values*. New Haven, Conn.: Yale University Press, 1951.

Bergson, A. "A Reformulation of Certain Aspects of Welfare Economics." *Quarterly Journal of Economics* 52 (1938): 310–34.

Lipsey, R. G., and K. Lancaster. "The General Theory of Second Best." *Review of Economic Studies* 24, no. 1 (December 1956): 11–32.

Samuelson, P. A. *Foundations of Economic Analysis*. New York: Atheneum Publishers, 1965.

———. "The Pure Theory of Public Expenditure." *Review of Economics and Statistics* 36 (November 1954): 387–89.

23

On the Economic Role of Government

Larry L. Wade

What are the most elemental positive axioms that can be stated concerning the economic role of government? This is a challenging question, no doubt, but one worthy of our attention only if it has first been established that it is a sensible one. Does the question, for example, presuppose that polity (power) and economy (welfare) can be or ever have been disentangled in past or future social associations? Or that some ideal balance between economy and polity can be discovered and maintained by good republican laws? If so, the question is best left to those prone to fantasy and illusion, to, in Alexander Hamilton's pungent phrase, "the reveries of those political doctors whose sagacity disdains the admonitions of experimental instruction." Power and economy are invariably connected, whatever Prince Kropotkin may have thought possible. On the other hand, if the fundamental axioms called for are to be condensed statements of the economic relations that all historical political systems without exception have had in common, we will be left with a rather small set: After all, some political leaders have been interested in economic affairs only to the point of securing their personal power positions, not always an expensive proposition. Immemorial norms and habit-backgrounds have typically determined patterns of production and distribution among undifferentiated communities, such as the Mende of Sierra Leone or the Nuer of the southern Sudan. To describe such economies as "governed" by political authorities in any sense applicable to modern political economies is to suck on a dry husk indeed. Evidently, then, some boundaries must be set to our organizing question.

Let us be practical and confine our attention to the role of steel and gold in complex societies. This is not a temporally limiting condition and would in principle encompass complex political communities from ancient times to the present, viz., from the Aztecs to the Australians. For our study we require only a socially differentiated and well-recognized political and administrative class holding a monopoly of violence over a population of significant size living in a more-or-less defined geographical space. In such conditions, we may speak of a "political system" or "government" or "state." These entities take awesomely diverse colors and forms, as do the economies that sustain them; so sundry are they that here we cannot enumerate all the major taxonomies advanced by the political historian: modern and premodern empires, autocracies, constitutional monarchies, theocratic, feudal, capitalist, welfare, fascist, or socialist states, military dictatorships, polyarchies, oligarchies, and so forth. To the political historian and political scientist, the ties between polity and economy are always central: On the most primitive plane, the question is invariably one of supremacy—will gold buy the army or will the army take the gold?

Neither of these outcomes is inevitable, but the question poses, arguably, the most basic problematic of government and economy. It sets the analytic train in motion. It introduces the problem of power, and it forces attention to its composition and incidence. Thus, to understand the economic role of government, one must understand power. The origin and etiology of power is a large subject and need not detain us here, but one must note that power is necessary to any complex social organization and thus long predates any philosophical discussion of it. In history's harsh chronicle, a coarse will to dominate through unrationalized violence is often inscribed as the basis of political society—the sports of rapine and pillage seem to have motivated the Mongol hordes. On other occasions, a sacred mission derived from prophecy and myth may serve as the catalyst for the structuring of political power—think of Moses. Less frequently, a voluntary contract between members of an incipient society may assign political roles and authority through an agreed-upon process—the Mayflower Compact may be the purest case in point. Once political societies and their regimes are established, their consolidations and transformations begin, as do their political and economic histories. But the point to be made is that, given the cacophony of political types and the parables that inspire and sustain them, one can say little about government's economic role as such. What one can say is that all governments once established, will seek with varying degrees of success to maintain at least as much social order as is deemed sufficient to maintain their own existence and legitimacy, and that within that order economic activity will, given the ingenuity of the species, necessarily take place. The emphasis that government as such will place on economic welfare, not to speak of the extent to which it can actually affect such welfare, follows no clear rule.

In part, this is so because the maledictions of rulers may lead them to a stunning obtuseness as to the material conditions in which their subjects actually subsist. Or effective social control may require maintaining the purity of the ruling theses against inevitable heretics and may well absorb the full attention of the guardians of ideology and doctrine to the neglect of mundane problems of social welfare. In other circumstances, even well-meaning political elites may abjure an interest in economics as attention is focused on the more profound problem of leading their subjects to eternal salvation or of laying the groundwork for the future secular utopia. In either case, government's role in enlarging economic welfare may receive little heed from ruling authorities. It also transpires that governing elites vary widely in their understanding and competence in economic matters, even when they are concerned about enhancing popular welfare. The spectacle of rulers captivated by bizarre economic theories and the consequent havoc wreaked on their economies is a common one; worse, having brought devastation to the population, they not infrequently redouble their efforts to realize their unreconstructed phantasma. Such apparitions are by no means confined to the unlettered and unsophisticated, such as the money cranks or the gold bugs who have provided endless amusement to economic historians. To take a case in point, the necessary failure of central planning by bureaucratic/ political processes in complex economies has by no means dissuaded certain abstracted intellectuals from its pursuit. Nor did mercantalism or autarchy lack their otherwise intelligent proponents.

Moreover, it often happens that the economic concerns of political elites are necessarily subordinated to more pressing problems. From the perspective of the political class, the social situation is one that requires constant equilibration. However social interests are denominated—whether as economic classes, religious sects, racial or ethnic groups, regional sections, or cultural traditions— centrifugal tendencies are always at work in political society. These factions may be bound together by many ties, including a shared even if troubled history, custom, awkward but real mutual economic interests, physical location, or political domination. Some rough reconciliation of these factions is necessary if the polity is to persist, and the search for a propitiating solution to the threat of instability is a constant concern of government. If one considers almost any complex society, political interventions to moderate cleavages involving capital and labor, occupational groups, geographical sections, religious confessions, races and nationalities, and so on, it becomes clear that economic policy is only a part, and sometimes a small part, of the social roles assumed by governments.

The accommodation of these interests is made more difficult when it is recognized that major groups and factions may themselves fragment, crackup, or fall into internecine conflict, confronting government with new challenges to its cohesion and stability. In some circumstances, lines of social cleavage may overlap to some important degree—class, religion, ethnicity, and geography, even national identifications, may run in the same "direction" (Northern Ireland is a splendid example); absent cross-cutting cleavages, the imperatives of incorporation and reconciliation may become so difficult as to absorb all of government's limited energies. At other times, conflict along one dimension may be so relentless as to preoccupy the government exclusively. One thinks of severe antagonisms between economic classes, or between two irreconcilable religious faiths. Again, government's economic role may receive short shrift in view of the overpowering problems which such disputes pose for governmental security. The dilemma of securing some measure of pacific relations among factions is compounded by individuals who challenge authority from a variety of directions and whose understanding is the trying task of the political psychologist. As

Harold D. Lasswell (1930) reminds us, much of politics consists of private affect displaced on public objects and rationalized in terms of the public interest. Governments must contend, therefore, with the inordinately selfish, the sinners, the alienated, the misfits, the violence-prone, the frustrated power-hunters, the truth-seekers of all persuasions, mettlesome artists, tenacious intellectuals bearing a thousand reforms, well-meaning but confused ordinary citizens, as well as sincere and responsible democrats. It is not unlikely that the Solzhenitsyn Problem received more attention from the Politburo at various times than did the Five-year Plan—not that either was particularly tractable.

Thus far, and for heuristic reasons only, we have spoken of government as a unitary actor, as a sovereign. In fact, such situations are increasingly rare, however much they may have defined, for example, the Age of Absolutism or Korea's Yi Dynasty, and even in such cases the foxes continually contemplated the lions. The Manchu rulers came to fear their eunuchs, and ancient kings their own sons. Nor have contemporary totalitarians been without intra-elite adversaries. Hitler was set upon, albeit unsuccessfully, by dissident military assassins. Beria died of unnatural causes induced by his fellow oligarchs. The dictator can take nothing for granted. Faced with a pressing need to thwart an inevitable opposition from below or within, his close examination of the people's economic welfare may appear an unwise distraction. Heaven's mandate is always at risk.

It does not follow that people fortunate enough to live under durable constitutional governments will experience intelligent economic management from public policymakers, although it is true that governmental persistence depends ultimately on a tolerable measure of economic success. The rule of law and parliamentary institutions that have tamed political power permit few deductions concerning the particular economic roles that government will assume. In principle, as Joseph Schumpeter (1950) pointed out, constitutional government is consistent with a very broad range of economic arrangements. These vary with, among other factors, political culture, social structure, national history, and level and type of economic development. But in all such systems, authority is scattered, whether between government and opposition, or by the separation of powers, federalism, and so forth. This redeeming safeguard against tyranny, however, is not without its consequences for government's economic performance.

Constant manuevering for institutional advantage and personal advancement in a pluralistic democratic order is a fixed summons to demagogues and opportunists who can frequently assemble a majority against what a prudent and experienced economist might consider objectively sound economic policies. It can be shown mathematically that self-interested democratic coalitions are inherently unstable. Few will be satisfied with any tax system, for example, since there is always the prospect that political action may reduce whatever levies the current fisc may impose. Politicians in search of applause from the crowd are not oblivious to this truth. Thus, public policies in democracies are always under siege, erratic, and, as an ensemble, inconsistent. Mercurial coalitions and shifting officeholders introduce volatility into the making and implementation of eco-

nomic policy. Therefore, predicting the economic roles that democratic government will assume is a nearly hopeless undertaking, especially if political culture
is splintered beyond some (imprecise) point and if the shifting combinations of
power factions reflect that condition.

The logicians of social and public choice have also provided instruction in
the inevitable disjunction between individual volitions and their aggregation by
democratic process. There are no rules by which even a well-informed and well-
meaning democratic government can tap a social consensus on some unknown
but surely broad and important range of policy questions. Indeed, there are no
rules by which such a government could itself rest unambiguously on the diverse
preferences of the restless individuals who populate democratic society—even
if one charitably grants the premise that incoherence is not an invariable characteristic of those preference orderings. Professor Kenneth J. Arrow (1951) has
proved quite correct in this regard.

It should not be concluded, however, that no predictions at all can flow from
the flux and confusion of the democratic order. It was Alexis de Tocqueville,
the first great student of mass democracy, who plotted most presciently the likely
future economic role of popular government: growth and centralization, a result
intended by no one but accruing inevitably as fitful and ambitious individuals
conclude that to "increase their comfort at the expense of the public treasury
strikes them as being, if not the only way, at least the easiest and most expeditious
by which to escape from a condition they no longer find satisfactory" (1969,
p. 633). Popularity-chasing politicians acquiesce, with the result that the "sphere
of the central authority extends insensibly in all directions" in a fruitless effort
to accommodate, with limited means, "demands which multiply without limit"
(p. 672). The reverberating economic inefficiencies need not be stressed, being
all too obvious. In any case, they do not provide the most tragic corollary. Claims
that "can never be satisfied" lead to a "permanent opposition" that may at
some point "seek to overthrow the constitution and give new shape to the state."
The ironic outcome is the collapse of democracy itself and the demise of those
politicians who have sought to concentrate on themselves all the desires generated
by the opportunities of mass political participation. Tocqueville observed wryly
that "One day they will discover that they have put their own power in hazard
. . . and that it would have been safer and more honest to have taught their
subjects the art of looking after themselves" (p. 634). True, there was some
chance that the growth of enlightened as opposed to myopic self-interest might
curb these tendencies and preserve both liberty and democracy, but there is no
gainsaying the philosopher's skepticism on this score.

Purblind self-interest is aided and abetted in these processes by the melioristic
belief that popular government, somehow to be led by benign, public-spirited,
and uncommonly competent policymakers, can "solve" all manner of social
"problems" including economic ones, and must do so to guarantee peace,
security, freedom, justice, morality, equality, fairness, fraternity, solidarity,
growth, progress, happiness, and an interesting life. Every day and in every way

the world would get better and better if government were more responsive, properly constituted, compassionate, or if more people would "participate." The inquiry comes full-circle: democratic government in the world as it is must cope with wildly inconsistent and often foolish visions and philosophies to the necessary neglect of more studied analyses of economic policy (excepting the occasional Thatcher factor).

For these reasons, government, whatever degree of autocracy or democracy may characterize it, may be closely or weakly linked to economic activity. It is no great help, for example, to say that all governments of whatever stripe must supply some quantity of public goods sufficient to support economic activity, else how are we to live? This is only trivially true. Neither the Dalai Lama's Tibet nor Haile Salassie's Ethiopia were much concerned with economic development or the provision of public goods, as road-weary travelers can attest. The Samurai clung to their warrior code as the feudal system eroded, contemptuous of practical measures by which to arrest their economic decline. The just price of the medieval theologians was poor supply-side economics, but then stimulating trade and maximizing production were not part of their particular optimization strategy.

To be sure, the modern period is one in which governments around the globe regularly reassure their populations that new economic ideas, plans, and programs are being prepared to resolve whatever economic afflictions seem politically relevant at the moment. This being so, perhaps the search for fundamental axioms bearing on the economic role of government could profitably be confined to the contemporary era and to the pervasive if not yet universal recognition by political elites throughout the world that economic welfare is a matter of the highest priority for their subjects or citizens, the odd ascetic excepted, and regardless of whether government can do much about it. All political decision makers carry economic theories in their heads. Whether it will be convenient or feasible to implement their theories, however insightful or uncultivated, is a constant question with an uncertain answer. After all, it is one thing to have a theory and quite another to do anything about it: action may agitate the opposition or prove inconsistent with the policymaker's own interests. The superb actors who populate the political arena are also altogether capable of advancing economic programs they know secretly to be mischievous or unworkable, but this fact may be thought less important than winning votes or preserving existing dispensations to potentially unruly interests. Indeed, current economic follies are maintained for precisely those reasons. Examples could be given without number, but readers will have their own favorite candidates. Of course, every state will have an economic program if only by default or inertia, but one can say little about its precise configuration except retrospectively or in very gross terms (there are probably some means of exchange and at least a few roads, for example) *unless* some historical or political information is supplied. Government as such has few necessary economic functions. Of course, one finds significant differences between the contemporary economic roles of government in, say, the Marxist-

Leninist societies in Eastern Europe, the liberal democracies (polyarchies), and more oligarchical systems (say, traditional or military regimes) and their relative reliance on state/bureaucratic versus market allocative processes or their respective patterns of resource use. For example, Alexander J. Groth, Larry L. Wade, and Alvin D. Wiggins (1984) used discriminant analysis to predict the political regime-types of 91 countries very accurately (96 percent correct classifications), based on twelve measures of each country's allocative patterns to industrial development, transportation, education and culture, consumer services, and feminism. One may discern real differences in the government's economic role in rich versus poor societies, or in traditional versus modern ones. Such empirical comparisons and distinctions are the subjects of comparative economics and politics. They are interesting and important but, as far as once can tell, do not address our cardinal question, which concerns government as such.

What, then, can be said about the "fundamental economic role of government?" Very little, it would seem. The reason, at bottom, is that economic policy is a "byproduct" of power. Economics is something government may address when its more fundamental challenges have been more or less met and when economics is seen as an appropriate governmental concern. There is no mystery as to what the first task of government has always been, and no one has expressed it better than James Madison in *Federalist 51*: "In framing a government which is to be administered by men over men, the great difficulty lies in this; you must first enable the government to control the governed." (And, Madison added immediately, if it is to be a decent government, you must "in the next place oblige it to control itself.") As suggested here, it is an open question whether government, having secured social order, will turn its attention to economic matters, but even if it should, new political contests will soon divert its attention back to the problem of maintaining itself. Again, economics will receive only backward glances from authorities anxious to evade the ubiquitous foxes in search of power and advantage.

This chapter has shunned the normative form of its initial query, but if it has identified any home truths about government and politics, certainly some prescriptive implications may be drawn. Most obviously, those who believe that government can be the primary engine of economic efficiency and equity have the burden of explaining, not merely asserting, just how this might be possible: social control, the first task of any government, has always required actions inconsistent with intelligent and virtuous economic policy. That government is rare enough that can reconcile social interests more or less peacefully and that is so constrained in its own behavior by rules and traditions that tyranny is not threatened. A decent government's economic role must be a relatively modest one, and a decent economy requires a decent government. This lesson is part of the great relearning that may be occurring now on a rather broad and even international scale, but it is far too early to advance such a proposition except in the most tentative terms.

REFERENCES

Arrow, Kenneth J. *Social Choice and Individual Values*. New York: John Wiley, 1951.
De Tocqueville, Alexis. *Democracy in America*. Garden City, N.Y.: Doubleday, 1969.
Groth, Alexander J., Larry L. Wade, and Alvin D. Wiggins. "Classifying the World's Political Systems: A Resource Allocation Approach." In A. J. Groth and L. L. Wade (eds.), *Comparative Resource Allocation*. Beverly Hills, Calif.: Sage, 1984.
Hamilton, Alexander. *Federalist 28*.
Lasswell, Harold D. *Psychopathology and Politics*. Chicago: University of Chicago Press, 1930.
Madison, James. *Federalist 51*.
Schumpeter, Joseph A. *Capitalism, Socialism and Democracy*. New York: Harper & Row, 1950.

24

The Economic Role of Government as a Constitutional Problem

David K. Whynes

In this chapter I have elected to interpret the economic role of government in an essentially normative fashion. I propose to inquire how one goes about deciding that which a government *ought* to do, as opposed to detailing that which governments actually *do* do. The investigation follows the conventional lines of economic theory, my purpose being to demonstrate that the role of government is extremely difficult to prescribe using such techniques. Incidentally, the normative focus, precludes a discussion of positive theories of government functions in historical societies, for example, the Marxian interpretation of the state as a creature and instrument of the economically dominant class.

Since the beginnings of the modern period, the orthodox approach to the analysis of the proper role of government has posited the existence, at some time in the past, of human beings to whom government was unknown. Such beings were autonomous and autarkic individuals, self-regarding, self-sustaining, and self-centered, being possessed of a number of natural rights. One day, or so the story goes, these individuals became conscious of certain inadequacies in their otherwise utopian existences, inadequacies devolving from their realization that they were actually neither autonomous nor autarkic. Conflicts over resource usage were arising, and conditions of self-sufficiency were not prevailing. All these troubles caused our heroes to enter into a social contract among themselves to regulate their interdependencies. Society emerged by translating individualism into catallaxy, a nexus of managed and ordered interindividual exchange relationships. The government consequent on this contract had the function of providing, on the basis of legitimacy backed up by force, the social environment in which exchange could flourish. It became the umpire of the catallactic game, policing the avenues of commerce.

Over the centuries different contributors to the contractarian tradition elaborated and embellished different parts of the story. The threat of individual life and limb which prevailed in the ungoverned "state of nature" was, for example, a peculiarly Hobbesian emphasis. John Locke and, after him, Adam Smith, focused on the preservation of property and the regulation of exchange which the contract offered. Although he all too often appears nowadays disguised by differential calculus, the human agent modeled by contemporary neoclassical economics can also be identified as originating within the contractarian tradition. *Homo economicus* holds private rights, he exercises the prerogative of free choice, and his dealings with others are thus catallactic in essence. This view of social structure and, *pari passu*, of government, is recognizable in the "minimal state" theories of modern philosophers such as Robert Nozick (1974).

It is important to appreciate that the definition of government in this contractarian model goes hand in hand with the identification of its function. Following the logic of the contract, a government is an institution whose will is sovereign over the will of any one individual or that of any coalition of individuals. It follows that, in secular societies at least, such a government must be in possession of the means of violence, given that violence forms the ultimate mundane sanction. Any government that did not monopolize the means of violence would not remain the government for long, because it would be supplanted by a coalition exercising superior power. Defense and internal policing must accordingly become the necessary and sufficient economic functions of a government in such a social structure. This logic applies even in Nozick's "ultraminimal state," in which the defense of the polity does not necessarily *have* to be provided. However, if it is provided, it has to be provided by government, citizens being at liberty to opt out of being defended.

As R. A. Musgrave and A. T. Peacock (1967) have appreciated, the economic analysis of government in the contractarian economy simply involves the establishment of criteria under which the citizenry pays for defense and policing services. In the nineteenth century, the favored criterion became taxation according to "ability to pay," translated by John Stuart Mill into "taxation so as to inflict equal sacrifice." Within the liberal economic tradition, there was accordingly no need to consider the benefits of government spending whose existence was dictated by necessity.

From the end of the nineteenth century onward, economists began to consider seriously whether the appropriate economic role of government might actually be larger than the role suggested by the "minimal state" model. Adolph Wagner (1883), for example, gave notice of the replacement of private economic activity by collective organization, observable historically. This he took to be indicative of a "law of increasing expansion of public, and particularly state, activities" (p. 8). At the time of the identification of this "law," economists were not particularly well equipped to understand why government provision should necessarily represent a form of economic organization superior to the market. Wagner's case seems to have rested strongly on notions of the necessary complementarity and interdependence of public and private activities throughout the process of economic development and on the possibility that state employees would be in receipt of nonpecuniary remuneration (honors and job security), making them cheaper to employ and thus more cost-effective. In more recent times, however, economists have come up with an impressive list of "market failures," theoretically plausible sets of circumstances for which it can be demonstrated that purely catallactic outcomes are neither collectively nor, most importantly, individually optimal. Prime candidates in this respect would be:

1. Decreasing cost production, where Pareto-optimal marginal cost pricing can only be attained under loss-making conditions.
2. Cases of the production of commodities with public characteristics (nonrivalness and nonexcludability).
3. Cases in which the consequences of bilateral contracting between individuals impinge on nonconsenting third parties (externalities or spillovers).
4. Instances in which individuals run the risk of making the wrong decision owing to imperfect information.
5. Circumstances whereby micro-level rational decisions induce suboptimal macro-outcomes, implying the desirability of supra-individual economic management.
6. When the distribution of income derived from exchange is deemed unjust under nonmarket-based ethical criteria (Bator, 1960; Whynes and Bowles, 1981).

Whether or not these possibilities are empirically relevant depends on the historical context of the society in question. Even so, modern Wagnerians would presumably wish to attribute the phenomenal growth of the public sector in nominal market economies to the accumulation of market failures—technological, economic, and social changes have all given rise to problems that cannot be resolved by market allocation and that are accordingly the proper responsibilities of governments. Thus, it might be argued that technical progress has generated more and more externalities requiring regulation, that the rapid development of capitalism in an international context necessitates government support for industry and overall economic direction, while the decline of traditional support structures such as the family means that the state is obliged to take charge of individual risk management (Self, 1985).

The belief that government now possesses more than simple definitional functions adds a further dimension to the analysis of public finance. Equitable taxation can no longer be reduced to the question of ability to pay because, most likely, individuals will benefit or lose differentially from any given government policy. Such a policy, be it a prohibition or the provision of a particular level of supply, will normally apply equally to all, and citizens will therefore be, in A. Breton's phrase, "coerced" (Breton, 1974). The individual's demand for public activity is therefore a function both of the net cost or net benefit of the activity to that individual and of the share of the costs that other individuals are willing to incur in order that the activity might be undertaken. Governments supply, and tax, according to such demands.

We thus arrive at a simple conclusion, namely, that the economic functions of government are those which citizens are willing to pay for. Unfortunately, this argument itself poses a further problem, as was recognized some time ago by Knut Wicksell (1896):

If the individual is to spend his money for private and public uses so that his satisfaction is maximised, he will obviously pay nothing whatsoever for public purposes. . . . Whether he pays much or little will affect the scope of public services so slightly, that for all practical purposes he himself will not notice it at all. Of course, if everyone were to do the same, the state would soon cease to function (p. 81).

The resolution of what is nowadays termed the free-rider problem is, as Wicksell recognized, essentially political. The resolution requires, first, that all public spending decisions be also taxation decisions, that is, expenditure programs cannot be initiated without consulting citizens over their shares of the cost. Second, "provided the expenditure in question holds out any prospect at all of creating utility exceeding cost, it will always be theoretically possible, and approximately so in practice, to find a distribution of costs such that all parties regard the expenditure as beneficial and may therefore approve it unanimously" (pp. 89–90).

Let us pause for a moment and consider whether our argument has rested on the correct premise. The contractarian approach is founded on methodological individualism, government being established to serve private interests in a public fashion. Suppose, however, society is not so structured. Suppose there exists, as H. Ritschi (1931) believed, a parallel dimension of community, a dimension of nonmarket values. Human needs in such a dimension are collective and are met collectively:

between the community and its members there is no reckoning of what is given and what received, no specific compensation nor any excogitation of general rewards. For the means needed for common purposes and aims, the public economy appeals to the citizens' spirit of sacrifice and demands their property and life without reward. . . . The contributions and obligations must be legally determined and laid down (p. 240).

A communal model of economic organization is represented, in more recent times, by the work of social administration theorists such as Richard Titmuss (1970).

Economic agents in these two worlds clearly have quite dissimilar characteristics. However, what seems particularly intriguing about the two approaches is that, in order to identify the appropriate tasks of government, both require an essentially constitutional theory of the state. Both concede that governments might initiate any given economic policy provided that the decisions are reached in the proper procedural fashion. The issue in either case is therefore one of political legitimacy. It accordingly follows that the fundamental economic role of government is whatever the citizens of a legitimate state will sanction.

Thus far, our thinking has been theoretical. Let us accordingly confront these theories with the reality of modern government in capitalist economies; here we encounter a most substantial problem. As A. J. Simmons (1979) persuasively argues, the logic of political obligation in historical societies is tenuous. With the exception of interindividual bonds established via contract (for instance, the deliberations within the Rawlsian "original position"—Rawls, 1971), "citizens generally have no special political bonds which require that they obey and support the governments of their countries of residence" (p. 192). The conventional arguments for legitimacy, such as tacit consent *a la* Locke, the principle of fair play, natural duty, and Socratic notions of gratitude—all are found wanting when tested. This realization is consistent with the principle adopted by Wicksell. Moreover, it holds true, it seems to me, even if one accepts, say, Rousseau's strong assertion that social decisions are always superior to individual ones, because such superiority is itself a function of the legitimacy of the manner in which such decisions are made (Rousseau, 1968). Citizens of modern states do not, with rare exceptions, enter such states as a result of bilateral contract. In consequence, the citizen's acceptance of a political system or a government economic policy is an essentially pragmatic, as opposed to a principled, decision; it is one based, in R. P. Wolff's phrase, on "prudential self-interest" (Wolff, 1970, p. 18).

A further problem results from the realization that government resolutions of market failure are not, in themselves, costless. First, governments are personal, not impersonal, institutions. They comprise a relatively small elite granted, even within the minimal state context, a substantial amount of power. As Thomas Hobbes appreciated, the granting of power to individuals does not carry with it the guarantee of prudent or socially optimal usage. Second, the political structures of modern industrialized economies are oligarchic. This was recognized at the turn of the century by the "heirs of Machiavelli"—Vilfredo Pareto, Gaetano Mosca, and Robert Michels (Hughes, 1967)—and has since been given substance by the work of public choice theorists in the wake of A. Downs (1957). In economic terms, oligarchy translates to oligopoly, implying limited scope for consumer sovereignty in the political marketplace. Third, the bureaucratic form of policy implementation in modern states facilitates rent-seeking on the part of the bureaus themselves (Niskanen, 1971), bureaucrats becoming analagous to Ricardian landowners in their control of the "means of administration." Factors such as these lead modern liberal economists such as J. M. Buchanan (1977) to conclude that "a significant . . . part of the observed growth in the public sector can be explained only by looking at the motivations of those who secure direct personal gains from government expansion" (p. 6). Fourth, an element of the fundamental logic of government intervention can be called into question by accepting the Austrian interpretation of governments as having no gifts of foresight beyond those accorded to other groups within society. Thus, Hayek states: "If man is not to do more harm than good in his efforts to improve the social order, he will have to learn that . . . where essential complexity of an organized kind prevails, he cannot acquire the full knowledge which would make mastery of the events possible" (Littlechild, 1986, p. 79). Finally, in the absence of consent, individual responses to government policies can be strategic. Unless policy policing is total, economic agents can respond to government initiatives found privately unfavorable by actions that might, *in extremis*, vitiate the government's action.

Citizens of all democracies are presumably concerned that their governments are both legitimate and efficient. This proposition would appear to follow regardless of ideology as long as one retains some premise of accountability. (In a society where a specific government gains its legitimacy simply by virtue of its being the government, its role, functions, powers, and relative efficiency would not be the subject of debate). However, from what has been discovered thus far, neither legitimacy nor efficiency can be regarded as probable descriptors of contemporary governments. This being the case, what are the options?

Regarding the growth of the state as a problem leads liberal economists at least to argue that governments, and therefore the problem, should be made as small as possible. Defining "smallness" is no simple matter, however. Restricting the volume of resources controlled by government without doubt weakens the government's impact and acts to minimize potential inefficiencies. On the other hand, a small state (in expenditure terms) can still be powerful if its strength is exercised through regulation rather than provision. In terms of intrusions on the citizen's lifestyle, it is not immediately clear that, say, the public provision of health care represents greater government strength than legislation governing land or motor vehicle use. Liberal states can be rendered totalitarian purely as a result of legislation and policing; in equivalent fashion, there is no requirement that collectivist states require the central provision of goods as part of their definition of collectivism. Pleas for attaining smallness in expenditure terms also appear to ignore all the factors that have made governments large in the modern period. Being essentially mythological, the contractarian model fails to encompass the historical dynamics of the accumulation of state power, a process that appears difficult to reverse.

These matters notwithstanding, there seems no reason to believe that a small government is what any particular society would want. Even under Wicksell's formulation, citizens might be democratically disposed toward granting a legitimate government a considerable degree of responsibility for resource management. The point at issue *vis-à-vis* liberal economics is the conflation of outcome and procedure—in that a government, it is held, acts against people's interests if follows that its influence ought to be minimized. In truth, however, the argument is not one of outcomes (economics) but one of procedures (politics), that is, of deriving a legitimate means for articulating preferences. A legitimate government can do anything that it, and the citizens, want it to.

What might be concluded from these reflections on the fundamental economic role of government? In the first place, the long-recognized distinction between the twin functions of government—as a regulator to police exchange and as a provider in cases of market failure—seems valid. Second, in the real world pragmatics determine all. If one is predisposed toward seeing both markets and governments as imperfect methods of resource allocation, then the choice between the two is determined by the extent to which the practical performance of either is likely to depart from an optimum. At its simplest this amounts almost to an article of faith—would one prefer to entrust one's welfare to a private entrepreneur or a government employee? Finally, the nub of the theoretical argument is constitutional. The concept of the proper role of government presupposes a proper determination of government. Such a proposition is not, of course, an invitation to inefficiency because citizens certainly have an interest in seeing their resources well employed. The issue, however, is not whether certain sections of the economy should be privately or publicly operated a priori but whether the specific government, together with its policies, is held legitimate in the eyes of the citizens. If it is, it can potentially do anything; if not, it should clearly do nothing.

REFERENCES

Bator, F. M. *The Question of Government Spending*. New York: Harper & Row, 1960.

Breton, A. *The Economic Theory of Representative Government*. Chicago: Aldine. 1974.

Buchanan, J. M. "Why Does Government Grow?" In T. E. Borcherding (ed.), *Budgets and Bureaucrats: The Sources of Government Growth*. Durham, N.C.: Duke University Press, 1977, pp. 3–18.

Downs, A. *An Economic Theory of Democracy*. New York: Harper & Row, 1957.

Hughes, H. S. *Consciousness and Society*. London: Macgibbon & Kee, 1967.

Littlechild, S. C. *The Fallacy of the Mixed Economy*. 2d ed. London: IEA Hobart Paper 80, 1986.

Musgrave, R. A., and A. T. Peacock (eds.) *Classics in the Theory of Public Finance*. London: Allen & Unwin, 1967.

Niskanen, W. A. *Bureaucracy and Representative Government*. Chicago: Aldine-Atherton, 1971.

Nozick, R. *Anarchy, State and Utopia*. Oxford: Basil Blackwell, 1974.

Rawls, J. *A Theory of Justice*. Cambridge, Mass.: Harvard University Press, 1971.

Ritschl, H. "Communal Economy and Market Economy." In Musgrave and Peacock, pp. 233–41.

Rousseau, J.-J. *The Social Contract*. London: Dent, 1968. (First published Paris, 1762.)

Self, P. *Political Theories of Modern Government, Its Role and Reform*. London: Allen & Unwin, 1985.

Simmons, A. J. *Moral Principles and Political Obligations*. Princeton, N.J.: Princeton University Press, 1979.

Titmuss, R. H. *The Gift Relationship*. London: Allen & Unwin, 1970.

Wagner, A. "Three Extracts on Public finance." In Musgrave and Peacock, pp. 1–15.

Whynes, D. K., and R. A. Bowles. *The Economic Theory of the State*. Oxford: Martin Robertson, 1981.

Wicksell, K. "A New Principle of Just Taxation." In Musgrave and Peacock, pp. 72–118.

Wolff, R. P. *In Defense of Anarchism*. New York: Harper & Row, 1970.

25

Diverse Approaches to the Economic Role of Government: An Interpretive Essay

Warren J. Samuels

I. INTRODUCTION

This chapter interprets and integrates the foregoing efforts to identify the most important aspects of the economic role of government. Section I presents certain preliminary materials; Section II identifies and interprets the themes that pervade the contributions; and Section III presents the conclusions.

Economic policy—the economic functioning of government—is not solely an intellectual matter. Intellectual elements abound in the making of economic policy, but that process is largely the exercise of power, selective perception, and belief (ideology), political psychology and mobilization, and so on. To Vilfredo Pareto, policy was, in modern language, a function of three sets of variables: power, psychology, and knowledge. Each is a function of the other and, especially, of the belief used to manipulate psychology in order to influence power and, thereby, policy.

Two types of theories and models are found in the social sciences and related fields: conflict and harmony. Analysts who prefer a harmony model of the economy and society often apply a conflict model to government whereas conflict theorists apply their approach to both government and the rest of society.

Policy is in part a matter of the definition of reality, with reality especially defined both in terms of and with regard to the economic operations of government. Economists, political scientists, and others have attempted to make sense of the functions of government, contributing thereby to the definition of reality and to the policymaking process, the latter if only indirectly. John Stuart Mill, for example, distinguished between the *necessary* and the *optional* functions of government. Gabriel Almond, a political comparativist, concluded that every political system performs five functions: political socialization, political recruitment, interest articulation, interest aggregation, and political communication. Carl Auerbach, a lawyer, identified three functions of law in society: the allocation of decision-making power between the nominally private and public spheres, and within the private sphere, and the adjustment of conflicting claims. Robert Solo, a political economist, has also identified three functions of government, but they are very differently formulated: the ordinary, or housekeeping, function, for example, national defense, police, and fire protection; the compensatory or offset function, whereby government attempts to adjust or correct for problems originating in other spheres, for example, unemployment and inflation; and a planning–programming function, in which government organizes activities and finances private enterprise in certain areas, such as the NASA space program.

Two characteristics of these taxonomies are, first, the need to distinguish analytically between the general formulation of a function and the attribution or determination of substantive content thereto; and second, the importance of the decision-making process through which is determined, first, that a function will indeed be undertaken and, second, of what precisely it will consist. It is an important matter, for example, for government to assume a conscious macroeconomic stabilization function; it is quite another important matter for government to determine the relative importance of protection against unemployment and against inflation.

A variety of different approaches to the economic role of government have been followed. Indeed, it is likely that any individual's view thereof is a composite of several of these approaches. The principal approaches may be briefly identified as follows.

1. *Government as an exogenous black box*: Government is perceived as operating outside or above the economy, operating perfectly and without having to make decisions. What it does is a matter of how the black box is internally programmed. Government is outside the economy, above economic conflicts and the messiness of human decision making, automatically producing the correct and best possible result or solution. Too know ''government'' one would have to penetrate the black box, which is exceptionally recondite and impenetrable. Thus, government can and indeed must be accepted as such; one does not have to worry about decision making, for it is automatic, correct, and above politics.

2. *Government as a neutral extension or aggregation of private choice:* Government is not outside the system, but it is nonetheless neutral, above the fray of economic conflict. Government serves as a neutral aggregation process through which private choices are made and aggregated, with government not imposing its own preconceived solutions to problems. To know and understand what government does, one has only to study the exercise of private choice, as government gives effect to the totality of such choices.

3. *Government as a nonneutral decision-making or preference-aggregating process*: Government is seen as an extension of private choice, an arena in which private choices are in part made and aggregated, but one in which the results of aggregation are themselves a matter of the exercise of choice in structuring and conducting government. Government is not neutral because, through the exercise

of past and other present choices, it has been structured to favor certain interests and outcomes rather than others. Government channels decision making or preference aggregation because it has been (re)formed to do so. Different governmental power structures produce generally different structure-specific policies or problem solutions.

4. *Government as an instrument of the powerful*: Government is within the system and not neutral, being rather a tool of those at the top of a hierarchic structure. What government does is dependent on the uses for which the powerful choose to employ it. There is close interdependence between government and the powerful: Among other things, the powerful use government to establish, reinforce, and extend their hegemony; and government both functions selectively to determine the powerful and depends for its authority on the legitimacy accorded by the powerful. Property, for example, is thus the already established interests that certain persons or groups have had secured as such through government. Property is protected not because it is property, but property is property because it is protected; and government is the process that determines which interests will be protected.

5. *Government as an instrument with which to check the power of the powerful*: Government is seen as open to the interests of the otherwise powerless, for example, those without property. Government is recognized to be a means of reinforcing the power of the already powerful, whose power may well have been and indeed likely was the result of other, past actions of government. It is also seen as a means by which the power of the already powerful is checked in the interests of those who are otherwise relatively powerless, perhaps in the name of new conceptions of justice, perhaps a wider definition of individualism or of freedom, and so on. New forms of property rights, or their equivalents, arise as the power of older rights is checked and protection newly given to other interests, which become property because they too are protected.

6. *Government as the source of problems, if not of evil, in society*: Government is identified not as the solution to a problem(s) but as either generating or constituting the problem itself. Others might perceive government as controversial because intractable socioeconomic problems tend to become matters of government policy, and because government has to make choices and thereby generates the problems and incurs the ill will consequent to the opportunity costs its choices entail. Advocates of this view, however, contemplate that without government the problems themselves would not exist.

7. *Government as the source of progress*: Government is identified as perhaps the principal means through which solutions to problems are worked out and the conditions or the substance of whatever is taken to constitute progress is achieved. Instead of no good, and only bad, being associated with government, here that which is perceived as good is attributed to government. Instead of using the term *politician* pejoratively, here it is used honorifically. Government is seen, perhaps as part of the problem (for example, through

past misuse of government), but also and most certainly as a means of solving the problem.

8. *Government as part of the necessary framework of the market*: The market-plus-framework approach is probably the dominant paradigm in the disciplines of history, philosophy, law, and the social sciences, including economics. It maintains that the market exists within a framework of legal and nonlegal institutions that both form and work through the market. By government or law is meant all the institutions and processes of government; by nonlegal institutions is meant custom, mores, religion, morality, and so on. At least four distinctive analytical problems arise with the market-plus-framework approach, problems on which individual formulations of the approach take positions: (a) the conceptual separability of "market" and "framework:" (b) the relative weight to be given to the legal and nonlegal elements of the framework: (c) the static versus dynamic character of the framework, that is, the role to be given to legal and/or nonlegal social control as a mode of change of the framework itself; and (d) the coherence of any distinction between "framework filling" and other, "nonframework filling," "particularistic interventions" by government.

Characteristics similar to those attributed earlier to the taxonomies of government function also apply here: (1) The necessity to distinguish analytically between the general formulation of an approach and the attribution of substantive content thereto. (2) The importance of the decision-making process by which are determined, first, that a particular approach will indeed be followed and, second, of what precisely the approach will consist. It is one very important matter, for example, to recognize the necessity, indeed inexorability, of the legal framework of the market; it is quite another and very important matter to determine whether the antitrust laws or certain alterations of the law of property constitute framework-filling legal change of law or pejorative particularistic interventions. It is one matter to identify government as a preference-aggregation process; it is quite another and a very important matter to identify the preferences as well as the processes by which preferences are (re)formed and (re)aggregation takes place. In all these and still other matters, the operation of selective perception is paramount, for example, as to precisely what about the economically relevant actions of government is "inexorable"—as are also the forces at work in society influencing the practice and direction of selective perception. In all these and still other matters, as with the several taxonomies of government functions, substantive content must be worked out—even to that which is attributed to government as either an exogenous black box or a neutral extension of private choice.

Sections II and III discuss the so-called legal-economic nexus, the social space wherein the details of both economy and polity are formed. Four models identify and locate in such a context certain fundamental aspects of the economically relevant actions of government, certain processes in which government willy nilly is involved, models to which in practice the principle of selective perception also applies.

Model 1

Consider the representation of the economic process given by the conventional diagram in which the production possibility curve is juxtaposed to an actual social welfare function to yield at the point of tangency the putative socially optimal allocation. There are at least four processes at work underlying this diagram about which conventional practice makes restrictive assumptions, assumptions about things which in practice must be worked out. In making these assumptions, economists both limit and channel their results, but in the real world government is involved willy nilly in each of the four processes. The four processes are those by which (1) the values on the axes, (2) the shape and location of the production possibility curve, (3) individual preferences, and (4) power structure are worked out.

The four processes may be discussed as follows: First, the process by which is determined which values (commodities or goals) are to be represented on the axes, the values between which choice has to be made. When a politician states that ''such-and-such is the issue in this election,'' he or she is in effect endeavoring both to get a particular value on the social agenda and to have it weighed heavily relative to a competing value(s).[1] The values dealt with are worked out through markets, private and group choice, and politics, that is, in part through government.

Second is the process by which is determined the shape and location of the production possibility curve, which governs the tradeoffs that have to be made. Economists have not studied this matter extensively, though they understand that both shape and location are influenced by population size, quality of the work force, quantity and quality of natural resources, level of technology, and so on— factors that change and are themselves in some or many respects a matter of policy. Consider the production possibility curve relating price stability and employment levels. Whatever governs the empirical Phillips curve tradeoffs will help govern the slope and location of this production possibility curve. Among the factors governing the empirical Phillips curve are inflationary expectations (and whatever governs them), the relationship between employment security and productivity, the relative power of managements and workers in arriving at wage rates, central bank money supply policy, other government policies, and the pricing practices of business-people.

Third and fourth, inasmuch as the actual social welfare function (in contrast to one assumed by the analyst) is the product of individual preferences weighted by power structure, are the processes by which, first, individual preferences and, second, power structure are formed.[2] Economists have not studied either process very much, but in order to reach determinate solutions they make assumptions as to how these processes—and the values ensconced within them—work out. Individual preferences are formed and reformed on the basis of experience and subjective perception of experience, encompassing both socializing and individuating processes. The power structure is not given once and for all time. It too is formed and reformed, in part through processes endogenous to the economy narrowly defined and in part through broader processes.[3] In each respect, government is involved.

These four processes are truly fundamental economic processes. They also interact with each other. In the case of each process and its interaction, government is involved. These processes are at the heart of the legal-economic nexus.

Model 2

Consider the usual context in which the concept of opportunity cost in economic analysis is conducted: choice from within a given opportunity set. Economists properly and usefully tend to assume that economic agents know their interests and act so as to promote them: the rationality assumption. The foregoing analysis of the social welfare function has highlighted the process, neglected by the simple rendering of the rationality assumption, by which preferences are formed. However, economists also tend implicitly to assume that individuals will practice constrained maximization *within their opportunity sets*; in other words, they will assume *given* opportunity sets. In so doing, assumptions are made about what in the real world has to be worked out. The fact is that individual opportunity sets are the product of an extraordinarily complex set of interacting processes—and government is an important, indeed intrinsic, part of these processes, as both a dependent and independent variable.

The problematic, process character of opportunity sets is indicated by the following model, which applies to the economy and to all two- or *n*-party decision-making situations. Let Alpha be an individual economic agent and Beta either another individual agent or the sum of all other agents. An opportunity set by definition is comprised of all the operative alternatives available to the individual actor and between which he or she can choose. The respective opportunity sets of Alpha and Beta are the result, for present purposes, of three sets of processes: power, self-choice, and interaction. Each opportunity set is a function, first, of power: participation in decision making and the bases of that participation, such as legal rights. Included within power in the form of rights may be the right to attempt to have government (courts, legislature, executive) change the relative rights of Alpha and Beta. But overall one's opportunity set is derived from one's power in the form of rights, for example, one's wealth or property.

The development of one's opportunity set over time is a function of the choices one makes at various points in time from within one's opportunity sets as they exist at those points in time. The quality of one's portfolio decisions, for example, will affect one's income and wealth and thereby *pro tanto* one's future opportunity set. There is an interaction between legal social control and one's decisions insofar as the path of one's opportunity set is concerned. Thus, insofar as knowledge is a basis of power, legal control over the use in trading of insider knowledge will affect one's choices and thereby one's future opportunity set. Given one's rights, knowledge, persuasive ability, and so on, however, the range and content of one's future opportunity set will depend on one's substantive choices in the present and how they come to fruition in the future.

Third, one's opportunity set is also a function of the choices of others. When Alpha makes choices within his or her opportunity set, these choices can have an impact, either positive or negative, on the opportunity set of Beta, and vice versa with regard to the impact of Beta's choices on Alpha's opportunity set. One can call this mutual coercion, defined as the impact of others' choices on one's opportunity set and of one's choices on others' opportunity sets. Government, through its decisions concerning the definition, assignment, and use of rights, is a critical factor in the formation of opportunity sets and the exercise and consequences of choice within them. But government itself is an object of the exercise of rights within opportunity sets in order to influence future opportunity sets. Government is both a dependent and an independent variable in the process of forming the structure of opportunity sets. In such manner, government is part of the legal-economic nexus.

Model 3

Consider the problem of order which is defined as the continuing resolution of the conflicts of freedom and control, continuity and change, and hierarchy and equality. "Order" can be defined in terms of particular configurations or resolutions of these conflicts. That is what is done by making assumptions in order to generate particular solutions in the context of the foregoing models. One can alternatively focus on the processes involved in working out the three conflicts, including the subtleties involved in their ongoing resolution. Moreover, it is true both that government is involved in the ongoing working out of solutions to the three conflicts comprising the problem of order and that the problem of order applies to government itself. These matters are worked out in the legal-economic nexus.

Model 4

Consider a broader model, in which the economic process is understood as producing policy, that is, effective choices, and policy is explicated as a function of power, knowledge, and psychology variables, perhaps as developed by Pareto. Each of the three is a set of diverse variables that can be variously modeled, and the three interact. The point is the same: given that the economy comprises, or can be understood and analyzed as comprising, such a complex and kaleidoscopic process, government is involved in the (re)production of power, psychological states, and knowledge (belief), as both an independent and dependent variable, that is, as both cause and consequence.

Resident within each of the foregoing models is the evolution of the power or rights structure of the economy. There is, like it or not, no question of establishing the power structure once and for all time; nor is there any question of establishing the legal foundations of the economy (rights and so on) once and for all time. Both are subject to redetermination and are continually being worked out. The power structure is revised in part through private trade and its Pareto-optimal results, and the legal foundations thereof are altered through legal change of legal rights. It is only by foreclosing both the evolution of power structure and the related dynamics of legal change (for example, by assuming the status quo and, in some cases, pejoratively treating the processes governing legal change as "intervention" and "rent seeking") that government can be dismissed and ignored—either creating or reinforcing exceptionally narrow and misleading understandings of power and of the dynamics of legal change. However, this foreclosure is rarely total; in practice, it is highly selective. The belief or pretense that government is unimportant, ineffective, or immoral is almost always selective. As such, it is part of the process of inevitably selective legal change; it is part of the processes that mark the legal-economic nexus.

II. ANALYSIS OF THE CONTRIBUTIONS

The foregoing contributed chapters clearly and unequivocally demonstrate the multiplicity of different perspectives that can be had on government at what is intended to be the most fundamental level. The fact of this diversity is itself suggestive. Because there always are alternative perspectives, one must be rather diffident in accepting as final and conclusive what any one writer says. Moreover, the different approaches taken by the various writers can collectively and in juxtaposition to each other enable us to penetrate more deeply into the most fundamental questions, processes, and issues pertaining to the economic role of government but without any necessary conclusivity.

As my own chapter should be taken to suggest, one must be especially wary about the language used in discussing the economic role of government. Consider the phrase used in the title and logic of this volume: "the economic role of government." It seems to define reality in terms of two entities, two subsectors, or two processes, each having an independent and otherwise autonomous existence, the economy and the polity. The implication is that whatever the economic role of government may be, the economy is, or is otherwise (a weaker position but in the same direction), self-subsistent and independent of government, and vice versa. My chapter espouses a contrary view, namely, the existence of a more fundamental legal-economic nexus in which certain behavior is simultaneously legal and economic, in which the two nominally different processes are really aspects of one fundamental process, or in which there is a sphere in which the two processes come together, and thereby qualifies the meaningfulness of any idea of the self-subsistent existence of either economy or polity.

The central element of this legal-economic nexus is *governance* in the sense of a process in which important decisions are made, whether by legislatures, courts, and/or administrative agencies; or by giant manufacturing corporations, cartels, trade associations, pension funds, major banks, and so on; or by alliances of governmental institutions and private organizations. One can speak, then, of private property as manifesting a disaggregation of sovereignty; and of "private government" and "public government" in which the key in certain respects is the division of power between what is nominally private and public, and in other respects the practices of governance per se. In other words, when considering the loci of important decision making, one cannot restrict analysis solely to official government. On the other hand, whether one affirms two separate but interactive processes or one process with two aspects is a matter of modeling design and should not necessarily be taken to be conclusively descriptive of the real legal-economic world—though it is often compelling to do so!

Let us now examine and interpret the contributed chapters, in part to discern what they may be taken to mean—with due regard to the evident fact that different writers attempting this interpretive task likely would discern different lessons and produce different interpretive results. This is a matter of both infinite regress and the hermeneutic circle: infinite regress, inasmuch as interpretation can always be further interpreted (or deconstructed); the hermeneutic circle, because interpretation inexorably presumes its own foundation. Our task is to undertake interpretation carefully, while not pretending to conclusivity. Finally, I must apologize in advance for any misinterpretation or misapplication in this chapter of the contents of any of the contributions to this collection.

1. Government Is Important

Perhaps every author recognizes, if not emphasizes, the critical importance of government in the organization and control (in the structure, operation, and performance) of the economy. This is true for those who see both good and bad in government, for those who do not take decidedly normative positions on government, and for those who are generally negative about government (albeit typically for somewhat different reasons; contrast William M. Dugger and Dwight R. Lee, for example). Citing the critical importance of government as recognized in these chapters would be trite except for the pronounced tendency of the dominant Western ideology to treat government in negative terms, as something bad, perhaps at best a necessary evil; as ineffective if not dysfunctional; as unimportant except insofar as it misbehaves and is dysfunctional; and, *inter alia*, as a danger to freedom.

The chapter by Lee argues for a necessary role for ideology in the limitation of government power. It thereby affirms the putative importance of government, whether or not one likes what it does. In contrast, John E. Elliott, contrary to one version of Locke, is tempted to conclude that government is integral, rather than external, to the economy—that is, government is important in ways which the minimalist doctrine either neglects or obfuscates.

Neva Makgetla and Robert B. Seidman employ Dorner's taxonomy of theories that analyze how decisions come about within existing institutions and theories that call in question those very institutions. After a detailed exploration of the legal-economic nexus, they affirm the inexorable importance of government in economic affairs. They argue that every law or regulation delegates power, so that a key issue that arises is to whom and how should the legal order delegate a particular power? Because government ineluctably and pervasively intervenes, the issue is not whether it should nor in what arenas, but in whose favor it should intervene and in what form. (The reader will note my personal displeasure with models or terminology that use the concept of intervention, for the reason given above. But the term is used, and editors must be faithful to their contributors' conceptualizations, even when questioning them, especially when the authors were given complete freedom of expression.)

2. Close Empirical Description

Several authors work at a descriptive level very close to what they consider to be the more or less objective facts of empirical experience: James E. Anderson, Tom Bottomore, Jesse Burkhead, C. Lowell Harriss, Irving Louis Horowitz, Vernon W. Ruttan, and Larry L. Wade. (Of course, others, such as Walter Adams and James W. Brock, Dugger, Lee, Samuels, and A. Allan Schmid surely believe that their chapters closely reflect empirical reality.) Although they may be understood as writing within some particular paradigm or to be advancing inexorably theory-laden "descriptions," in comparison with some other authors, whose contributions are intentionally more theoretical or normative, these authors' respective contributions are relatively commonsensical and empirical, largely preferring to deal with description of what they believe actually happens in the economic role of government.

Among the points stressed by these authors are the historical fact of governmental activism in economic affairs, quite independent of ideology, coupled with enormous growth, perhaps more than is generally realized (a nuance drawn by Anderson), though perhaps the overall rate of expansion has slowed down (a query posed by Bottomore). Horowitz traces the ever-expanding role of government in part to what he perceives to be the infinite regress of equity demands, a secular demand for equity. His explanation is somewhat different from that of Lee, who focuses on the adoption of government programs through the activism of ideologues and their expansion through the enlisted interests of beneficiaries. Horowitz also traces the increasing economic role of government to the stagnation of the traditional classes, the expansion of administrative and service sectors, the growth of a huge bureaucratic and appointed class, and impulses to change generated by a mix of social-political-and economic factors (and not simply to demand-supply factors alone).

A further major point concerns the historical relativity of the economic role of government. Bottomore, for example, argues that the extent, nature, and modes of the economic role of government have varied over time and across systems and with the interests of specific social groups, especially classes, as well as with the political complexion of the government in power and historical cultural traditions; that it is therefore an evolutionary phenomenon; and that it requires necessary normative direction, a matter treated separately below.

Burkhead, too, emphasizes both the historical and evolutionary character of the economic role of government. He states that government's economic role is shaped by custom and tradition, though it is also changing owing to shifts in perceptions.

Elliott argues that the economic role of government varies with the historical evolution and circumstances of power and class structure, and is both a cause and consequence of cultural factors. These factors are increasingly classist in nature.

Flynn, whose analysis is particularly important with regard to the idea of a legal-economic nexus, emphasizes that, however modeled, the substantive content of the confluence of economy and polity is profoundly influenced by a society's underlying moral beliefs and cultural values, even though they may be so unrealistic as to be mythic in nature. Flynn emphasizes that an analyst's assumptions and tools will determine what is examined and measured as the "reality" with which government must deal and as government itself.

Harriss likewise stresses the cultural and historical nature of the economic role of government. He uses the framework figure of speech, stressing that resolution of the conflict of continuity with change of the framework is the great problem, and that no type of government policy is inherently fundamental in the sense of always being followed.

With regard to this point, Wade agrees, arguing that circumstances permit few deductions concerning the particular economic roles that governments undertake; and that constitutional government is consistent with a very broad range of economic arrangements, which vary with political culture, social structure, national history, and the level and type of economic development. Makgetla and Seidman also stress political structure.

Although several writers stress the need for close attention to government budgets, several others, for example, Burkhead and Horowitz, hold either explicitly or implicitly that consideration of the literal amounts of government spending by no means exhausts the economic role of government and is indeed perhaps not all that important. Schmid argues that budgets may be substitutes or complements to property and other rights: Some people's opportunities are derived from rights and regulations and others from the budget; and no one source is more or less "interventionist." He particularly stresses the notion that the rules of benefit–cost analysis and of the budgetary process are equivalent to property and other rights insofar as they govern opportunities.

Several other arguably empirical conclusions about the economic role of government appear to be made by many authors and are considered individually later in the chapter: the centrality of power, the necessity for normative direction (arguably, what the question of power is all about), the existence of fundamental dilemmas or conflicts, and the relevance of selective perception. A further conclusion, namely, the existence of a legal-economic nexus, is undoubtedly understood by several writers as grounded in empirically observable reality. But this could itself be adduced to either selective perception or the imposition of theory on facts illustrating one of the principal conclusions of this chapter—that the distinctions between positive and normative and between empirical and theory-laden discussions of the economic role of government are very difficult to draw in any conclusive, dispositive fashion. I stress this conclusion, despite my own strongly held analytical views.

There is therefore an important tension within the arguably empirical orientations: an emphasis on, *inter alia*, the historical and cultural variability of the economic role of government juxtaposed to the presence of some general conclusionary themes. Whether these conclusions are principally empirical or rely on underlying theoretical and/or normative structures is a further example of the interpretive problem noted in the preceding paragraph.

3. Taxonomies of Governmental Roles

Several writers responded to the basis question at least in part by articulating certain fundamental roles of government. Perhaps the most elaborate is that presented by Anderson, who identifies seven basic tasks or purposes constituting the fundamental economic role of government: (1) providing, maintaining and/or protecting the economic infra-structure; (2) various further collective goods and services; (3) conflict resolution and adjustment; (4) competition; (5) natural resources; (6) minimum access by individuals to the output of the economy; and (7) economic stabilization. Anderson also calls attention to the problem of differentiating the fundamental from the merely useful or convenient activities and/or those that serve the interests of particular groups.

Robin W. Broadway distinguishes two roles: collective action (1) to exploit gains from trade and (2) to improve equity.

Bottomore approaches the question of government functions differently, identifying several different levels at which government affects economic life: basic economic institutions, a managerial compensatory function, perceived national economic interests, international organization intervention, and structural change.

Elliott traces, analytically if not historically, the evolution of government functions against a backdrop of the evolution of class society. In the classless first stage of Locke's two stages of the state of nature, Elliott finds government adjudicating or arbitrating relations among individuals and protecting citizens against the threat of external invasion. In the further development of a classless society, perhaps along lines envisioned by Rousseau, government may attempt to prevent extreme inequality and may also attempt to perform certain collective actions as a straightforward community organization.

In Locke's classist second stage in the state of nature, government functions to protect the property of the rich and powerful against the perceived predations of the poor. But government also adjudicates conflicts among members of the ruling class, and protects the lives and liberties of all members of society against internal or external aggression. It may also engage in certain collective activities, such as the provision of public works. It may attend to common problems posed by the particular stage of economic development; policies clearly in the interest of the capitalist class as a whole; and policies that run counter to the interests of some components of the capitalist class, but that are essential to the long-run preservation of the private property system (all clearly a matter of selective perception). It does not, however, adjudicate between the owning and nonowning classes. Thus, according to Elliott, conservative defense of propertied interests often goes hand in hand with an economically active government.

Finally, in Elliott's view, a more complex set of functions is possible: protecting the property of the propertied, protecting the life and liberty of individuals of all classes, acting as impartial umpire among individuals and classes, and regulating (though not redistributing) property. Central is the transformation from adjudicating among the propertied class (and defending their interests against the nonpropertied) to adjudicating between the propertied and the nonpropertied. This last stage is due to the democratic revolution and features, in part, tensions between the efforts of the propertied to use government to obtain a more favorable distribution of wealth (as they have been doing all along) and the efforts by some to have government at least partly independent from social class relationships and economic circumstances in performing its economic functions—and the efforts by some to use government for redistributionist goals of a contrary kind.

Harriss identifies such functions as protection against domestic coercion of person and property and against outside enemies, provision of a facilitative framework and an economic infrastructure, promotion of competition, and, increasingly, alleviation of misery.

Horowitz has a somewhat different orientation, centering on defense and the praetorian guard of the ruling class versus the benefactor of the working masses, an orientation quite different from the more typical paradigm of liberal democratic states per se.

A quite different approach is that of James D. Shaffer, who first distinguishes between government involvement in the articulation of preferences and the organization of production and next identifies four generic functions of government: providing procedures for making rules, definitions of entitlements to output, rules for coordinating economic activity, and rules defining jurisdictional boundaries.

Somewhat similarly, Richard W. Tresch argues that two fundamental questions are involved in working out the economic role of government: what economic functions should government perform, and what economic decision rules should public officials follow in each area?

Also employing a very different approach is Dugger, who distinguishes between the predatory and parasitic operations of government, understood to be those in favor of the haves; and productive operations, in favor of the have-nots. The first is exemplified by the corporate state, and the second by the welfare state.

In the case of all these general articulations and taxonomies of governmental economic functions, it remains true that the substantive content thereof needs to be worked out. A good example of this point is Harriss's emphasis that a classic, fundamental function of government is protection of person and property but that "protection of property" is not a simple, clearcut matter, a point also made by Samuels, Schmid, and Shaffer. Shaffer also insists that government must be understood as a process of instituting the political economy and thus as a matter of power and conflict resolution, not as something static. Many writers seem to hold views congruent with Wade when he argues that government as such has few absolutely necessary economic functions and that its economic policy is a by product of power.

Several writers also identify sets of paradigmatic theories or philosophies of the economic role of government. Welfare economics is one such approach explicitly utilized by several authors (discussed separately below). (Boadway identifies within it three different approaches to using interpersonal welfare comparisons as a framework for decision making: social welfare function, property rights, and contractarian. He also distinguishes, as do several other writers, market failure and government failure approaches.)

Burkhead contrasts a Smithian noninterventionist from a neoclassical Samuelsonian formalist and interventionistically open approach.

Dugger adopts the dichotomy of predatory-parasitic and productive activities, said to be characteristic of government itself.

Elliott distinguishes between three "faces" or models of Locke: radical, conservative, and liberal, as constituting the analytical ballpark of modern discussion and analysis.

Flynn distinguishes between existentialist, Lockean-Smithian, and Aristotelian-Marxian approaches.

Horowitz uses a general taxonomy of minimalist, pragmatic, and maximilist perspectives.

Makgetla and Seidman present a complex dual taxonomy: three socioeconomic theories of development, namely, supply-side theory, basic needs theory, and socialist theory; and parallel schools of jurisprudence, namely, law and economics, liberal, and institutionalist.

Ruttan distinguishes between two types of argument and their respective theories: self-interest and ethical.

4. Liberal Democracy as General Context

Although several writers, such as Makgetla and Seidman, and Wade, discuss the economic role of government in regard to pluralistic and nonpluralistic, economically developed and nondeveloped, and autocratic and democratic countries, most seem to limit their analysis to liberal democratic states (such as Adams and Brock, Altman, Anderson, Boadway, Hirsch, and Rose, with Lee contrasting, for example, with Adams and Brock and with Dugger as to what constitutes both the nature and the normative problem of democratic states with regard to the economic role of government). Elliott, of course, is analytically more complex: to him, liberal democracy is but one of three Lockean models.

5. Power

Several writers maintain that one of the most fundamental things that can be said about the economic role of government is that it is functional with regard to power, as both a dependent and independent variable. To them the centrality of power is critical to understanding the economic role of government. This theme seems both pervasive and important to the authors themselves and to this writer—so much so that it warrants close attention.

Adams and Brock stress the importance of competition and the potential use of government to either restrict or promote competition. The fundamental problem, as they see it, is how to prevent private concentration of power controlling both the economy and the polity, and yet how to do so without creating an omnipotent government beyond control and accountability. In their view, government is inevitably used to control, abet, and/or ratify the structure of private power. The crux of government, in other words, is its involvement in the power structure and power processes of society.

For Andrew Altman, the relative strength of and relations between economic and political power, and the question of which of the two modes of power is more fundamental, are critical to our subject. One can stress economic power as being dependent on political power, or political as dependent on economic power, both presuming a one-way explanation. Although Altman also calls attention to their combination in what I call a legal-economic nexus, he does stress both that government reinforces and perpetuates the economic power of dominant economic classes and that economic power is an important lever for deploying state power.

One of the more elaborate treatments of the centrality of power, motivated in part by the author's own normative position, is Dugger's. Dugger argues that at the most fundamental level the state has but one function, to exercise power, and it can do so (as noted above) either predatorily or productively. By power Dugger means the ability to get people to do what you want them to do, whether or not they want to do it. To Dugger the state is an arena for power struggle and an instrument for power application. The question is whose interests are to be served by state power. In a manner reminiscent of the perspective that property is not protected because it is property but is property because it is protected, Dugger argues that to say the state has been captured by the vested interests is redundant, for it is the state that vests the interests in the first place. His principal point is that the forms of organized activity which the state decides to legalize, and the forms which it decides to ignore or criminalize, became extremely important in determining who can and cannot exercise power through collective action. The state is much more than a class mechanism, more than a dependent variable in a class equation of power; it is also a wielder of power on its own behalf and in its own right.

Interestingly, Dugger's view is in this respect not in conflict with that of Lee, who argues that power is critical to understanding government and that ideology is critical in either empowering or limiting state power. (I would prefer to say channeling.) Lee finds that ideological sympathy for an active economic role for government undermines the ideological control that the public can exert over government while increasing the need for that control—the importance of which is its implications for social power.

For Elliott, the economic role of government has to be comprehended not only in terms generally of power but also specifically of class. The fundamental difference, in his view, is between societies that are classless, strictly classist, and classist but with government not solely the instrument of the ruling class.

Alexis Jacquemin argues that neither economic performance nor the economic role of government is a matter of natural necessity but of power relations, including efforts by economic actors to modify their environment in their favor.

Makgetla and Seidman focus on law as a determinant of the structure of nominally private power. Every law or regulation delegates power, so that a key issue becomes to whom and how the legal order should delegate a particular power. A parallel proposition states that inasmuch as government ineluctably and pervasively intervenes in the economy, the issue is neither whether it should nor in what arenas but in whose favor to intervene and in what form. A further argument focuses on differential empowerment and the consequent allocation of resources producing the substance taken by economic development.

Shaffer's theme—that government is not static, not a given, but rather the process of instituting the political economy—centers on power and conflict resolution.

Wade neatly encapsulates the ideas of many contributors in his proposition that to understand the economic role of government one must understand power, for example, that economic policy is a byproduct of power.

Similarly, David K. Whynes (among others) contrasts the mythological contractarian model to the historical dynamics of actual state power.

An implication that seems to reverberate throughout most, if not all, the contributed chapters is that social, political, economic, and legal theories often obscure, and often are used to obscure, the fact of power. Thus, they serve as the instruments of decision makers or would-be decision makers who reinforce the lawtaking mentality.

6. Welfare Economic Approach

Not surprisingly, several writers have adopted in whole or part the perspective of applied welfare economics. More remarkably, all these writers stress the inconclusivity of the applied welfare economics approach to the economic role of government.

Anderson does not adopt the approach but levels strong criticism. He says that the widespread use of the theory of market failure is not without utility but that it does not help determine when government action is justified, that it depoliticizes economic problems by treating them as technical failures, whereas they involve strong distributional and other consequences (see below); that it does not help with values other than efficiency; and that because it does little to explain the adoption of the existing set of government policies it is at best a post hoc rationale rather than an explanation.

Boadway adopts the applied welfare economics approach, but he too finds serious fault with it. He finds that the use of hypothetical compensation as a test involves the accrual of losses as well as of gains and thus does not actually constitute a Pareto improvement. The implication is that efficiency alone cannot be the sole test of government policy, in part because of multiple possible Pareto optimal results. Boadway also argues that the property rights approach is presumptive, making existing property rights sacrosanct. He argues principally that government policies must inevitably be of two types: collective action to exploit gains from trade and collective action to improve equity. He concludes with a juxtaposition of public sector failure to market failure, with ensuing ambiguity and inconclusivity of policy implications.

Burkhead makes a number of corollary points (considered later in this chapter). Of present significance is his argument that benefit-cost analyses can be helpful but also positively misleading, as they necessarily involve selective perception and choice regarding whose interests count, for example, in regard to externalities. He also stresses that efficiency measurements are limited especially in regard to their failure to extend to distributional considerations, a matter of great importance because no government programs are distributionally neutral and economists cannot specify a "proper" distribution of income.

An argument comparable to those of Boadway and Burkhead is made by Flynn, who argues that efficiency may be reckoned in terms of either the existing distribution or a redistribution of rights, and that both approaches take positions on the normative status of existing rights or on rights as understood to exist.

Harriss argues that government ipso facto both conveys benefits and imposes losses, the great problem being to determine whether to preserve or to modify the legal framework and its distributional consequences.

Werner Z. Hirsch implicitly challenges the utility of the logic of Pareto optimality in rejecting the view (identified as Platonic) that all significant social questions must have one true answer and that these true answers are compatible with one another and form a single whole. Like a number of other contributors, for example, Schmid, Hirsch argues that the role of economists is to provide information with which decision makers can think about their goals and ends-means relationships and thereby make informed choices, and not to act as either ideologues or advocates. Lee, of course, has a diametrically opposed view of the role of economists.

P.M. Jackson, too, uses the applied welfare economics approach as his analytical framework. Jackson surveys the basic theory of the market, the case for unfettered markets, and the prescription for limited but important economic roles for government, noting that this is conventional for all economists except libertarians, for whom there is no logical foundation for public collective action. His principal argument is that both neoclassical theory and the market solution are incomplete. The economy is in fact non-Walrasian; there is widespread market failure; government allocation and stabilization functions are in fact possible, the governmental redistribution function (the problem of social justice) is central, generating nonunique Pareto optimal results; and there are no once-and-for-all-time answers. The situation is further complicated because of government failure. Economic theory is unable to provide unequivocal answers to questions of policy. In macroeconomics, Jackson also notes, first, that the modern argument for the ineffectiveness of public policy is based on the unrealistic assumptions of a Walrasian economy; and second, that instability is endogenous to the modern capitalist economy, and is not due to government alone. Jackson goes so far as to say that both Pareto efficiency and freedom, as products of the market, are true only for the most trivial and contrived systems.

Jacquemin maintains that the traditional invisible hand and freedom-centered arguments are insufficient against governmental activism in a world of strategic behavior by economic actors who seek to favorably alter their environment, including the behavior of others. The existence of both conventional market failures and strategic behavior severely limits both the neoclassical paradigm and Pareto optimality.

Rose argues that a meaningful political economy implies public policy appraisal by the standards of both political desirability and economic effectiveness. Effectiveness, he states, is a primitive concept in comparison with efficiency; yet a program must be effective before it can be evaluated for efficiency. Moreover, statements about the effectiveness of policy (and presumably their efficiency) are contingent. Richard Rose notes that economists tend to become partisan advocates of efficiency, asking questions about costs and benefits, and suggesting ways of using economic incentives and disincentives to achieve goals more easily and effectively than (for example) by administrative regulation. He also states that they have a commitment to the competitive market as an ideal, but that programs are defended by those who find them efficient and effective to secure their own political or economic ends—thus raising the key question of whose ends are to govern (provide the substance of) efficiency. In the absence of an answer to that question, the concept of efficiency is purely formal, except insofar as the economist adds selective implicit assumptions as to whose interests are to count.

Schmid points out another critical problem of the applied welfare economics approach: that the state is the process by which rights are learned and evolved, such that government is important in forming the rights that govern efficiency rather than in solely facilitating the achievement of a unique efficient result.

Schmid's approach, too, questions the fundamental coherence and conclusivity for policy of the applied welfare economics approach insofar as it begs the question of whose interests are to count through rights of one kind or another.

Tresch somewhat parallels Jackson in adopting the applied welfare economics approach and in surveying its basic components, especially Pareto efficiency, first- versus second-best policy rules, and so on. Consideration of the economic functions of government are fundamentally tried to whether the market can satisfy the interpersonal equity and Pareto optimality conditions. Its failure to do so offers a potential role for government to guide the economy along the paths of equity and efficiency. The problems, however, are, first, that the centrality of interpersonal equity conditions are the Achilles heel of normative public sector economics, because there is no convincing case for any particular social welfare function; and, second, that if narrow self-interest truly dominates policy decisions, only one fundamental economic proposition about the role of government seems possible, namely, that individuals and firms simply use the public sector as a vehicle for increasing their personal utilities and profits. Tresch does not find this proposition very uplifting (but several authors, perhaps especially myself, find it to be analytically and objectively very important). Tresch's analysis, reinforced by that of several other writers, casts serious doubt on the utility and dispositiveness of a corpus of analysis that either presumptively postulates particular policy goals (a particular social welfare function, or whose interests count) or denigrates the use by nominally private economic actors of government as an economic alternative in the search for utility, profit, or other advantage. Perhaps the juxtaposition of categorical assertions of policy goals to pejorative assertions about special interests is an inevitable characteristic of the processes of government—and something "fundamental" about the economic role of government, or about typical discourse pertaining thereto.

Finally, Whynes finds the supply of government to be a function of the demand for government, in part manifesting free-rider behavior. He also notes the Wicksell solution which combines spending and taxing decisions. His analytically more powerful finding, however, is that the fundamental economic role of government is a function of whatever its citizens will sanction.

7. Necessary Normative Direction

If efficiency is recognized to be purely formal, if some decision has to be made as to whose interests are to count, if government does whatever its citizens sanction, and, *inter alia*, if conflicts and ambiguities exist owing to the juxtaposition of putative market failure and putative government failure, then it is not surprising that many contributors explicitly or implicitly conclude that normative direction must necessarily be provided to government, that is, that government policy is neither preordained nor self-subsistent nor the product of an exogenous black box.

The basic point seems to be that whatever specific functions the government is used to performing, both the adoption and the instrumentation thereof requires antecedent normative premises that must somehow be provided. The economic role of government is in fact a normative matter. Various theories of politics or of the economic role of government provide some direction, however selectively and problematically. So do the ordinary processes of law and politics.

For Bottomore, insofar as the economic role of government is to be understood in relation to the interests of specific social groups, including classes, to the extent that these groups or classes dominate government they thereby provide the necessary normative channeling. Elliott delivers essentially the same message.

The same point is made more pointedly by Dugger: The use of the state on behalf of the haves or the have-nots is both important and normative. State power will be used to promote one set of interests or the other, and normative direction is mandatory. In such cases Dugger seems to suspect that the pretense that government is doing the right things, perhaps as an exogenous black box, functions to telescope "is" and "ought" and thereby obfuscates the inexorable introduction of normative premises by those who control the state, typically the haves—who are the haves because they have come to control the state in the first place.

For Flynn, underlying moral beliefs and cultural values are in fact the source or test of the rules controlling the economic role of government. Critical to him are the positions supported with regard to continuity versus change of existing rights or of rights as understood to exist. (There is the already noted question of whether moral beliefs and cultural values are determinants or merely rationalizations of decisions made on the basis of material interests or jockeying for power.)

Harriss recognizes the role of normative direction in determining both the essentials of government activity and the degrees of desirability thereof—for example, whether and how much to support government education, research, and alleviation of misery.

The most intriguing argument is made by Lee, who argues that the role of normative premises in political decision making creates both doubt as to the feasibility of limiting the economic role of government and concern over the consequences of not limiting that role. Because ideology-generated normative premises lead to the adoption of government programs which then, as he sees the matter, become captured and subverted by nonideological special interest groups; and because expanding the economic roles of government increases the need for public control of monitoring, but the programs become more responsive to special interest influence than to public interest concerns; because, in other words, ideological sympathy for an active economic role for government undermines the ideological control that the public can exert over government while simultaneously increasing the need for that control, Lee finds that some significant degree of ideological negativism is necessary to approximate the proper economic role for government. Lee would assert this argument, for example, in the interest of limiting what Jacquemin calls strategic behavior to use government to favorably modify economic actors' environments—though it is imaginable that Jacquemin could find in Lee's argument a pregnant example of precisely that behavior.

The importance of necessary normative direction for government's economic role is affirmed by Ruttan in a quite different way. The case for foreign economic aid requires normative premises, premises that can be and have been criticized from both right and left. The ethical (as distinct from the self-interest) argument for foreign aid underscores the necessity for some philosophical basis of policy and can take the form of one or another theory. For Ruttan normative direction is required to resolve such questions as the appropriate level of assistance, who should receive aid, the form aid is to take, and whether assistance should target institutional reform in the recipient country. The necessity of normative direction is underscored, not negated, by Ruttan's argument that the self-interest argument for foreign assistance is compromised by a hidden agenda, the normative premise in the hidden agenda providing, desirably or not, the direction for policy.

Tresch's treatment of applied welfare economics affirms the necessity of limiting or channeling normative direction for policy because of the general infinity of possible outcomes. In the real world government must work out the entitlements structure which, together with choice from within opportunity sets, produces the actually achieved nonunique Pareto optimal result in the market. This determination of rights must somehow be given direction. One senses that this is the most critical point that can be made with regard to government in the context of applied welfare economics, despite the apparent and ironic fact that the conventional rendition of that theory often does not make the point either explicit or central.

Wade makes the point in a different context. He says that rulers may display a stunning obtuseness as to their subject's material conditions; that political leaders may be interested in economic affairs only to the point of securing their personal power positions, seeking to maintain as much social order as is deemed sufficient to maintain their own existence and legitimacy; and that within that order economic activity takes place. Normative direction for the government's economic role, such as it is, is thus a product of leaders jockeying for power and efforts to remain in power in the face of both practical crises and the claims of political-economic dissidents and ideological heretics. The government's role in enlarging economic welfare need receive little heed from ruling authorities. But whatever government leaders do to sustain their authority will contribute to government's normative direction and the actually achieved Pareto optimal result in the market.

Whynes stresses the necessity of normative premises to guide the economic role of government, but he argues the difficulty if not the impossibility of prescribing those premises on the basis of conventional economic theory.

Several writers (notably Bottomore, Lee, and Whynes) identify the key role of public opinion in forming or sanctioning government economic actions. At least three writers discuss the broader question of the relationship of knowledge and power, together illustrating the different ways in which the relationship can be understood or modeled. Altman stresses that economic knowledge is a critical political factor. Rose argues that, within government, economists are expert advisers, on tap but not on top, as he puts it. Knowledge is an asset, but it confers neither legitimacy nor power. Economic knowledge must be marketed to decision makers. Shaffer argues, *inter alia*, that power and myth (a form of belief, or what is taken to be knowledge, as the basis of policy) are particularly important in defining rights to output, and that the rules of entitlement to ouptut resulting from inherited knowledge are most important.

Resident within this widespread emphasis on necessary normative direction are at least three other conclusionary themes or characteristics: tension between technique and subjectivity, the relevance of selective perception, and the attempt by contributors themselves (in part through the approaches they adopt or cite) to provide some necessary normative drive or substantive content to decision making. There is an even more pervasive general theme: that government is a process for working out both its general economic roles and the substantive content that each role is to have, and not something that is or can be preordained in advance. The three are considered next.

8. Technique Versus Subjectivism

There is a continuing tension among students of public sector economics between those who believe that policy is largely a matter of finding technical solutions and those who believe that policy is fundamentally a subjective, normative matter. This tension is not between mutually exclusive positions but between relative emphases; clearly, both are necessary to produce policy. Advocates of applied welfare economics generally tend to advance that approach as technically neutral and useful. But, as has already been discussed, many contributors to this collection affirm the subjective, normative nature of economic policy and the correlative limits of technical analysis per se.

Anderson specifically argues that the theory of market failure does not help determine when government action is justified, objecting that the theory focuses too much on ostensibly technical failures and not enough on distributional and other consequences.

Burkhead writes that complex budgetary choices have to be made; the problem is to determine the basis of choice. He is obviously not pleased with the formalized neoclassical approach to the public household which has an imaginary manager of each branch (allocation, distribution, and stabilization) pursue reasonably well-defined objectives—to the neglect of the process by which subjective and normative objectives, not the least of which is distribution, are in actual practice worked out. Similar ideas are present in the contributions by Harriss, Hirsch, Horowitz, Tresch, and Whynes.

Jackson seems to concur that economists are unable to provide definitive technical answers to the question of the location of the boundaries of government's economic role.

Lee's argument about the necessity of ideological negativism seems to amount to an argument in favor of the subjective view.

A somewhat different view is provided by Rose, who argues that politicians want from experts not so much neutral competence as relevant competence, as well as confidence in successful advice. The point, of course, is that such advice combines technique and subjectivity, both ex ante and ex post.

9. Selective Perception

In this chapter and in other writings, I have stressed the principle of selective perception: Freedom, order, continuity, change, rights, government itself, coercion, market failure, government failure, and other subjects ensconced within discourse on the economic role of government have multiple facets and can be and indeed are approached from different perspectives, such that different interpreters can perceive and use different meanings and reach radically different conclusions. The principle seems to be a major characteristic of discourse on the economic role of government, resulting in part in the inconclusivity of interpretations and policy implications. What amounts to this principle is amply evident in several of the contributions to this collection other than my own.

Adams and Brock, for example, denigrate the use of government to promote private concentrations of power and affirm the use of government to promote competition. They recognize the problems of (1) creating omnipotent governmental concentrations of power in the effort to combat private concentrations, and (2) whether particular government actions promote competition or the noncompetitive interests of other specific groups. (That is, actions restrictive of Alpha's power may facilitate Beta's power.) These are generally matters of selective perception, for example, when government is pejoratively "omnipotent," when government is promoting competition, and whether it is sufficient to say that markets are per se competitive quite independent of considerations of structure.

Burkhead notes that the economic role of government is continually changing, especially because of shifts in perceptions as to the appropriate division of resources between the public and private sectors.

Dugger's basic distinction between predatory–parasitic and productive, identified in terms of the conflict between the haves and the have-nots, is a matter of selective perception on at least two levels: first, as to the actual existence of the distinction and the conflict; and second, as to whether any particular action of government is predatory or productive, promotive of the interests of the haves and have-nots. As an example of the latter, government policies ostensibly aimed at helping the poor can also be perceived (on the political right) to further immerse them in poverty or (on the political left) to discipline and render the poor docile. In both respects, interpretation is a matter of selective perception, often involving quite subtle considerations of means, ends, consequences, and their interrelationships.

Harriss states that one constructive use of coercion through government is to protect humans against other coercion. In a world of mutual coercion, each element of which is capable of being selectively perceived and evaluated, it is not surprising that those private exercisers of private coercion against whom government coercion is directed will perceive government coercion pejoratively (but not their own), whereas those whose own coercive capacity government coercion is protecting against the private coercion of others will not perceive government coercion pejoratively but will perceive the private coercion of others pejoratively. Policymaking involves not only selective perception, but also an inexorable necessity of choice as to who can do what to whom. In a world of mutual coercion, it simply is not conclusive to call something coercive either analytically or pejoratively; the action in question must be understood in a larger context. But discourse is laden with selective perception, and power players attempt to influence discourse (public opinion) along selectively desired lines.

Horowitz, in distinguishing between minimalist, pragmatic, and maximalist perspectives, and in saying that they are less principles of government and more practices and policies of everyday decision making, also implicitly stresses the role of selective perception as to what constitutes, either in theory or in practice, policy that is minimalist, pragmatic, and maximalist.

This is illustrated in Lee's argument wherein he takes a selectively perceived position regarding the respective strength of idelogical affirmativism versus negativism, that is, on what is necessary to constitute the agenda of government's "proper" economic role. It is certainly Lee's premise that ideology can, and can be used to, influence perceptions about appropriate resource allocation within government and between government and the private sector.

Similarly, Schmid emphasizes the principle in his treatments of the formation of rights, of what is perceived to be "natural" and to constitute "damage," and so on.

10. Policy Contributions

One arguable characteristic of all the contributed chapters seems to be an intention by their authors that their analysis and insights make some contribution to both understanding and improving both the actual discourse and decision making pertaining to the economic role of government. This would be the case even if the authors did not have particular substantive policy goals in mind, as is the case with my chapter. But certain chapters are clearly marked by a distinctive normative drive on the part of their authors to make particular substantive contributions to the policy process.

This is manifestly the case with Adams and Brock and with Dugger, Adams and Brock affirming a conception of competition deemed necessary to what they consider a free enterprise economy, and Dugger affirming policies that he deems "productive" because they promote the interests of the have-nots. (Harriss, too, affirms the use of government, *inter alia*, to encourage competition and to curb and control monopoly.)

Makgetla and Seidman certainly assume and affirm government intervention in Third World countries to alleviate the extremes of poverty and oppression. Ruttan, perhaps less forcefully, also assumes the desirability of foreign assistance for economic development.

The normative drive is also evident in Boadway's premise that the objective of government should be to improve the economic welfare of individuals, that decisions should reflect individual preferences and wherever possible be decentralized to the individuals themselves. Of course, such a formulation is inconclusive because it does not stipulate anything about *which* individuals' interests are to be promoted. (After all, it can be argued that it is *only* the economic welfare of *individuals*—including those in giant corporations and big government—that can count; who else's?) But it does reflect a common normative individualist predisposition among economists, a disposition quite amenable to selective specification, for example, in stipulating either status quo or desired rights. This latter is another mode of participating in the policy process.

The most dramatic example is Lee, who affirms the promotion of ideological negativism to counter the consequences of those whose ideologies both directly and indirectly promote expansion of the economic role, especially the literal size of government. Lee seems clearly to understand himself as participating in the relevant decision-making process, hopefully to influence both discourse and policy. He seems to be essentially performing the ultimate high priest role, in which nineteenth-century liberal ideology and, arguably, bourgeois economic theory represents, at least in part, and always selectively used, an attempt to "limit"—really to channel—the economic role of government. It will not have escaped the reader's notice that Hirsch takes a diametrically opposite position, denigrating both the ideologically driven conduct of economists and the "research" results lacking scholarly impartiality and objectivity. To Hirsch, adoption of the high priest role compromises scholarly integrity and puts the scientific status of economics at risk. On the other hand, Altman notes two relevant concerns: Whether liberal democratic states can overcome government reinforcement and perpetuation of the economic power of a dominant economic class, and whether liberal democracy may limit the capacity of government to change the distribution of power (a limitation Lee would apparently enhance).

In this respect, the assumption by various writers of liberal democratic states as their frame of reference can be taken as either a normative premise or as a limiting device to exclude political systems that are either different or on which the author lacks expertise. Of course, what constitutes a liberal democratic state is another matter. Surely Dugger and Lee will disagree as to whether Lee's ideological negativism is predatory on behalf of the haves or promotive of freedom for all.

11. Fundamental Dilemmas or Conflicts

Closely related to the centrality of power, the necessity for normative direction
for the state, and selective perception is an identification of certain fundamental
dilemmas or conflicts at the heart of what must be worked out by and through
government insofar as important details of its economic role is concerned. Particular ideologies and positions on the substance of government's economic role
strongly tend to take positions on these dilemmas or conflicts.

As we have seen, Adams and Brock identify the related dilemmas resident in
(1) controlling private coercion without creating an omnipotent government coercive apparatus beyond control and accountability, and (2) protecting certain
parties from the anticompetitive behavior of others without promoting the noncompetitive position or behavior of the former parties.

Altman's account of the relative strength and relations between economic and
political power identifies dilemmas involving the perception of power per se
(which is raised or implied by perhaps all contributors) and one-way modeling
in the relationships between economic and political power.

Anderson juxtaposes a nineteenth-century view of freedom as the absence of
governmental restraint to a twentieth-century view as the absence of obstacles
to realization of desires coupled with a liberating role of government. Independent
of ideology, or of ideologically channeled selective perception, government
action that restrains Alpha may also liberate Beta; or the absence of governmental
restraint on Alpha may correlate with the presence of obstacles to the realization
of desires by Beta.

Burkhead argues that it is too simplistic to assert that public programs always
encroach and limit private economic activity or that government is the problem
and not the solution. Many public programs extend human freedom and contribute
to an improved standard of living; modern government is not simply a coercive
mechanism that restricts and confines. Government necessarily both encroaches
upon and extends human freedom, though typically (most dramatically in the
controversial cases) for different people. The policy question concerns who is
to be restrained and who is to be liberated, that is, whose interests are to count.
A normative, subjective problem of selective perception and choice inexorably
arises.

For Dugger, the basic dilemma and policy conflict derives from what he
perceives to be the basic dichotomy or dual nature of the state: The state is
predatory and parasitic, and it is productive; one exploits, the other nurtures.

For Flynn, the tensions are between the conflicting perceptions, even ideologies, of different stages, each with their putative economic functions of government. Belief systems from one stage are carried over into another stage, often
functioning for certain interest groups or classes. But perhaps the key tension
or conflict is between different classes in classist society, even when government
is not strictly the instrument of the propertied.

Flynn maintains that government is the product of a perennial dialogue within society concerning the reconciliation of the centrifugal forces of individualism and the centripetal forces of community—in accord with the underlying values of society, which presumably are themselves a matter of dialogue and subject to both revision and/or varied application. One form which this takes, emphasized in the Lockean-Smithian approach, is consequent to the tendencies of some to invade the rights of others. Who has what rights, and who can perforce do what to whom else, is precisely the dilemma or problem that must be worked out. An example is the conflict between views of property: one as an essential dimension of individualism and the other as a means to the ends of protecting the individual against government and/or other individuals. To simply affirm the glory of the institution of property is to beg the problems resident in the dilemma. Another complex example arises in assuming some distribution of rights, either the existing distribution of rights or some presumptive formulation of it, or a different, perhaps more equitable, distribution. Resident within Flynn's discussion is a point also made by Schmid: The use of law to protect the individual can give rise to the need to change the law to maintain that protection in response to changed circumstances and/or changes in what is necessary to protect individuals, but which gives rise to the further dilemma as to when a change of law is a change of means and when a change of end, for example, a change of the individual(s) whose interest is being protected.

For Harriss, too, a relevant dilemma involves the use of legal or governmental coercion to protect against coercion, including the choice of which private actor engaged in mutual coercion is to be restricted and the other ipso facto facilitated. This is a matter directly involved in determining, in the face of parties whose interests directly conflict, whose interest is to be protected as property or otherwise and whose is to be sacrificed. Harriss also notes a dilemma involving knowledge: that the "common man" cannot possibly know the details needed for many decisions (at least to the extent that the decision rests on technical details rather than subjective or ideological concerns), nor can he be sure whom to trust among the possible experts. Harriss concludes with still another problem: how to avoid a romantic dream world without renouncing aspiration.

Horowitz echoes several other contributors when he argues that the transformation from a pro-minimalist government to the welfare state involved a change not only in the economic role of government per se, but also in what is meant by government itself, namely, the prevention of discrimination and the exercise of justice. He also insists that policy choices are made within the parameters of system survival and equity claims, and not between an all-powerful economic role of government and a nonexistent role. The dilemmas of policy resident within these views are multiple, including, for example, having to choose between maximalist interpretations of government when protecting Alpha and minimalist (if not nonexistent) when protecting Beta.

Jackson notes the contradictory comprehensions that government is both part of the answer to a problem and part of the problem. He also notes the necessity of government, and perforce of politicians and laws, for both freedom and the market, and the necessity for constitutional and other constraints on politicians and bureaucrats—in part, the dilemma confronting anarchy without government with the Leviathan of big government (see also Adams and Brock). Jackson also emphasizes that limitations on freedom imposed by government in one dimension are necessary for the pursuit of freedom in other dimensions, that government action can expand positive freedom through limiting freedom, the problem being, which or whose freedom.

Lee centers on and attempts to provide a solution for the dilemma resident in what he perceives to be the fact that expanding the economic role of government increases the type of government activities that require detailed public control, but that are more responsive to special interest influence than to public interest concerns (a distinction the substantive content of which has, of course, to be worked out), undermining the ideological control that the public can exert over government while increasing the need for that control. Whether his proposed ideological negativism itself raises further dilemmas is another matter of considerable importance, for example, in regard to the claims of those who see ideology as a mask for certain special interests rather than others or the public interest. In addition it is not clear just where Lee's ideological negativism stands with regard to Schmid's argument that the protection of particular property or other interests may require change of law under altered environmental circumstances; or Samuels' argument that legal change of the interest to which government gives its support is not intervention, not "big government," in the sense of government intruding into a situation in which it hitherto has been absent. Determining when government action (or, for that matter, inaction) constitutes promotion or restriction of privilege is always a matter of selective perception and thus a policy dilemma. Finally, it is possible to see in Lee's proposal two quite different things that also pose a policy dilemma: narrow and myopic special interest manipulation of government in their own favor in the guise of limiting government, or participation in a more or less competitive market of ideas for control of government. As has been noted above, Lee's argument can be seen as functioning either in opposition to strategic behavior by interests or ideologues seeking to use government or as an example of that behavior.

Ruttan poses related dilemmas: the inherent contradiction when donor pursuit of self-interest also harms the recipient country, the perhaps more general conflict between the self-interest and other arguments and hidden agendas, and/or the use of self-interest and other arguments more as a cynical effort to develop domestic constituencies for foreign assistance than a serious economic or political rationale. Ruttan also identifies a dilemma that is not restricted to questions of foreign assistance: when the scope of political and economic interdependence is not coextensive with national boundaries, so that the decision-making group is not co-extensive with the cost-incurring and/or benefit-receiving groups (a matter also implicit in Lee's analysis).

As we have seen, Schmid argues that when government prohibits a de facto act allegedly causing damage, it may be seen as carrying out its initial intended distribution of rights or as changing it. He also stresses that when government limits Beta's options, it is defining Alpha's rights, whether as rights per se, regulation, or liability. These are truly fundamental and ubiquitous dilemmas of perception and of policy.

Wade obviously echoes several other writers, such as Adams and Brock, when he invokes the Madisonian insight that government must be first enabled to control the governed and next obliged to control itself—the problem being, of course, that different putative private rights holders or claimants will perceive the situation quite differently, for example, Schmid's Alpha and Beta.

12. Legal-Economic Nexus

Perhaps because, in order better to comprehend the economically relevant operations of government, I am sensitive to considerations that political-governmental-legal, and economic–market processes are not fully separate, self-subsistent orders, but rather constitute twin aspects of a fundamental legal–economic nexus, I found evidence for such a view in several contributions. More importantly, several contributors directly focus on the idea of a legal–economic nexus as their answer to the question, what is the most fundamental thing that can be said about the economic role of government? In addition, and not surprisingly, they find the core of this nexus to be power.

The idea of a legal–economic nexus is implicit in Adams and Brock's treatment of the question of whether government is to promote and protect competition or to eliminate or channel competition. Here government will be responsive either to certain interests or to others, an instrument for certain policies or for other policies. Government is both a dependent and an independent variable, both consequence and cause. The legal–economic nexus is implicitly that sphere of decision making wherein such decisions are made.

The question of a legal–economic nexus arises in Altman's juxtaposition of two one-way explanatory models: one in which economic power is dependent on political power and another in which political power is dependent on economic power. He calls attention to the relative balance of forces and conditions of success of each. He notes a political emphasis in which attitudes toward the status quo often dominate, with economic power subject to political control either to limit or to make use of government as a mode of change; and an economic emphasis, in which government is seen as reinforcing and perpetuating the economic power of dominant economic classes, in part because economic power is an important lever for deploying state power, and in part because political power–government is normally subordinate to economic power.

Burkhead, who emphasizes the centrality of the budget in understanding what government actually does, says that the economy has an impact on the budget and the budget has an impact on the economy. Not unlike Altman, he notes the dual relationships or flow of force. Burkhead also observes that private markets do not allocate resources but rather send signals, derived from the institutional and power structures and the choices emanating therein, which govern resource allocation. On the other hand, the government budgetary process generates a very different kind of signal but a signal nonetheless. An implication of his analysis is that there is a core of human action focusing on government, not least importantly on the budget, some aspects of which are arguably political and others economic, but which constitute fundamental allocative decisioning that is at once both political and economic. The budget, then, is at the core of the legal–economic nexus, but perhaps either is not the core itself or does not entirely constitute the core.

For Dugger, state power is the ability to exercise social control over the behavior of individuals either directly through the state's own mechanisms or indirectly through other institutions. But state power itself is influenced by forces and institutions outside the state, for example, class. The forms of organized activity which the state decides to legalize, and the forms which it decides to ignore or criminalize, become extremely important in determining who can and cannot exercise power through the state. The state, according to Dugger, is a class mechanism, but it is much more than a class mechanism. The mechanisms of the state are important in their own right, pursuing the interests of state officials against each other and in allegiance with class interests or with special interests. The state is a dependent variable, but it is not solely a dependent variable in a class equation of power. It is also a wielder of power on its own behalf and in its own right. The legal-economic nexus by implication is the location wherein is determined who controls the state and the uses to which the state is put.

For Elliott, government in all societies is integral to the economy and in a classist society is at the core in which polity and economy are jointly and mutually determined under the aegis of culture and class, with the culture itself influenced by class.

Flynn directly attempts to identify and penetrate the legal–economic nexus. He states that there is an obvious chicken and egg problem: Which came first, government or economy? What are the fundamental assumptions of the economic role of government from which economic analysis (and presumably the economy itself) proceeds, and what is the role of economics and the other liberal arts (and presumably other nominally private power players) in defining the background roles and rights from which the determination of governmental institutions proceeds? Flynn argues that we must abandon linear thinking and recognize that the answer is neither and both. Government is the product of tensions between power-concentrating and power-diffusing forces, between individualism and community, with the community effectively dominant through underlying cultural values and moral beliefs. As for the riddle of the economic foundations of government and the governmental foundations of the economy, it is not a case of either economics determining the role of government or of government determining either the economy or the role of economics, but each serving to define the other in light of cultural heritage and the values which that heritage defines, with both culture and values changing (like rights) themselves in the process.

Thus, to Flynn the legal–economic nexus is driven by (more or less changing) moral beliefs. But it is especially the case that the economic and the political are not independent and self-subsistent: Each is involved in the determination, the definition, of the other. The legal–economic nexus is the social space and process wherein that mutual definition takes place. Part of that mutual definition includes the determination and assignment of rights, including property rights.

Harriss makes somewhat the same kind of point in a more general way when he argues that governments are the means (human institutions) which human beings use to achieve objectives and that it is misleading to personify "government" as an entity with the power to act as an agency independent of the people who make choices. (This view parallels my earlier point that it is not enough to affirm that individual preferences are to count without saying something about the distribution of power which weights the preferences of different individuals, some in and some out of government; that is, whose interests are to count.) The legal–economic nexus is the sphere wherein these determinations are made.

Horowitz implicitly raises the idea of a legal–economic nexus when he calls attention to the process by which government has become transformed from the praetorian guard of the ruling class to the great benefactor of the working masses. System survival rather than economic equilibrium (as he puts it) is the hallmark of government, but most fundamental is the legitimacy of government itself, including the imposition and critique of the equity bases of government. According to Horowitz, the existence of a noneconomic core is exactly what one means by a democratic system—a view that is not strictly contradictory to the idea of a legal–economic nexus but that affirms the importance of government and of what is achieved through government.

Jackson, on the other hand, in saying that the central problem is determining the boundaries of the public domain, or the limits to the economic role of government, seems to infer that political and economic processes are, at least in some respects, separate and self-subsistent. However, the problem of boundaries and limits also arises in connection with the idea of a core legal–economic nexus.

A presumption of a legal–*economic* nexus may be of a self-subsistent economic sphere *in some sense* different and separable from the legal–political sphere. The pervasive problem, however, seems to be the enormous opportunity for selective perception in identifying the categories of the economic and the political, respectively, when arguably the legal–economic nexus is holistic, and it is only our perception that there are two intertwined processes. As Robert Heilbroner and others have argued, it may be one of the consequences of market economies that polity and economy *appear* to be separate and autonomous orders or processes. In other words, there is a difference between the actual legal–economic nexus and both our perceptions of it and our mode of discourse about it. Of course, the substantive resolution of the problem of order (for example, the substantive achievement of the pattern of freedom and control) derives, to some extent, from constitutional and other policies giving affect to selective ideological beliefs in separate political and economic orders, a view likely congruent with Lee's argument.

Schmid echoes Flynn in arguing that the dichotomy of "private" versus "public" loses easy meaning. Interdependence is never left to work itself out "naturally" by government silence and absence. What is "natural" about government is a matter of selective perception. Where there is capacity for interdependence, there is government, as in the case of rights, regulation, or liability. For Schmid, then, the state has a central position in the determination of whose preferences count, through helping to govern the resolution of conflicts owing to interdependence. This position is guided by pressures from nominally private actors and institutions. Government is neither exogenous nor transcendent but is responsive to the parallelogram of forces brought to bear on, constituting it, and operating through it. The legal–economic nexus exists at precisely that social space wherein government responds to outside forces and generates solutions to problems with outside impacts.

For Schmid, too, more is involved than an initial determination of entitlements followed by the nightwatchman. Factor endowments cannot address all sources of human interdependence and are therefore necessarily ambiguous. The state is the process by which rights are learned and evolved, in part in response to changing circumstances of interdependence, perhaps to change rights in order to change entitlements, perhaps to modify rights in order to maintain some original distribution of entitlements. The legal–economic nexus exists at that social space where problems of legal change of legal rights are worked out— even when the goal is to maintain the integrity and economic significance of existing rights.

Schmid also says, reminiscent of Burkhead, that the same is true of budgets as alternatives to property and other rights. Some economic actors acquire their opportunities from rights and regulations and liabilities imposed on others, and others acquire theirs from the budget. Thus, the rules of benefit-cost analysis and the budgetary process are instrumentally equivalent to property rights insofar as they govern, or are used to govern, opportunities and distributive and allocative results.

Shaffer, like Harriss, succinctly makes much the same general point when he argues that the behavioral rules of the total system are both a product and an input. The legal–economic nexus exists at that social space wherein behavioral rules of law are both output and input and wherein government and economy are an "organic unity."

A parallel but different point is made by Tresch when he argues that the success of actual policy initiatives depends on the behavior of economic actors, which itself depends on conditions that may themselves be influenced by government. The critical point made by Tresch, is, however, that, nonnormatively, the economic role of government is one in which economic actors (individuals and firms) use or attempt to use the public sector as a vehicle for increasing personal utilities and profits. Government is an instrument available for use or an arena in which its use is fought over and worked out. Nominally private determination of the nominally public must be joined with the nominally public determination of the private (for example, through rights), in a process in which, therefore, both are not so much or not only mutually interactive but also mutually defining—or perhaps, better put, commonly defined.

Tresch does not find this nonnormative conclusion very uplifting, but he does state it forthrightly. Interestingly, he observes that the public sector really has no other useful function to perform if people have no interest in maximizing social welfare. This view seems to give a privileged position to exchange leading to nonunique Pareto optimization and to neglect, if not to deny, the role of legal change in (re)determining the rights on the basis of which social welfare "maximization" (universal Pareto optimality) is achieved. The legal–economic nexus is at the center of that process.

Wade also attempts to go beyond the idea of two separate and self-subsistent processes or orders. He argues that it would be fantasy or illusion to presuppose that polity and economy can be or ever have been disentangled—even though some political leaders have been interested in economic affairs only to the point of securing their personal power positions. On the one hand, says Wade, all governments, once established, will seek with varying degrees of success to maintain at least as much social order as is deemed sufficient to maintain their own existence and legitimacy, and that within that order economic activity necessarily takes place. Economic policy is only a part, and sometimes a small part, of the social roles consciously assumed by governments. Government, whether autocratic or democratic, may be closely or weakly linked to economic activity (though here Wade seems to refer principally, if not exclusively, to deliberative, rather than effective, policy. This is always a matter in part of selective perception). On the other hand, much of politics consists of private affect displaced on public objects and rationalized in terms of the public interest.

Finally, we may note Whynes' statement, perhaps parallel to Flynn's emphasis on the role of moral beliefs and cultural values, that the fundamental economic role of government is a function of whatever citizens will sanction. The legal–economic nexus is in this respect the social situs wherein government action and public opinion come together and are mutually defined.

III. CONCLUSION

What, then, are the most fundamental things that can be said of the economic role of government? Let me suggest a few, building on the foregoing.

1. Economy and polity are not self-subsistent but can be seen as either mutually defining or arising in the legal–economic nexus. This nexus is a continuing, explorative, and emergent process through which are worked out ongoing solutions to problems such as whose economic and other interests are to count and which economic and other performance results are to be pursued. Whether or not one accepts the concept of the legal–economic nexus, the emphasis must be on process, on working out, on problematicity—in short, on the process by

which actors who are simultaneously both economic and political actors themselves work out solutions to problems that are simultaneously both political and
economic and that simultaneously form the achieved economy and polity, the
process to which particular ideologies and particular policy analyses and/or proposals are but particular contributions, the process by which solutions in the real
world to the four models surveyed in the first part of this chapter are worked
out.

2. Critical to this process is the role of the social belief system. This belief
system provides part of the basis on which policy is made; belief governs the
definition of reality which influences policy. The belief system is itself an object
of control and manipulation, as economic actors attempt to influence policy by
controlling the relevant definition of reality. It is true that beliefs are a function
of power, in part that they are weighted by power structure; and that power is
in part a function of belief. One aspect of this dual process is the creation and
maintenance of the belief that the legal–economic system is given, above politics
and policy, in efforts to abort certain users and certain uses of government.

3. There is a great variety of interpretive systems that arguably can be called
close to legal–economic reality, whatever one means by "reality:" different
taxonomies of, different philosophies of, and different approaches to the economic role of government, as well as different formulations and uses of the four
models surveyed in the first part of this chapter, and so on.

4. The central concept is power: power in government, power in the economy,
the determination of power in each, the mutual interaction, and especially the
simultaneous and/or mutual definition of economic and political power. Power
governs both whose interests count and performance results, including those
results deemed (on the basis of exchange within existing rights) Pareto optimal.
Power also governs opportunities to change power in one sphere or the other.
The legal–economic nexus is the social space wherein power in one sphere is
brought to bear on the other, in the process of mutual redefinition; or wherein
the power of both simultaneously originate and are indistinguishable except
through selective perception.

5. The economic role of government requires normative direction; it is not
determined exogenous to society or to the individual, and it is not self-subsistent
or self-determining. The legal–economic nexus is the social situs wherein the
determination of the normative direction of the economic role of government is
worked out, including the ongoing resolutions to the various policy dilemmas
identified in this collection.

6. A critical principle is that of selective perception, ultimately derived from
the multifaceted and kaleidoscopic nature of politico-economic affairs, as illustrated, for example, in the four models surveyed earlier and variously emphasized
and/or exemplified in the various contributions to this collection.

7. Given the status quo configuration of rights and other bases on which
economic interests and opportunities rest—which, it is to be emphasized, can
be specified or defined in various ways—the critical question of the economic

role of government is legal change of legal rights, legal change of the interests to be given protection and putative effect by government. Again, this is not intervention in a situation in which government hitherto has been absent. But it does involve the problematic continuing redefinition and reassignment of rights, owing in part to changing values, changing power structure independent of government, and, *inter alia*, changing environmental circumstances, such as technology, demography, and knowledge of consequences.

One can contemplate a model in which the configuration of legal rights is determined by the structure of private power and changes more or less as and in response to changes in the structure of private power. But it is equally possible and instructive to contemplate a model in which the structure of private economic rights is determined by the configuration of political power and changes more or less as and in response to changes in political power. As Flynn and Schmid, for example, would put it, legal and economic power are mutually interactive and mutually determining, neither self-constituting nor self-subsistent. In a sense, legal power is a function of economic power, and economic power is a function of political power. Legal change of legal rights must be understood in this complex, larger context.

It is also possible to contemplate the problem of legal change of legal rights as existing at the very center of the legal–economic nexus, the location wherein both the nominally economic and the nominally legal-political are simultaneously worked out.

Lee's use of ideological negativism would be a contribution to the process constituting the legal–economic nexus. To some, however, it would constitute the selective reinforcement of the status quo against legal change, whereas to others it would involve the affirmation of freedom and a correlative check on the power of government, and to still others a selective use of government as such. The point is that at stake is the problem of continuity versus change of the distributional consequences of government activity, which may be present whether or not one takes what Lee calls an ideologically negative stance. The legal–economic process is ongoing, and only within certain selective assumptions can one give privileged status to status quo rights (however selectively these are perceived) over "rent-seeking" legal change.

Legal change of legal rights seems to be the central subject of the economic role of government, or at least the operative question on which all discussions ultimately are brought to bear. "Fully defined" rights are an impossibility in practice. It is the law-and-economics equivalent of the auctioneer and pre-reconciled prices in neo-Walrasian general equilibrium theory: It assumes as given what in fact has to be worked out in practice. It is simply not possible to fully define rights, because we cannot know all the present interdependencies with respect of which rights have meaning; and, moreover, because we cannot know the details of technological, demographic, and other changes and all the future interdependencies with respect to which presently defined rights will have economic significance and other meaning. We are faced with the problematic nature of rights as well as the inexorable necessity of government having to choose between conflicting rights' claimants as conditions, perceptions, and values change. This is true when government pursues, or is used to pursue, legal change of legal rights in order to attempt to reinforce the interests it sought to protect through its initial definition and/or assignment of rights. It is also true when government pursues, or is used to pursue, legal change of the interests to which it will give its protection.

8. The partial disjunction between those schools of public sector economics which emphasize that policy is largely a matter, respectively, of technical details and of subjective judgments is very important in comprehending the various perspectives which analysts take of the economic role of government. While that disjunction is only partial, a matter of emphasis, the difference in emphasis is important.

The conflict between technical details and subjective valuation arises not only in policy analysis but in actual political administration as well. One arguably can identify a partial disjunction between government administrations that are driven largely by ideology and those that are motivated by a preoccupation with technical details. Again, the difference is one of emphasis, though an important one: Administrations driven by ideology must translate their principles into specific policies (legislation, court decisions, administrative rules); and those manned by technical experts without overt and conspicuous ideological commitments must have their technical solutions to problems driven, at least in part, by normative premises such as those found in various politico-economic ideologies.

In short, the fundamentals of the economic role of government are not simple and obvious. Perhaps that is the most fundamental statement that can be made about the economic role of government. But this carries the implication that the various ideologies, schools of economic and political thought, and decision-making techniques are by their very nature limited and, with regard to the tautological relationship between their respective premises and policy implications, presumptuous. Indeed, they are not conclusively dispositive of the issues to which they typically are addressed, or not so without additional selective perceptions and antecedent normative premises.

The economic role of government has to be worked out. It can be neither encapsulated in a few glorious propositions nor set down in concrete once and for all time. The legal–economic nexus is where it is worked out. Accordingly, in understanding the fundamentals of the economic role of government, it seems helpful both to transcend ideologies wherein certain agendas of government are and others are not perceived to constitute government; and to commence inquiry with the straightforward, and not necessarily cynical, premise that government is an instrument available to whomever can control and use it and/or an arena in which the details of use are worked out. Perhaps only in this way can our common love–hate relationship with government be transcended for purposes of analysis but not repealed for purposes of policy participation.

NOTES

1. The politician is trying to get (re)elected and thereby seeks to identify with values which he or she believes can be or are held by the voters (or sufficient of them to win election). Politicians do two things in this process relevant to the discussion in the text: First, they help form voter preferences; and second, they serve as conduits or vehicles for whatever preferences voters come to act on. Politicians will try to reform voter preferences to be consistent with their, the politicians', own preferences or principles and also to "rise above" their own principles so as to better comport with the preferences of the voters (such as they cannot reform) so as to gain reelection. (In the latter case, the objective function of the politician is obviously not solely to advance his preferences or principles but to gain [re]election, period.) As indicated in the text, these are all very complex processes. The principal characteristics of relevant reality are that neither the politicians nor the voters have well- or conclusively defined sets of values or preferences and that it is very difficult for them to be effectively communicated. It is also true that communication (information provision) is asymmetrical.

2. This is not an hypothetical social welfare function as designated by an analyst, even one who intends to represent the actual function extant at the time and place. The combination of individuals with preferences for certain values and a power structure that weights those preferences across individuals (that is, determines whose preferences count) *in effect* yields the actual social welfare function. The discussion is not intended to be a mechanistic representation of reality but a tool indicative of what is going on in society.

3. As further indication of the complexity of these (and other) processes, consider the situation in which the power structure does not change but the beliefs of the (hegemonic or decisive) power-holders change, thereby changing the decisional outcome. The more general problem arises with the use of the fourth model presented in the text, in which an outcome can be explicated in terms either of power, knowledge, or psychological factors, such that the analyst has to assess the relative weights of the three factors. There are, of course, also definitional and modeling problems, such as defining moral suasion (leading to a change of belief) as a form of power.

Selected Bibliography

Arnold, Thurman. *The Folklore of Capitalism*. New Haven, Conn.: Yale University Press, 1937.

Arrow, Kenneth J. *Social Choice and Individual Values*. 2d ed. New York: John Wiley, 1963.

Bartlett, Randall. *Economic Foundations of Political Power*. New York: Free Press, 1973.

Baumol, William J. *Welfare Economics and the Theory of the State*. Cambridge, Mass.: Harvard University Press, 1952.

Beck, Morris. *Government Spending*. New York: Praeger, 1981.

Burrows, Paul, and Cento G. Veljanovski (eds.). *The Economic Approach to Law*. London: Butterworth's, 1981.

Cardozo, Benjamin N. *The Nature of the Judicial Process*. New Haven, Conn.: Yale University Press, 1922.

————. *The Paradoxes of Legal Science*, New York: Columbia University Press, 1928.

Clark, John M. *Social Control of Business*. 2d ed. New York: McGraw-Hill, 1939.

Cohen, Felix S. *The Legal Conscience*. New Haven, Conn.: Yale University Press, 1960.

Commons, John R. *Legal Foundations of Capitalism*. New York: Macmillan, 1924.

Dahl, Robert A., and Charles E. Lindblom. *Politics, Economics and Welfare*. New York: Harper, 1953.

De Schweinitz, Karl, Jr. *Industrialization and Democracy—Economic Necessities and Political Possibilities*. New York: Free Press, 1964.

Downs, Anthony. *An Economic Theory of Democracy*. New York: John Wiley, 1957.

Frank, Jerome. *Law and the Modern Mind*. New York: Coward-McCann, 1949.

Friedmann, Lawrence M. *A History of American Law*. New York: Simon & Schuster, 1973.

————, and Stewart Macaulay. *Law and the Behavioral Sciences*. 2d ed. Indianapolis: Bobbs-Merrill, 1977.

Friedman, Wolfgang. *Law in a Changing Society*. 2d ed. New York: Columbia University Press, 1972.

Galbraith, John Kenneth. *The New Industrial State*. Boston: Houghton Mifflin, 1967.

Hale, Robert Lee. *Freedom Through Law*. New York: Columbia University Press, 1952.

Heilbroner, Robert L. *Behind the Veil of Economics*. New York: W. W. Norton, 1988.

Hirsch, Werner Z. *Law and Economics*. 2d ed. Boston: Academic Press, 1988.

Hurst, James Willard. *Law and the Conditions of Freedom in the Nineteenth Century United States*. Madison: University of Wisconsin Press, 1956.

Kelman, Mark. *A Guide to Critical Legal Studies*. Cambridge, Mass.: Harvard University Press, 1987.

Knight, Frank H. *Freedom and Reform*. New York: Harper, 1947.

Lindblom, Charles E. *Politics and Markets*. New York: Basic Books, 1977.

McConnell, Grant. *Private Power and American Democracy*. New York: Alfred A. Knopf, 1967.

Mercuro, Nicholas (ed.). *Law and Economics*. Boston: Kluwer, 1989.

————, and Timothy P. Ryan (eds.). *Law, Economics and Public Policy*. Greenwich, Conn.: JAI Press, 1984.

Miliband, Ralph. *The State in Capitalist Society*. New York: Basic Books, 1969.

Miller, Arthur Selwyn. *The Modern Corporate State*. Westport, Conn.: Greenwood Press, 1976.

————. *The Supreme Court and American Capitalism*. New York: Free Press, 1968.

Page, Benjamin I. *Who Gets What from Government*. Berkeley: University of California Press, 1983.

Pound, Roscoe. *Social Control Through Law*. New Haven, Conn.: Yale University Press, 1942.

Robbins, Lionel. *The Theory of Economic Policy in English Classical Political Economy*. London: Macmillan, 1953.

Samuels, Warren J. (ed.). *The Economy as a System of Power*. 2 vols. New Brunswick, N.J.: Transaction Books, 1979.

————. and A. Allan Schmid. *Law and Economics*. Boston: Martinus Nijhoff, 1981.

————. and Arthur Selwyn Miller (eds.). *Corporations and Society*. Westport, Conn.: Greenwood Press, 1987.

Slichter, Sumner H. *Modern Economic Society*. New York: Holt, 1928.

Smith, Adam. *An Inquiry into the Nature and Causes of the Wealth of Nations*. New York: Modern Library, 1937.

Unger, Roberto Mangabeira. *The Critical Legal Studies Movement*. Cambridge, Mass.: Harvard University Press, 1986.

Vincent, Andrew. *Theories of the State*. New York: Basil Blackwell, 1987.

Index

About the Contributors

WALTER ADAMS is distinguished university professor (economics) and past president, Michigan State University. He was a member of Attorney General Herbert Brownell's National Committee to Study the Antitrust Laws (1953–1955) and has appeared frequently as an expert witness before congressional committees. His books include *Monopoly in America* (1955), *The Brain Drain* (1968), *The Structure of American Industry* (7th ed., 1986), and *The Bigness Complex* (1986). His articles have appeared in the *American Economic Review* and a number of other journals. He has served as visiting professor at the major universities in France, Italy, Austria, and Germany.

ANDREW ALTMAN is associate professor of philosophy at George Washington University. He specializes in legal and political philosophy, and his articles have appeared in *Philosophy and Public Affairs* (1986) and *Legal Studies Forum* (1986).

JAMES E. ANDERSON is professor of political science at Texas A&M University. Previously, he taught at the University of Houston and Wake Forest University. His research interests include the presidency, the policy process, antitrust and regulatory policy, and agricultural policy. He is the author of *Politics and the Economy* (1966), *Public Policy-Making* (1984), and co-author of *Managing Macroeconomic Policy: The Johnson Presidency* (1987).

ROBIN W. BOADWAY is professor of economics at Queen's University (Canada) and specializes in public economics, welfare economics, and cost-benefit analysis. He is the author of *Public Sector Economics* (2d ed., with David Wildasin), co-author of *Welfare Economics*, co-author of *Canadian Tax Policy*, and editor of the *Canadian Journal of Economics*.

TOM BOTTOMORE is emeritus professor of sociology at the University of Sussex. His main interests are the history of social thought, Marxist theory, classes and elites, and processes of social development. Among his published writings are *Sociology* (3d ed.), *Elites and Society*, *Political Sociology*, *Theories of Modern Capitalism*, and (as editor) *A Dictionary of Marxist Thought*.

JAMES W. BROCK is professor of economics at Miami University (Ohio) and specializes in public policy toward business, antitrust policy, and the structure of U.S. industry. He is coauthor of *The Bigness Complex* (1986) and numerous journal articles. He is currently writing a book on mergers, takeovers, and leveraged buyouts.

JESSE BURKHEAD is Maxwell professor of economics, emeritus, Syracuse University. He has published widely in public finance, with emphasis on public expenditure. He has written *Government Budgeting* and co-authored *Public Expenditure*. He is editor emeritus of the journal *Public Budgeting & Finance*.

WILLIAM M. DUGGER is professor of economics at DePaul University, Chicago. He is the author of *An Alternative to Economic Retrenchment* (1984) and the editor of *Radical Institutionalism: Contemporary Voices* (Greenwood Press, 1989). He has written numerous articles and reviews on institutionalism and corporate capitalism. His latest book is *Corporate Hegemony* (Greenwood Press, forthcoming). He has served as the president of the Association for Institutional Thought and as president of the Association for Social Economics.

JOHN E. ELLIOTT is professor of economics and director of Political Economy and Public Policy at the University of Southern California. His professional interests are the history of economic thought, comparative economic systems, and contending perspectives in political economy. He is the author of *Comparative Economic Systems* (1985), *Marx and Engels on Economics, Politics, and Society* (1981), and numerous journal articles.

JOHN J. FLYNN is Hugh B. Brown professor of law at the University of Utah, specializing in the fields of antitrust, regulated industries, corporations, constitutional law, and legal philosophy. He is a coauthor of *Free Enterprise and Economic Organizational Antitrust* (6th ed.) and a companion volume, *Government Regulation*. He is a frequent contributor to law reviews and authored a chapter in *Corporations and Society: Power and Responsibility* (Samuels and Miller, eds., 1987). He has also served as special counsel to the U.S. Senate Judiciary Committee and its former Subcommittee on Antitrust.

C. LOWELL HARRISS, professor emeritus of economics, taught at Columbia University from 1938 to 1981. His teaching and research have embraced most aspects of government finance—and political economy and ''policy'' aspects of economics and politics. He also served as economist for the Tax Foundation, Inc., as an associate of the Lincoln Institute of Land Policy, and as executive director of the Academy of Political Science. He is the author of numerous books and hundreds of articles on a wide range of economic topics.

WERNER Z. HIRSCH is professor of economics at the University of California, Los Angeles, specializing in the field of law and economics, public finance, and urban economics. He is the author of *Urban Economic Analysis* (1984) and *Law and Economics: An Introductory Analysis* [2d ed.] (1988) and is a frequent contributor to economic journals and law reviews.

IRVING LOUIS HOROWITZ is Hannah Arendt distinguished professor of sociology and political science at Rutgers University. Among his major works are *Three Worlds of Development* (1965, 1972), and *Beyond Empire and Revolution* (1982). He has served as visiting professor at such major institutions as Stanford, Princeton, and Wisconsin, and taught development policy at the University of Tokyo, the Hebrew University in Jerusalem, and the University of Buenos Aires. He was the founding editor of *Studies in Comparative International Development*.

P. M. JACKSON is professor of economics and director of the Public Sector Economics Research Centre at Leicester University, England and research director of the Public Finance Foundation, London. He is the joint author of *Public Sector Economics* (4th ed., 1989) and author of *The Political Economy of Bureaucracy* (1982). He has also contributed many articles in economics journals and is currently carrying out a major research project covering the growth of the United Kingdom's public sector over the post–1950 period.

ALEXIS JACQUEMIN is professor of economics at the Université Catholique de Louvain, Belgium, specializing in industrial organization, and law and economics. He is the author of *European Industrial Organization* (1977), *European Industry* (1984), and *The New Industrial Organization* (1987), and the editor of the *International Journal of Industrial Organization*. He is currently economic adviser at the Commission of the European Community and member of the Advisory Board of the Japanese Research Institute of the Ministry of International Trade and Industry.

DWIGHT R. LEE is the Ramsey professor of private enterprise economics at the University of Georgia, at Athens. His primary professional interests are in public finance and public choice. He is co-author of *Regulating Government: A Preface to Constitutional Economics* (1987), and has contributed articles to a number of journals. During the 1988–1989 academic year, he was the John M. Olin visiting professor at the Center for the Study of American Business at Washington University, St. Louis, Missouri.

NEVA SEIDMAN MAKGETLA is assistant professor of economics at the University of Redlands. She is co-author of two books on southern Africa and author of various articles on African and development economics. Her principal research interests include development economics and economic policy, particularly in the African context.

RICHARD ROSE, director of the Centre for the Study of Public Policy at the University of Strathclyde, Glasgow, Scotland, is known on both sides of the Atlantic for his pioneering work in the application of social science concepts to problems of government. He has been a visiting fellow at the Brookings Institution, the American Enterprise Institute, and the International Monetary Fund, and at universities in the United States, Germany, and Italy. Among his recent publications are *Understanding Big Government*, *Public Employment in Western Nations*, and *Taxation by Political Inertia*.

VERNON W. RUTTAN is a regents' professor of economics and agricultural economics and an adjunct professor in the Hubert H. Humphrey Institute of Public Affairs at the University of Minnesota. His research has been in the fields of agricultural development, resource economics, and research policy. He is the author of *Agricultural Research Policy* (1982), (with Yujiro Hayami) *Agricultural Development: An International Perspective* (rev. ed., 1985), and with Anne O. Krueger and Constantine Michalopoulos), *Aid and Development*.

WARREN J. SAMUELS is professor of economics at Michigan State University, specializing in the history of economic thought, law and economics, and public utility regulation. He is the author of *The Classical Theory of Economic Policy* (1966), *Pareto on Policy* (1974), and editor of *The Chicago School of Political Economy* (1976), *Corporations and Society* (1987, with Arthur S. Miller), and the annual *Research in the History of Economic Thought and Methodology*. He is writing a book on the use of the concept of the invisible hand.

A. ALLAN SCHMID is professor of agricultural economics, Michigan State University, working in law and economics, public choice, and benefit-cost analysis. He is the author of *Property, Power, and Public Choice* (1987), *Benefit-Cost Analysis: A Political Economy Approach* (forthcoming), and, with Warren Samuels, *Law and Economics: An Institutional Perspective* (1981).

ROBERT B. SEIDMAN is professor of law and political science at Boston University. He has taught extensively at universities in Africa, most recently for three years at the University of Zimbabwe. He spent 1988–1989 teaching at Peking University on a Fulbright Fellowship. He is the author of *The State, Law and Development*, and author of over a hundred law review articles.

JAMES DUNCAN SHAFFER is professor of agricultural economics at Michigan State University. His work has focused on issues of food systems organization and performance in the United States and in less developed countries, especially related to governance institutions. His article in *Cooperative Theory: New Approaches*, USDA, (July 1987), pp. 61–86, illustrates this interest.

RICHARD W. TRESCH is associate professor of economics at Boston College, specializing in public sector economics. He is the author of *Public Finance: A Normative Theory* (1981) and, more recently, *The Massachusetts Personal Income Tax* (1986), a monograph prepared for the Massachusetts Special Commission on Tax Reform. He is currently writing a Principles of Economics text.

LARRY L. WADE is professor of political Science at the University of California at Davis. His fields of research include political economy and American and comparative public policy. His recent publications have focused on the geographical basis of economic voting. His current research aims at developing a new tariff map of the United States based on congressional voting patterns.

DAVID K. WHYNES is senior lecturer in economics, and co-director of the Community Policy Research Unit at the University of Nottingham, in the United Kingdom. His current research interests center on economic aspects of social policy, including control of illicit drug use and homelessness. He has published in the fields of development, political economy, and public economics, for example, *The Economic Theory of the State* (1981), *Comparative Economic Development* (1983), *What is Political Economy?* (1984), and *In Defence of Welfare* (1985).